PEOPLE HACKER

PEOPLE HACKER

CONFESSIONS OF A
BURGLAR FOR HIRE

JENNY RADCLIFFE

GALLERY BOOKS UK

First published in Great Britain by Gallery Books UK,
an imprint of Simon & Schuster UK Ltd, 2023

Copyright © Jenny Radcliffe, 2023

The right of Jenny Radcliffe to be identified as the author
of this work has been asserted in accordance with
the Copyright, Designs and Patents Act, 1988.

1 3 5 7 9 10 8 6 4 2

Simon & Schuster UK Ltd
1st Floor
222 Gray's Inn Road
London WC1X 8HB

www.simonandschuster.co.uk
www.simonandschuster.com.au
www.simonandschuster.co.in

Simon & Schuster Australia, Sydney
Simon & Schuster India, New Delhi

The author and publishers have made all reasonable efforts
to contact copyright-holders for permission, and apologise
for any omissions or errors in the form of credits given.
Corrections may be made to future printings.

A CIP catalogue record for this book
is available from the British Library

Hardback ISBN: 978-1-3985-1899-5
eBook ISBN: 978-1-3985-1900-8
eAudio ISBN: 978-1-3985-2258-9

Typeset in Perpetua by M Rules

Printed and Bound in the UK using 100% Renewable
Electricity at CPI Group (UK) Ltd

MIX
Paper | Supporting
responsible forestry
FSC® C171272

CONTENTS

INTRODUCTION

Definition: 'Social engineering is the manipulation of human factors in order to gain unauthorised access to resources and assets: the active weaponisation of human vulnerabilities, behaviours and errors.'

JENNY RADCLIFFE, 2022

Social engineering is the pre-eminent component of the overwhelming majority of cyberattacks today. Whether the goal of a threat actor is to directly perpetrate fraud, harvest credentials or install malware, at some point a human being must be coerced into taking an action on the actor's behalf. As a recent article for industry specialist Gartner stated, 'Human error continues to feature in most data breaches',[*] while numerous other industry analysis continually points to social engineering as being integral to most other security breaches.[†]

---

[*] Susan Moore, '7 Top Trends in Cybersecurity for 2022', Gartner, 13 April 2022: https://www.gartner.com/en/articles/7-top-trends-in-cybersecurity-for-2022

[†] See for example, Proofpoint's '2022 Social Engineering Report': https://www.proofpoint.com/sites/default/files/threat-reports/Proofpoint_Threat_Research_Social_Engineering_Report_2022.pdf

In their 2022 report on current cyber security threats and trends, PurpleSec (a cyber security company based in Washington) stated:

> In the broad world of cyber attacks, 98% involve social engineering on some level. It could involve masquerading as a trusted contact to encourage an employee to click a malicious link or email, pretending to be a reliable banking institution to capture login credentials, or similar activities designed to gain entry into target systems.
>
> Once trust is established – which is the social engineering part of the equation – other attacks can occur. Whether it be the distribution of malware, identity theft, or anything else, social engineering was essentially the gateway.[*]

Different analysts and organisations give varying, but always extremely high, percentages attributing the vast majority of breaches to this human method of attack.

Social engineering as a component of cybercrime, cons and scams is an enduring security issue. It is essentially a psychological hack. It is difficult to protect against because people will always be vulnerable to mistakes, manipulation and errors in judgement that allow a criminal to find their way into our lives whether on a personal level or as part of a bigger corporate or social network.

The consequences for victims can be devastating, with everything from the theft of our personal data and finances, to enormous legal, reputational and financial damage to organisations.

[*] 'Cyber Security Statistics: The Ultimate List of Stats, Data & Trends for 2022', PurpleSec: https://purplesec.us/resources/cyber-security-statistics/

Breaches initiated by social engineering include some of the most widely reported attacks in recent history, including the WannaCry hack of 2017, a ransomware cryptoworm enabled because vital software system updates were forgotten or ignored by operators.

The Colonial Pipeline hack of May 2021 shut down one of the largest and most vital oil pipeline systems in the United States, causing President Joe Biden to declare a state of national emergency and deem the attack a national security threat. Access to the company network was gained through an exposed password on a VPN account.

While security technologies do much of the heavy lifting in terms of screening out attacks, the ones that get through can often be attributed to human error or negligence; a culture of blame in organisations that prevents employees reporting suspicious behaviour; direct manipulation, often through bribery and/or coercion of employees; or insider threat, when someone within a firm, through mistake or malice, enables or assists outside attackers.

The security industry battles such threats every day with technology, awareness training and testing, but human beings are part of almost every system, and human beings are not perfect, a fact that is all too exploitable by criminals.

While the larger attacks make headlines, smaller more personal tragedies occur every day. The elderly couple who lose their life savings in an investment scam; the businesswoman who fell for a romance scam and paid thousands to a non-existent boyfriend 'trapped' in a foreign country and needing a quick exit home; the small bakery owner whose Instagram account was hacked, resulting in the loss of five years of photographs of the 'cake of the day' and her entire online network of customers. Tragedies such as these sometimes seem insignificant in the greater scheme of things, but they are devastating to individuals who not only lose money but also their trust in human nature, their joy of life, their happiness. They almost always feel stupid to have fallen for scams, or to have been careless with a password, or not to have noticed that the caller was fake. They often find it hard to believe, even after the evidence is presented to them, that they were fooled. They lose confidence in their own judgement.

I am part of the industry that tries to protect people from these threats and the miserable aftermath for both corporate and individual victims. Along with a network of specialists, I put together simulated attacks on businesses in order to demonstrate what could be done by malicious individuals intent on targeting an organisation or individual for criminal gain. We take an attacker's perspective and replicate a criminal attack up to the point of harm in order to educate and strengthen the client's security systems. If we can find a loophole, a way in, then so could 'the bad guys'. We find it, exploit it, and then help them patch it.

There are many thousands of individuals engaging in this business of testing security defences, a process known as penetration testing: from small contractors like myself, to larger organisations and businesses each with their own specialism and skills. The intention of penetration testing is to demonstrate attack vectors and methods and then advise clients on how to harden their defences to prevent actual criminals from doing the same thing and stealing or damaging assets.

My work and methods are notable because I do not rely on technical means of infiltration. Apart from extensive online research, I work almost exclusively with human behaviour and characteristics and use these behavioural traits as levers to uncover security gaps and investigate weaknesses. I'm not unique in this, but the level of specificity that I deploy is rare in this industry.

Most penetration testers use technical hacking methods to find exploitable gaps in the security of a firm's computer network, the bulk of which can be done remotely. Whereas I specialise in the physical infiltration of client sites, and the construction and scripting of approaches to individuals in order to extract information, whether that be via email, text or bogus social media contacts, or even in person.

This has led to my online moniker of 'people hacker' and my description as an ethical con artist and burglar for hire.

This book is about how I came to have the unusual career I do today. When I began to think about writing about my job, I soon realised I needed to go into some detail about how I found I had an aptitude for this kind of work thanks to some of my experiences growing up, as well as describing some of the more interesting and exciting jobs I have done. I wanted to show the variety of the work a social engineer might be asked to do as well as explain how some of the cons are put together, in order to teach a wider audience something about prevention.

I also felt it was important to demonstrate that there are many different paths to a career in security, as well as many different specialisms; that not every job is technical in nature and diversity of all varieties is an advantage in the industry.

I also wanted to show that, despite what popular culture might have us believe, there isn't always a clear distinction between the 'good guys' and the 'bad guys'. That sometimes, in order to defeat a criminal you have to be able to think and move like one, and that choosing the right path is not always straightforward.

*

This book is about my life and work and because it is reality, as opposed to TV or film, the stories can be messy. I don't always know exactly what is going on for a client when I take a job, and my methods don't involve too many explosions or abseiling down buildings, although I don't deny that the job can be both dramatic and dangerous at times.

There are sometimes questions left unanswered in the book, and not every job is perfectly run or polished in its execution. I've made many mistakes and encountered people and situations that seemed illogical, bizarre even, at times as well as done many jobs that were less than remarkable, and too routine to include here.

I've hesitated to write down all of the stories. There are many people out there who have much slicker and more professional operations than I do; large teams, who always work to tight contracts and use the latest technology. I still don't work like that. I recruit from my network for the skills a job requires and we try, wherever possible, to keep things simple.

Apart from changing some details and masking identities to protect clients and myself, I have related truthfully, to the best of my recollection, what happened on the jobs described in this book. If the gaps are frustrating then I apologise. It frustrates me too, but I have learnt that things are not always neat and tidy, especially when human nature is involved, and that also, most particularly, includes myself.

PROLOGUE

A mixture of amusement, fear and incomprehension flashed across the faces of the nine suits sitting in front of me. Although they had asked me to break their security systems, like many before them, they hadn't really expected me to do it so well.

Be careful what you wish for.

I'd taken them through the report, accompanied by a slide deck that had outlined, with pictures, how we had bypassed their expensive systems, got around the locks, fences and guards and had wandered around their premises. I'd gone into their offices, planted twenty-five business cards in and around their site, made myself a coffee in their kitchen and photographed key information about their company.

I'd just taken an hour outlining the process. How I'd spent a couple of weeks outside and around their premises watching the routines and patterns of their staff. How I'd got to know their security guards online, watched them at a distance and singled out the ones who were easily distracted or just not very vigilant. I had noted the ones for whom this was just a job, like any other; who would take a nap or read the paper, doing the minimum to get paid without paying a lot of attention.

I'd selected a good time to tailgate past the dopiest guard, gained access to the site then hidden in a janitor's cupboard for the rest of the working day, until almost everyone had gone home, and I could wander about freely.

I told them how I'd had various calls with cleaners, secretaries, middle management, and even the suits themselves, under different pretexts and guises over the last month so that I knew which offices to target, those most likely to yield the best information. Information that, depending on who took it, could be used variously to sell, copy, coerce or bribe.

Then I had explained how I had walked out of the cupboard, and taken many photographs, downloaded samples of computer files, walked around their site, pretty much wherever I wanted, and pinned flyers up on the staff noticeboard with bogus sites and emails, lethal if anyone acted upon them. I'd looked through desks, opened cabinets, and even gone up to the roof and spent some time taking in the view. All without being questioned or stopped – or even really noticed – by their security team or any of their staff.

The young managing director looked very uncomfortable. He had seen me speak at an industry conference a couple of months earlier and had been both impressed and amused by my talk. I mean, a professional burglar from Liverpool, who can break into high-security sites? Generally talking her way in, using that working-class humour and charm, and bobbing around nicking stuff? How funny is that?

I guess it's funny until it happens to you.

He had enjoyed my anecdotes from the job, tales of running around on rooftops and foiling security measures and had approached me later, at the networking dinner, and asked me to do a test on one of his company sites. They'd invested a ton of money in their security, and he doubted I could get through, he said, but he wanted me to try. Just me, and on my own; he wanted 'the best'.

I've two specialisms: one is physical infiltration, aka burglary, and the other is (broadly speaking) psychological 'persuasion' techniques. As he spoke to me, I watched him turn on the charm. I was sure it usually worked very well. It's not often someone tries to manipulate me so blatantly; attempts at smooth talk and flattery tend to fall flat. Game recognises game, and I had a lifetime of persuading people to do what I wanted. Most people were more direct with me, instinctively recognising that you should never play a player.

He handed me a glass of champagne, but I wasn't impressed, and gave him my stock answer for when I am turning down this type of enquiry, an answer that is, at least partially, true. I'd told him that I had more or less retired. That these days I did far less of the actual 'job', and focused more on education, on spreading the word to anyone who will listen about how to avoid being victims of social engineering. I'm now more often to be found giving keynotes, doing training and working as a legitimate consultant with my clients, in broad daylight, than conning my way into organisations or breaking into buildings. It's rare and expensive for me to rob you these days, I say; I train younger and fitter legs and minds to do what I did for the last forty or so years. There are plenty of firms out there who can help you to test your security, it doesn't have to be me.

He pressed a little more, so I explained how my knees are shot to pieces from many falls, and that I'd had enough excitement to last me a lifetime. I told him that now I mostly sit in front of my laptop writing, giving interviews about scams and cons, or give classroom training, showing others how to do the job or defend against its methods. I spend time with clients showing them how they might make things difficult for those people who would do the same things as me, but with malicious intent. I've settled into a comparatively quieter life; the anecdotes are getting thinner on the ground. I do only a few jobs a year, just to keep me current.

He looked at me and smiled. 'I've connected on LinkedIn. Look at our site and get back to me. It will be fun.'

The next day when I read his message, curiosity got the better of me and I looked at the office site he was talking about and did a little digging. It was about as secure as a children's playhouse, and he was offering me a very decent pay cheque to do it. Sigh.

I'd staked out the office, on and off, for a couple of weeks. Watching the site by night and day, at weekends and during work hours, I'd collected intelligence online about the company and its culture to see which pretexts might work best with his staff and suppliers. I'd covered my office walls in pictures of the building, and the key players in the firm, and I'd noted in what ways they were connected, looking for possible routes in both physically and psychologically.

Who was in charge? What were the people like? Did they socialise together? Who hated whom? What was happening at strategic level? What was happening at staff level? Who had personal problems? Who was having an affair? What department had the most valuable information? What did they value? What did they protect? Everything.

I'd decided I didn't even need to use a crew and would, as requested, work alone. It was a standard site with standard security and standard operational procedure. I could do it alone and had turned up and timed tailgating past the security guard without them giving me so much as a second glance.

It felt a bit lazy. Before any job I prepare thoroughly, working out a good back story with both online evidence and often physical props to back me up. I have well-rehearsed and plausible reasons to be at their premises, and I ensure I know enough about the organisation and its key players so that if I *am* stopped, I can waffle my way out of the situation fairly easily. Imagine the professional embarrassment if I was caught out by something basic for the want of background work. My ego wouldn't be able to handle it.

On this occasion it had not looked like a complicated job, and I had picked the easiest way in, through the front door. My research and surveillance had revealed likely insecure premises with negligent and unobservant staff, so I didn't worry too much about getting caught and I didn't need to pay for preparing a crew to help me. In truth I was used to working mostly alone, and if things changed tactically while I was inside, I trusted myself to improvise and handle things on the ground. I had the experience. My rough calculations estimated this as being approximately the six hundredth building I had broken into in my life so far.

For some of them I even had permission to do so.

Mr Champagne's site had indeed proved to be a basic enough job, and while there hadn't been a specific project or concern for me to focus on, what I had found was dangerous enough in the wrong hands. As is often typical, they had spent a lot of money on both digital and physical defences, but the humans who operated these systems were, like us all, occasionally care-less, tired or forgetful and vulnerable to persuasion, influence and deception techniques.

Security guards waved me in without the appropriate passes or documentation several times because I had convinced them I was expected on the site. The first time I told them I was there to measure the floor in the conference room for 'the new carpet fitting'. Complete with a clipboard and pen, a folder of carpet samples and a T-shirt with a convincing logo, they hadn't dug deeply when I failed to produce a contact name within the business, had bought the line that I was supposed to just get on with the job, and let me through the gates and into the site.

Once inside, I'd wandered around, moving in and out of offices, rifling through drawers, taking photographs of open computer screens and pocketing any keys or passes I found lying around, or otherwise unsecured. Although a couple of people had spoken with me, all my interactions had been brief and cordial. No one had asked me for identification or queried why I was there. I was friendly, looked busy, had a plausible story and didn't look threatening. I suspected that, as is very often the case, most people either didn't notice me at all, or decided very quickly that as I didn't look like a threat, then I wasn't a threat. They carried on with their day, got on with their job and didn't give me a second thought.

I'd returned the same evening, this time in office clothes, and used one of the stolen passes to try to move through the gates at reception, and back into the building. I'd waved at the guard and wearily raised my eyes, looking every inch the tired executive, annoyed at having to return to work at a late hour and preoccupied with working life. The guard smiled back and when the pass, perhaps now reported as missing, failed to give me access, he had beeped me through anyway without any questions.

The front entrance successfully breached, I tried the back door a few days later, this time in a high-visibility vest and carrying a cardboard box marked as special delivery. The guard at the back had asked me to sign a book to show I was in the building and then told me where to find the office of the recipient. I'd told him it was a recorded delivery and I needed to put the box into the hands of the IT guy who needed it urgently.

I'd signed using an alias and was shown to the elevator giving me access to the office floors, the guard helpfully explaining that the IT department was on the fourth floor. I'd wandered around a bit and found some passwords written on Post-it notes stuck to the side of computer monitors, pocketed some documents I found abandoned on printers, showing financial information and meeting agendas, before opening the box and depositing various items contained within it around the building.

A couple of covert cameras hidden in innocent-looking water bottles, some keylogger cables that sent every stroke on a laptop to a device back at our offices enabling us to see passwords, login information and anything else typed into the keyboard attached to the computers, and a Wi-Fi router device known as a 'pineapple' that could intercept their networks. This was a test, but had I had malicious intentions the information these devices could now gather would be enough to intercept, block and disrupt the private data and communications of the company. Even assuming that the digital protection the firm had installed on their system was working and blocking malware, or detecting suspicious activities on their network, we would still be able to see the passwords as they were typed into individual computers and could bypass the tech that way. If that didn't work, I'd just try what was written on the Post-it notes.

Fundamentally, it is human error that makes a company vulnerable to hacking, scams and criminal activity. This firm had spent the money. They had the gates, they had the software, the anti-malware, the virus-checking technology, but if no one stops a friendly face from wandering around their site and taking what might be useful, they are exposed to whatever malicious activity a criminal might devise to attack them.

From the lack of checks by the security guard, to the careless abandonment of passes, the open computers and written passwords, to the lack of challenge or checks of a stranger on their site, it was the people, as it so often is, who were their biggest risk, and the sad thing was that it wasn't even their fault.

People have to be seen and valued as the most important part of a security programme. No amount of investment in technological defences or fancy technology matters if you don't make your people aware of their role in security. They need to be trained to understand how they contribute, made aware of the risks of giving others access to their accounts and information, and know how to report issues and prevent problems.

It must be made clear to them that writing passwords down or leaving a computer open is dangerous: what use is technology to prevent computer infiltrations or hacks if the criminal doesn't even have to break in? They need to be told that challenging a stranger in their offices is OK, even if they get it wrong and stop a legitimate colleague or customer in the process, because a criminal doesn't necessarily look or behave like a criminal, and that unauthorised access to data and private information may be enough to bring an organisation down.

The information I gained access to that day was worth millions in the wrong hands, which could mean anything from criminal gangs to malicious hackers, corporate espionage and even hostile state actors.

Reputational damage, identity theft, financial losses, attacks on commerce, critical infrastructure, political processes and countless smaller, more personal losses, are all facilitated in worryingly increasing numbers by the mistakes and manipulation of us human beings, every day, and often in spite of the firms we work for spending huge sums on other, more tangible, methods of security.

After all, it was easy to buy a new 'magic box' tool and tick a compliance clause to show that you take security seriously. It may even go some way to help your firm claim some insurance money when you are breached, but it is much, much harder to work with the people and really care about protecting them, and by default your firm, from having their humanity exploited by someone who does the same job as me but with the intent to do harm.

Mr Champagne and his company had made these typical mistakes. They had invested large amounts of money on physical and technical defences, but when it came to educating their people, they fell short. It wasn't malicious, or even intentional, but by neglecting to educate their staff they were vulnerable.

Now it was my job to tell Mr Champagne and his board all of this. To show them how I had got into the site and managed to gain access to all of the things that they needed to keep private. To explain how their investments in security were not yet adequate to protect their business, their employees and themselves from malicious individuals. To explain how they could be attacked, coerced, breached and exposed in countless ways, ways they could imagine better than I could, because they, like everyone else, were vulnerable to social engineering, being 'hacked' through the mistakes or manipulation of their people, rather than by technical or digital means.

It was almost impossible to stop it completely, but they had to try. They needed to make themselves a harder target, starting, as everyone does, with their people. It was a bitter pill to swallow, and hard to accept, even in the face of the evidence I was about to show them, including the information we had gathered, legally and easily, on every single one of them online.

They watched and listened as I explained how I had got into the site, increasingly uncomfortable as I clicked through pictures of exposed desks and open doors, screenshots of confidential databases and financial data, business strategies and sensitive intellectual property. Finally, I handed each of them a sealed brown envelope with their name on the front.

'These envelopes contain the information we found about each of you online. We will destroy our only copies in forty-eight hours. We suggest you take a look and decide if you want it out there. It's your call, but please ask yourselves what a malicious individual might do with what we have found. If you need help hiding or deleting it, please just let us know. We are not saying that there is anything illegal or untoward in any of these files, but your personal details and information are always worth protecting, especially online. These files are intended to help you make decisions about what can be found out about you as individuals, and act as you see fit to limit or control it.'

About a minute passed in silence and then one of them looked at me and spoke.

'Very much "mission accomplished", Jenny, thank you.' A smartly dressed woman in heels and expensive glasses sniffed, avoiding my eyes. I mentally recalled my notes on her: Human Resources. White BMW, two cats, lonely, gets a bit drunk with her best mate on Fridays in a wine bar about a mile from the site. Allegedly hates her ex, according to her social media posts, but I suspect she would run back to him in a heartbeat, given the number of texts she sends him.

'We'll be in touch soon to discuss the improvements you have suggested to the site, and I think, rather quickly, about some awareness training.'

The others nodded, breathing deeply and exchanging glances.

'No problem.' I turned and pressed the off button on my clicker and closed my laptop, the screen behind me going black.

'Just one more thing before you go.' I knew they were about to ask me, because I get asked it all the time, and sure enough. 'I was just wondering. How on earth did you get into a job like this?'

I

FANCY AN UPGRADE?

'How's Hong Kong?'

'Hi, Frank. It's busy, I've spent money. How are you?'

'I'm fine. Are you travelling home tomorrow?'

'Yes. Flight is at 10.20 or something—'

He cut me off. 'Are you flying economy?'

'Yes, they put me in coach, the cheapskates.'

'Do you fancy doing me a little favour? I'll fly you home from Asia, business class. Bit of spending money as well?'

Frank was an old client who contacted me from time to time to carry out special tasks for him. Entirely separate from the large US corporate which constituted my regular employer at the time, he popped up occasionally with interesting and challenging jobs for me to undertake. He paid very well and quickly, and was the first client ever to offer to pay me for physical infiltration work. I never met him and could only guess at who he really was, but it seemed fair to assume he was, or previously had been, involved with the intelligence services.

For a start, he always seemed to be able to find me, even when my travel arrangements had changed at the last minute, or if I'd been suddenly diverted to a different hotel or city. I was travelling extensively in my legitimate role for my employer, and there were many times when I'd get a call within an hour or so of a reroute or schedule amendment that only I or the admin team at my office knew about. Then there was the nature of the jobs he asked me to do that were focused not on general or even specific security assessments, like my other clients, but more about finding pieces of written information, or weird details on a target.

I'd been dressing for dinner and packing my bulging suitcase when the call had come through to my hotel room. This was before the days of social media, when even a cursory glance at someone's accounts shows every bar they have ever visited, and every burger they ever ate. People post their entire lives on social media these days, from the routes they jog every day, to the places they work, who they socialise with, what causes they support, their friends, family and hobbies. Nowadays it is easy to find out everything about someone with a few clicks of a mouse and some targeted searches. Back then, it was only people like Frank who could easily find you.

Most importantly, Frank is my oldest and most regular client and I'd learnt to trust him over the years. I didn't know an awful lot about him. He was formal and polite and spoke calmly and without any regional accent. He sometimes used military acronyms and slang, telling me to 'bimble' around for a while, or that he would call me when I had 'yomped back to Blighty'. I never knew for sure, and it didn't seem polite or appropriate to ask him any specifics about his background. I made many contacts through Frank over the years, mostly law enforcement and former military, and I felt, rather than really knew, that he was on the 'right side', whatever that was.

My own legitimate, public career was going well; just shy of a decade into my working life I was a senior manager and an accomplished negotiator, with a Master's in business and a decent-size team reporting to me at a Fortune 500 firm. I travelled extensively for work and was on track for promotion, but I'd never stopped my side-hustle of burglary and investigation. Over the years the frequency of this other work ebbed and flowed, but if a job came in – an office that needed checking, a building to get into, a person to scrutinise, a security system to breach – I was nearly always up for the task. Normal work was often crushingly dull in comparison, but I did value it, so I worked hard at both careers.

I was doing normal, corporate work day-to-day – leadership programmes, qualifications, managing my team, navigating office politics and business travel – while also agreeing to various social engineering and security assignments whenever and wherever the offers came through. And they often came through Frank.

In those days, before the cyber security industry was worth an estimated $3tn globally, when 'penetration testing' did *not* mean checking the efficacy of security systems, what I did was not considered a respectable profession. It certainly would have done nothing for my legitimate career prospects, longer term. My family would have been worried, my friends incredulous, if I had even begun to describe what I did in my 'other job' in any real detail. At the time, I saw what I did for Frank and others as a way of earning occasional supplementary income through sometimes questionable means. It was also an exciting part of my life that I felt very few people would understand, let alone accept, and that might also get me into trouble. By and large, I kept it to myself out of caution and self-preservation. I saw no advantage in going public with the news that, aside from being a procurement manager for a large corporate, I was also a burglar for hire.

This time, I'd been on a standard business trip, auditing

and negotiating contracts with the suppliers in the Special Economic Zones of China and having meetings throughout Asia with new and potential suppliers. We'd been to China, Thailand and Taiwan, and now had a few days in Hong Kong tying up loose ends before our flight back home to the UK. I was supposed to be heading back to Manchester with my colleague Ginger Chris on the following Saturday morning.

It had been productive from a procurement and negotiation perspective, uneventful and good-natured. Ginger Chris was clever, good-humoured company and we'd enjoyed sightseeing and shopping in Hong Kong, before planning a final dinner and leaving for the airport the next day, a Friday.

When the request came in from Frank, it was a chance to see a different city and make some extra cash. I'd agreed to it very quickly and without much thought. Frank likes his luxuries and always books me into fabulous accommodation. Additionally, I hadn't ever been to the city he was talking about and after weeks of corporate discussions and contracts with my colleagues and suppliers in Asia, I was up for a little solitary mischief.

Little job, I thought, *spoil myself at the hotel, do a little shopping, decent flight home. Sorted.*

It would be no problem to go home a couple of days later than originally planned. Work didn't need to know; I wasn't due back in the office until Tuesday and could claim a dodgy stomach. I could tell Ginger Chris the same, that I was resting and was on a later flight. It would be easy money and something of a working holiday. I took a few notes on the little pad next to the hotel phone as Frank outlined the job he needed me to do.

He explained that he had an old acquaintance who thought that his house was 'impenetrable' and was being a bit too cocky about it. He told me that, despite these claims, the house wasn't especially well alarmed, guarded or even inhabited most of the time, and that it would be an easy matter to get in, leave a note on the guy's desk to prove he was wrong, and be back and drinking cocktails within an hour or two. He gave me a couple of details of the general location and description of the target's house.

It had sounded simple, which should have rung alarm bells, but I'd agreed readily and spun Ginger Chris some line about overbooked flights and a grumbling stomach at dinner. I'd then landed in the location and grabbed a taxi to an expensive hotel in the fanciest part of the city. When I checked in, the front desk handed me an envelope which I opened in my room. It contained the remaining part of the address of the target building and a note.

'*Check if this name xxxxx is written inside his leather address book in the desk. If you don't find the name then don't worry about leaving the note and just get out. Enjoy business class.*'

When I first heard about the job it had seemed very straight-forward, a standard night's work, although 'standard' rarely exists in what I do for a living. As I unpacked, I thought some more about the job. The guy who owned the house had obviously authorised the break-in, at least at some level, or I wouldn't have been asked to do it, would I? Not my business what was going on between them. I didn't feel it was my job to ask questions, and honestly I wasn't actually that interested. Frank likes his games, I'm not even a part of them, he's never steered me wrong in all the years I have known him.

I'd told him I would scope the house out that night, and then do the actual job in the early hours of Sunday morning. I'd had a rest and a shower and, after a brief wander around the area, some dinner and a few phone calls, I was ready to go.

Wearing a pair of black jeans and a plain long-sleeved black T-shirt, I tied my hair back into a long braid, took off all my jewellery and picked up a cheap-and-nasty plastic keyring torch at the little shop in the reception of the hotel. I got the concierge to hail me a taxi and asked the driver to head to a golf club which was at the end of the residential street on which the target's house was situated. The driver dropped me off, and I noticed that plenty of cabs and rickshaws were queued just around the corner, a little way from the entrance to the club. *Perfect,* I thought, *I'll grab one when I get back; it's only reconnaissance, it shouldn't take long.*

I walked down the gravelled drive and out of the gates. Soon I was strolling down a long, winding street of colonial-style mansions, most of which were set back from the pavement behind high walls and railings. I could see glimpses of cars and occasionally had to walk around a fallen bloom from a tree branch on the pavement, but otherwise there were very few signs of the lives beyond the perimeter fences and gates of this weirdly sterile but clearly affluent area.

The noise of music and conversation from the golf club gradually faded as I walked, but it still carried over the large stretch of water that flanked the entire street on my right-hand side. The evening light was fading fast and the moon was rising large in the sky. I was enjoying the walk and could smell cooking, garlic and ginger, and the slightly pungent scent of drains and greenery in water as I made my way further down the road.

I was looking for names or numbers on the houses and becoming a little concerned, noticing that many of them had no means of identification whatsoever. I thought I might struggle to find the target, but I needn't have worried. After about three-quarters of a mile the buildings started to change, getting bigger and more lavish than the ones nearer the golf club. I felt I was getting closer and started to look for a house matching Frank's brief description.

I knew the target as soon as I saw it in the distance. With its pale pink-washed walls and high black gates, it was hard to miss. A monstrosity, in my opinion, but my opinion didn't count. I slowed my step to get a better look and peered through the gates into the property beyond. The house had at least three floors and was designed in a colonial style, all columns and white marble. With lush greenery and exotic blooms framing the building on either side, there were trees and shrubs lining the drive which led to the front of the building and a large carved black front door. The place lacked a heartbeat, as if no one was at home.

Looking up and down the street, there was no discernible sign of life. I could hear a couple of large dogs barking in the distance, but other than that it was eerily quiet, which was likely why I could still hear the golf club noise whispering away in the background. It was the most lavish ghost town I had ever seen, and it had a strange, lonely feel to it. *You could scream or be run over here,* I thought, *and no one would hear you.* There was almost no traffic and not so much as a duck, much less a boat, on the stretch of water over the road. I looked again at the house and saw no sign of any alarms or lights.

The large iron gates were, unexpectedly, standing slightly ajar. I thought about what Frank had said. This guy didn't seem to bother much with security, which was fine, but odd to say the place was impenetrable as well? I wondered what he meant by that; how could it be secure with no visible security measurements? With nothing to act as a deterrent, what on earth was giving Frank's acquaintance that level of confidence?

A couple of cars appeared at the vanishing point of the street and passed me on the road. Not wanting to look suspicious, I began walking again for a few metres until they disappeared, and then bent down to fiddle with my shoelaces before turning back for another look which confirmed my initial impressions. The house didn't just look quiet, there were absolutely no signs of life at all. The gardens were neat and clearly professionally maintained, but there was no hint of human life around that property. It looked empty.

I moved closer to the gate and squinted down the line of the wall from the gatepost and along the right-hand side of the house. I could make out large French doors on an upper floor with a flight of stone stairs curving up to meet them from the gardens at ground level. Otherwise, the side of the house had relatively few windows, and was in comparative shadow. That would do nicely.

Satisfied with my research, I headed back to the golf club without incident and, as the last of the pink evening light rapidly faded, I grabbed a taxi outside the club and watched the moon as we drove back into the city and to my hotel.

I went up to my room and drank a bottle of water, switched on the TV and lay back on the bed. So, it was on, tomorrow night. I would wait until the early hours, get a taxi to the golf club, do the same walk, and sneak in through the gates. I'd use the side stairs to get to the French doors, open them, by force if necessary, and gain access to the house. Frank had told me the study was on the ground floor near the front of the house, so it would take me only a few minutes to do what was needed. I'd need the crappy torch and something to act as a crowbar, but otherwise I'd be in and out in less than fifteen minutes. Then I could relax.

I ran a bath and added some bubbles, but as I undressed, I looked at myself in the mirror. Screw it.

I put my crumpled T-shirt back on and, without allowing myself to think too carefully, I replaced my recently discarded socks and Converse on my feet. I grabbed the bottle opener from the mini-bar and slid it down the inside of my trainers, along with a Post-it with the note Frank had told me to leave on the desk if I found the name. I hooked the torch over my fingers, turned the TV on and walked towards the door without glancing at myself in the mirror. The job was on.

Years of doing this type of work have made me superstitious. I have lots of rituals and routines that I have come to follow on physical infiltration jobs, persuading myself that they will ensure not just a successful assignment, but also as incident-free a job as possible. Similarly, there are protocols to be followed in terms of planning and preparation. One of the most basic rules of thumb is that once a plan has been established, it is wise to stick to it. Follow the plan to victory. Stick to the plan. I was about to break that rule.

This is true, even though the ability to adapt a strategy and improvise is vital when you are inside a target site. It is so, so important not to keep chopping and changing details in the master plan unless you really must. You pick a course of action and then commit to it. You absolutely need a plan A, plan B and even C and D covering a variety of eventualities. However, all of them should still be variations on a central and well-thought-out theme, if possible, as once on site everything else tends to change and tactical adaptation is always necessary. You need to give yourself as few things to think about as possible. Changing significant aspects of any plan points to it being flawed in the first place, or worse a lack of faith in the original intelligence or research.

A clear and obvious element to the plan is safety. Absolutely non-negotiable and fundamental to every job is to make sure that somebody, somewhere, knows where you are, when you are working, and when you are likely to be back. That way, if something goes wrong, alarms can be raised, search parties deployed, poker hands declared, etc. Changing something as basic as the date and time of a job is rarely advisable, especially as a last-minute decision, and especially without telling your team you have done so. These days I'd never even consider such a move, it would be amateurish and dangerous, a rookie error.

However, to learn from your mistakes you must first make them.

I left the key in my room, slammed the door and took the stairs down to the lobby. I walked through the shop and out through the door to the bellboy outside and he flagged me a cab. I got in and gave him the address of the golf club. Why wait around for a day when you can get this done now? *Carpe diem* and all that? My impatience is a devil on my shoulder. One of many. The cab had weaved through night-time traffic, going past markets and crowded clubs, before finally pulling up outside the familiar golf club entrance. The club was louder and busier than earlier and as I retraced my steps towards the gates and glanced at my watch, it was already past 11 o'clock.

The moon was high over the water, and once again the walk to the mansion was quiet and devoid of life and noise. The night air was hot, and I was on edge with the surge of nervous energy I always felt before a job like this. My body felt jittery, and I cursed that I hadn't brought something sugary with me to calm me down (sugar helps boost your brain a little to better cope with stress in the short term, so it's useful to have some sweets stashed on these types of jobs).

I consciously suppressed a fleeting thought that this was a mistake and to head back now. I wouldn't normally forget to bring things I used on a job, and what with the pathetic torch, not telling anyone where I was, and changing my mind at the last minute, I was being impatient and sloppy. Not only that but this neighbourhood was giving me the creeps with its lack of life and animation. I paused for a second, but then sternly told myself it was just nerves and to get on with it. I even laughed a little internally; maybe the bath will still be warm when I get back. *That,* I thought, *would be some sort of record.*

I could hear nothing but crickets and the gentle lapping of the water just beyond the road as the house again came into view. No lights on inside. No lights on in most of the houses for that matter, I noted in passing, but the moon was bright, and there were streetlamps lining the road. There were still no cars moving along the road and there were no boats on the water. This was the quietest, most sanitised neighbourhood I had ever seen: no bins, no cats, nothing. Just as well, I told myself, less chance of being seen and the moonlight would help with visibility.

I walked up to the gates, hesitated for a couple of seconds, and walked through. Nothing. I threw a little stone towards the front door. No security lights went on, no dog barked at the noise. It was clearly and obviously empty. The best course of action now was simply to get in and out as quickly as I could.

I walked briskly and quietly around the side of the house and stopped at the bottom of the stone stairs leading up to the bay window area I had noticed earlier that day. A glance through a downstairs window revealed a darkened dining room with a few pieces of white A4 paper on the table and many more scattered on a wooden floor; there were no lights I could see on inside the building and no movement, but it wasn't too difficult to make out the room beyond the window in the moonlight. I stooped down and pushed the torch underneath the gravel next to the house to pick up later.

I moved along the wall and up the stone staircase at the side of the house. I stopped in front of the bay windows and knelt. Reaching inside my trainers, I pulled out the bottle opener that

I had taken from the hotel mini bar, its garish hotel branding somehow out of place in the moonlit night. I was about to insert it between the handles to force the doors when I heard a telephone ring somewhere inside the house. I froze and squinted again through the glass.

I could just about make out a bedroom with an unmade bed but few other notable features. Not so much as a book on the bedside table or a picture on the wall. *No one lives here,* I thought; *they sleep here sometimes, maybe use it as a base of some sort, but not tonight.* The phone trilled away inside the house, but I heard no steps running to answer it, saw no movement from my vantage point on top of the staircase. No lights switched on inside. This place was definitely empty. Good.

The ringing stopped and I waited a second before lifting the bottle opener again to the handles. Before I could apply any pressure to force the door, I remembered the fundamental rule that security only works if you use it, and that people often did not. The guy couldn't be so cocky that he didn't even lock the doors and windows, could he? Does he think that no one would dare rob him? The thought occurred that this might well be the truth and that proceeding, if this was the case, would be a very bad idea indeed. I thought I'd try anyway.

I put the bottle opener between my teeth and tried the handle. Pushing down gently, I heard a soft click and the door swung quickly and heavily open, blasting me with the breeze of air-conditioning. *Impregnable, my arse!* I thought, placing the bottle opener down carefully and wondering idly if the guy was being ironic and thinking how much Frank would enjoy hearing how easy this one had been.

Stepping through the windows, I trod carefully at first, waiting for an alarm, listening for movement. None came, and I relaxed a little as I walked through the empty bedroom, and through the open door onto a U-shaped landing overlooking a large, modern entrance hall lit by moonlight coming through the windows. I moved quickly along, past bedrooms and some closed doors, before trotting down the staircase and into the hall. It was unadorned and pretty much empty, save for a large display of slightly faded flowers in a black vase on top of a wooden plinth at the bottom of the stairs. They seemed out of place against the utilitarian sparseness of the rest of the house. *The purpose of this bouquet is to be admired, to be looked at,* I thought, *and yet no one even sees it — what a waste.*

I moved towards the front of the house, the rubber soles of my shoes squeaking as they gripped the hard flooring. The first door I tried was to the right of the enormous front doors; it opened silently and I could see I had found the right room on my first try.

My feet sank into thick carpet as I tiptoed into what was clearly a study and looked around. This room had an atmosphere that was entirely different to the rest of the house. It smelt nice, vaguely of incense, or maybe sandalwood. In the centre of the room there was a huge, illuminated fish tank, behind which was a long narrow desk with some papers and a coffee cup on its surface, while bookshelves with ornaments and decorations lined the walls.

This room, at least, looked lived in.

A gigantic, throne-like swivel chair was parked behind the desk at an angle. I plonked down in it, my feet barely touching the floor, and it rotated lazily clockwise in a well-oiled trajectory. Then I smoothed my hands across the leather-writing tablet in the middle of the desk. Reaching down, the desk drawers were locked, but some likely looking keys were in a glass bowl next to a phone on my right. I tried a couple of keys in the lock, and soon it turned smoothly enough. I pulled open the top drawer and looked inside.

I rifled through the contents, pricking my finger on some push pins as I went; there was some money and cigarettes alongside the stationery in the first drawer, but nothing of note. I was three drawers down before I found what looked like an address book. With the multicoloured fish in the tank watching me as they swam between fizzing bubbles, I scanned the pages for the name Frank had given me.

Most of the writing in the book was made up of oriental characters, so the few English entries stood out and I found the name quite quickly. Smiling, I got the Post-it out from my shoe, sorting it from the few notes I had tucked in as well for the fare home, and laid it carefully on the desk. I checked back at the name in the book and noticed a tiny spot of my blood on its otherwise pristine pages and rubbed the spot with my finger. This only made the splat worse, so I hurriedly closed it and shoved it back in the drawer. I locked it, replaced the keys and stood up.

I took a moment to look around. This was a weird sort of job. Watching the fish for a moment, I mused on what was really going on; I didn't like to admit it, but I was starting to get the feeling that this was some sort of joke or maybe a bet between Frank and the owner of the desk. I wondered idly, as I turned back into the hall and paced across the wooden flooring towards the flowers, whether perhaps he had told the person he could get into his study and had been disbelieved. *Maybe that is why I am here,* I thought, reaching out to touch the petals on a lily that had seen better days – Frank did like his mystery and his games. This would be a real win for him over his cocky friend. Not my concern, though, I was just doing my job. I noticed orange pollen on my hand and I absent-mindedly wiped it on my thigh, staining my black jeans as I turned towards the staircase to leave.

I was maybe three stairs up when the hall behind me was suddenly illuminated by a powerful set of car headlights pulling into the drive and stopping just outside the front door. It sounded like at least two cars pulling up, doors slamming and deep male voices speaking in rapid Chinese. I went immediately into fifth gear, running back up the stairs and darting along the landing. I rushed to the bedroom and ran as fast as I could to the windows I'd come in through. I heard the front door open and then footsteps and conversation in the hallway. In that moment, stood in the bedroom in front of the windows, I knew that this wasn't a joke or a prank at all. Quite what it actually was I could only speculate, but I know a serious security crew when I see or hear one, and even with the limited information I had I knew that these men were definitely some sort of security. This was an unauthorised entry, at least tonight, and I was completely screwed if they found me.

I bolted through the windows and half-fell down the stairs, twisting my ankle awkwardly and half ripping my shoe off as I stopped. I froze. I could clearly see two large 4×4 vehicles in the driveway. Reflected in the rear windscreen of the car closest to me I could see that there were two large men in black suits standing at the bottom of the steps to the front door and looking into the house. I could hear them speaking into radios and placing their hands on bulges just above their hips under their jackets. They looked armed, highly efficient and seriously pissed off, and they did not look like police. They wouldn't have any sympathy or sense of humour at all if they caught sight of me.

I needed to hide but there was nowhere obvious, so I crept down under the staircase and dashed across the gravel path, wincing at the slight crunching noise of the gravel beneath my feet. I moved sideways into the garden area with the plants and trees parallel to the stairs and dropped to my hands and knees, hugging the wall that curved around the side of the garden, leading to the gates. I lay down among the bushes and tree trunks, hoping for some cover in the shadows while I waited for them to leave, or otherwise had an opportunity to crawl towards the gates and slip away while they were inside.

I hoped I was pretty much shielded by the shadows, and the moonlight meant that I could see them fairly clearly moving in and out of the front door, back and forth to their cars, whose engines were still running where they had been abandoned in the drive. In the distance I could hear the music from the club drifting over the lake and my mouth went dry as I wondered if I could ask them for help if I made a run for it and they chased me. I decided that would be a very poor last resort.

After a few minutes, their voices faded and the light went on inside the house behind me. I lifted my head to scan around me. One of the cars was parked at a strange angle, almost but not quite blocking the gates. I started to inch along the wall, wondering if I could squeeze around and slip away. I had dragged myself a few feet and wasn't far from the gatepost at the end of the fence when I heard a metallic click. Suddenly, the engine of the car, which was by now just a foot or two from my head, growled loudly into life. I hadn't noticed a third guy, the driver, and he was rolling the car a little further into the drive nearer to where I was lying against the wall. I pressed myself face down into the soil, hoping that I would blend into the undergrowth and shadows of the garden, with my dark clothes and hair.

The car stopped rolling, and I heard the guy get out and move over to the gates, shutting them with an ominous clang now just a few feet in front of me. I froze and mentally ditched the idea of running away, but I thought I would wriggle back further away from the gates and wait for them to leave, hopefully without locking the gates. What seemed like an eternity passed and I continued to lie very still against the wall. It was so uncomfortable, and I was bent at a strange angle. It had all gone very quiet, and my left arm was starting to hurt. I needed to move it from underneath me before it went completely dead.

As my head moved a fraction, I felt some resistance and I realised that my hair was caught on something. Thinking it was a branch, I reached awkwardly and slowly around the back of my neck, grabbed my braid, and slowly gave it a speculative pull. It was stuck fast. I turned my head around an inch or two as far as I dared and glanced past my arm to try to see what the hell had caught my hair so fast. Then I saw the problem. The back wheel of the car had backed over the very tip of my braid, which was stuck fast underneath, about twelve inches from my head.

I almost screamed out loud and tried to think what to do. I could have pulled harder, of course, but the movement might well have attracted the attention of the driver. I hadn't realised the car had come so close to me! If it moved even slightly it might hit me, crush my stupid impatient head. I had to chance it and I put an aching hand around my hair and got ready to tug.

I froze again as I heard more steps on the path approaching the car. I braced myself, terrified, certain that they would either see me, or reverse the car over me, but then I heard a car door open, then slam shut while the two heavies spoke frantically to each other, the remaining guy leaning into the car window. One of them spoke into his radio. I heard crackling and tinny responses to his words, but the intensity was dropping along with the speed and volume of their speech. Maybe they were finishing up?

I had soil in my mouth, but I pushed myself down into the ground even further and tried another frantic pull on my hair.

I felt a sharp pain as a few strands came out, a couple more tugs and it would come free. I steeled myself to try again but I was starting to panic and suddenly felt very cold. My hand went very weak, my gut started to churn, and I felt sure I was about to black out. My mouth was dry and gritty from the soil, and I started to gasp uncontrollably for air, my noisy breaths masked by the sound of the engine running a foot from my head.

If I get away with this one, I thought, *I'll retire,* I mean I hadn't even charged extra for the job! I'd done it because Frank had offered to fly me back home business class! I'd sold myself so cheap! I'd done it because it seemed easy and exciting. I'd done it because, as ever, I was bored when I wasn't doing this job. I idly wondered what the headline would be when they found my body. 'Woman's body found in swamp' maybe?

Suddenly, and not for the first or last time, the ludicrous way I make my living hit me. The exhaust fumes were making me nauseous and the light-headedness came in another wave. Against all reason and sense, I felt the urge to giggle.

Then, the talking stopped. I heard the clinking of metal and imagined they now had their guns drawn. I heard footsteps walking away and up the few stairs again to the front door. Then two sets of footsteps came back, I heard a few more words before the men jumped into the cars. I grabbed my hair and pulled hard in a panic as I heard the car doors slam and the engines revving. I knew that if they reversed the car my head would be crushed, but before I even had the time to process this my hair came loose, and I thudded clumsily towards the wall as the two cars roared off through the gates, which must have at some point been opened again, and away into the street beyond.

It was suddenly very quiet again. I waited for a couple of seconds before forcing myself to get up shakily from the soil.

There were twigs and leaves hanging off my clothes, my hair and face were covered in dirt, and I had a big chunk of my own hair clenched tightly in my fist. I still felt like I was going to throw up and I started at a bug on my T-shirt, gave a rasping cough and tried to spit onto the soil from a bone-dry mouth. There was a me-shaped impression in the ground next to the wall. I hastily kicked the flattened bit so it wasn't so obvious, and without checking anything else I moved around the gate post, and hopped unenthusiastically on my sore ankle out of the gate and into the deserted street outside.

I breathed a sigh of relief as I climbed into a taxi outside the golf club. I was happy to get away, but my thoughts were dark as the cab moved through the night and I let myself think about what had nearly happened, about the risks I had taken so casually. I decided, as I have done many times, that this would have to be my last job. I'd used up my nine lives for sure this time. I was going to get a drink and a bath, go home tomorrow and I was never going to break into buildings for money again. I was done.

Tears streaked quietly down my face as the driver took me back to the hotel, but looking back, I can't say now exactly why I was crying. It might seem obvious to say that I was in shock. Frightened, with bumps and bruises, and even ashamed that I had been so stupid and naive. However, if I had to guess I would say that while all of these things were true, I think the real reason I was upset was because at that moment I believed that I would never do the job again. I was crying because I thought I was done, I'd made a stupid mistake by going in too early when nobody could have bailed me out, broken some basic rules and now I would, very likely, never be hired for the 'fun stuff' again.

I was dishevelled and dirty. I could feel scratches across my face and my T-shirt had a couple of rips on the front and sleeves, patches of dirt and pollen all over my jeans. If the driver wondered what I had been up to he didn't show it, keeping a professional friendly silence on the way back. I started to tremble with adrenalin as my system recalibrated. I really, really needed sugar.

We pulled up outside the hotel and I got out, saying a tired 'thank you' as I shoved crumpled notes into his hands and walked through the revolving glass doors and into the lavish hotel reception. I knew I looked a sight, and a less expensive hotel might have questioned me, but the most expensive hotels absolutely do not raise eyebrows at their customers, no matter what they look like, and Frank had put me in a *very* expensive hotel.

Even though a glance at the clocks in reception told me it was 3.15 in the morning, I walked straight to the empty bar and asked the pristine bartender to make me something 'very alcoholic that a kid would drink'. A colourful sugary concoction was put in front of me and barely touched the sides as it disappeared far too quickly. The sugar/alcohol settled me a little and I ordered another, with a beer as a chaser. I started to feel waves of relief as the barman grabbed the beer and reached for the bottle opener to open it. Oh my God. The bottle opener!

I reached into my shoe, but I knew it wasn't there. I'd left the bottle opener, with the hotel logo on it, somewhere at the job! And, for that matter, that stupid torch was buried under a few leaves and rocks at the bottom of the staircase. *Shit.*

I motioned to the barman for my tab, but he waved me away, winking at me in a manner that suggested he recognised someone having a bad day. I drained the beer, grabbed the cocktail, and made my way to the lifts, my mind racing. The corridor to my room seemed endless and I imagined the security guards rocking up at reception and asking if anyone had been acting strangely that night.

I pointedly locked the door to my huge hotel room, unplugged the stone-cold bath, drank an entire bottle of mineral water and ran myself another tub full of hot water. I poured all of the gels and lotions, regardless of what their actual function was supposed to be, under the running water and felt afresh the scratches stinging as I sank into the water. I was approaching the too-tired-to-care stage and decided that I was overreacting. It had been a legitimate job after all, and I wasn't a criminal, just a day early. I was catastrophising. I'd done my job, all sorted. Enough drama. The alcohol was helping, as was the warm, fragrant water and I dozed, topping up the water once or twice to keep it hot.

Afterwards, I fell asleep in my towel on top of the bed and woke up with a sore neck and my head on a damp patch made by my wet hair, large amounts of which had come off in the bath. I looked in the mirror. I looked like hell and I was starving; it was 3.30, I had slept for ten hours.

Frank had paid promptly, as he always did.

I never found out what the arrangement had been with his associate, but I assumed that the note I left on the desk had some meaning for them both. It would at least serve as some explanation of my presence in the house. Presumably upon its discovery, the owner would know that it was Frank, rather than some unknown adversary, that had breached his property. Frank would have proved a point about never taking security for granted, they would have laughed about it over drinks in an expensive bar next time they met, and the guy would have beefed up his security and not been as cocky in future.

Had I waited until the agreed infiltration time, twenty-four hours later, at least one of the security team would likely have been alerted at the last possible opportunity, to a potential security test at the site that night. While no security team is ever exactly pleased when someone gets past them, they are compelled to treat a security consultant with permission to attempt an infiltration very differently to a random burglar. Perhaps Frank knew someone on the security team personally and was planning to tell them or the owner at the last minute that he had asked someone to test the security measures that night so they knew it wasn't a real break-in. Either way, any notice of the job would have to be given at the last possible moment out of necessity, otherwise security would be prepared and the whole thing would be pointless.

Whatever the reason behind the job, I had to assume that some part of the plan included letting that security team know that I was, at least on some level, meant to be there. I had to assume that Frank was ready to rescue me if I really needed it, and that I was only in real danger because I had jumped the gun on timing. If this wasn't the case then the job was genuinely unofficial, criminal and dangerous and I couldn't afford to believe that Frank would ask me to do something like that, regardless of what it meant for my safety.

I never asked him for the details, in case it was some sort of joke, or worse a bet of some sort, but when we spoke, he clearly knew I'd gone in earlier than I had planned and that the bottle opener I had left behind had been found. I assumed that once the message on the Post-it note was discovered the owner had known to contact Frank and he would have then explained what had happened.

For most jobs the timing is important but isn't usually this crucial, the response not usually this harsh, the consequences not potentially fatal. Sticking to the scope and agreed parameters is important, but my life wouldn't normally be in danger if I strayed slightly beyond those lines. This time, however, had been different and my going in a day earlier than planned meant that, to all intents and purposes and certainly as far as that armed security team was concerned, I actually *was* a burglar and would be dealt with as such.

I got the feeling Frank was disappointed I'd been so cavalier about the job, even though he never specifies how I am to approach a target or makes comment on the methods I used. He could sense that I felt I had been stupid and was reflecting it back at me in his usual understated way.

I was disappointed in him too. He'd sent me into a dangerous situation and hadn't warned me about what I was walking into. It might have been handy to know just how dangerous this one was and that the timing was critical, if I didn't want to be met with an armed response. Although I fully accepted responsibility for my impatience, I didn't appreciate the lack of heads-up as to what I might be facing, and although nothing was explicitly mentioned about it between us, it was over a year before we spoke again. When we did, I was surprised and pleased to hear from him, but I told him I needed to know one thing before we could move on.

'Frank, you know in Asia . . .'

'Mmm . . .'

'It wasn't legit, was it? I mean the guy didn't authorise the job. It wasn't just the timing, was it? I was on my own, wasn't I?'

'Of course,' was the response, and we never spoke about it again.

THE LION AND THE LIGHT BULB

There was a soft breeze that night outside the zoo fences. It carried a musty, farmyard smell, mingled with the distant whiff of fish and chips and the happy sounds of the busy fairground in the distance. I hung on to my toy torch and reached up to take my cousin's hands so he could push me over the fence and into the grounds beyond.

It was summer, I was almost nine and this was my first real break-in.

Liverpool in the early 1980s was not exactly a hive of opportunity. Successive government policies, coupled with economic problems, had left the great northern city in a state of bad decline with very limited opportunities for its residents. Unemployment and crime were rife at the time, and there was a sense of hopelessness and despair pervading working-class communities throughout the country. Liverpool had been hit particularly hard.

My dad had been ill and was no longer working, and my mother was working long shifts in a local grocery shop. Money was scarce, but if you had asked me, I would hardly have noticed. I don't remember ever wanting for anything, and I don't recall ever having an empty stomach or a shabby piece of clothing, testimony I suppose to the resourcefulness of my family and the kindness of the community we lived among.

What was lacking at the time, and not just where I grew up, was a sense of danger and rules to govern what children got up to. It seems crazy to think about it now, but we really did go out to play in the summer holidays for hours on end without phones, sun cream or cycle helmets. I'd say it was a more innocent age but that might just be my nostalgia kicking in, because where I lived was not exactly quiet.

There was the time when the three grown-up sons of a neighbour came home to find their dad beating up their mother and so decided to kick him to death. They didn't quite succeed as someone eventually called the police, but only because there were 'little kids watching out of a neighbour's window'. The rest of the street had closed their curtains and refused to intervene, as he was well known for domestic abuse and was getting what most felt he deserved. Where I lived you didn't grass or call the police unless absolutely necessary, and even then, anonymously and with limited information.

Then there was the strange man who lived at the bottom of the road whom the kids were told to avoid, and who flashed you if he caught your eye. There was the patch of wasteland next to the pub where a bonfire known locally as the 'eternal flame' burnt most nights, continually fuelled by everybody's old furniture and rubbish. There was even a dead dog stiff as a board chucked on it one time. Two blokes with tears streaming down their faces placing it among the flames, and all of us kids stood around watching. It was a tough neighbourhood, but full of kind, helpful people who looked after each other to the point of naivety, until the time when they decided not to and then you were out.

I was eight years old the day I got kidnapped. It had been a long hot summer and I had been playing at the top of the street with a friend for some of the morning. We were climbing on top of some lockups at the end of the street and throwing a ball around, sizzling in the sunshine and singing daft little songs when a woman approached us. She seemed full grown to us, but I later discovered she was actually only a teenager, about seventeen years of age, who lived with her parents nearby but was left alone for extended periods while they worked away and looked after elderly relatives. She came up and asked us if we were thirsty and offered us both some orange juice, so we followed her into her house.

We had a glass of juice each and then went and sat on some sofas. I could see other kids playing in the schoolyard opposite through the net curtains draping the window of the front room. We could hear music playing somewhere in the house and she left us momentarily to turn the volume up. When she came back she asked us if we liked the song. I remember the song now, but I can't bring myself to type its title. Suffice to say it was a pop hit with a melancholy theme, and a female vocal which repeated the same lines endlessly throughout the short track. As kids do, we started dancing and jumping around the room, and before too long we were out of breath and sat down.

The music was still blasting out but there was no more conversation and my friend said she was heading home. I got up to follow her, but the girl looked at me sadly and asked if I really needed to go. I said I'd stay for a bit and smiled at her. I heard the front door slam shut and watched my pal skip past the front window and head home.

'What's the matter?' I asked her.

'Let's just have a dance,' she said. 'That will make me laugh and cheer me up.'

So, I started to dance again, in as goofy a way as I could

hoping to make her laugh, although her expression had changed, and she wasn't smiling anymore. Before too long I realised that the same song was playing repeatedly. It was starting to be a bit annoying, so I asked her to change it. She left the room and turned the volume up even more, but she didn't change the track. When she came back, I shouted to her over the noise that she needed to turn it down. But she just sat down and didn't answer me.

In that moment I knew I was in trouble. I remember fear gripping my stomach in a cold flush and my mouth going dry. She wasn't listening to me, and she wouldn't do as I asked. I moved towards the door, but she jumped up quickly and slammed it shut.

'Keep dancing,' she said.

'No.'

'Yes.' She pushed me roughly back into the middle of the room.

So, I started to dance again, facing away from her, and looking out of the front window at the kids playing in the schoolyard. I remember trying to think how I could get out of the situation and run home to my mother. The windows were fixed, and she was sitting near to the door. She was an adult, at least in my child's eyes. There was no way I could overpower her. *Think.*

I stopped.

'Dance,' she said.

'I'm tired.'

'I don't care.'

'I need the toilet.'

'No.'

I moved towards the door, and she stood up and leaned against it. The song was playing again, confusing me, and making me panic. I felt hot and sweaty and suddenly very frightened.

'I want to go home.'

'No.'

'I want to.'

'*No!*'

I started to cry, and my knees felt weak, so I sat on a chair. She came over and dragged me back to my feet. 'Dance.'

'*No!*'

She grabbed my arms and started moving them around. Kicking at my feet to move them, but I was sobbing by now. Deep down I knew she meant me real harm. I could feel in every part of my bones and especially in my stomach that I might not get out of this. She was treating me like a doll, and I was in her control. I slumped to the floor and had my head in my hands.

She left me there and went and sat on the sofa near the door. I looked at the pattern on the carpet. Floral against a dark blue background, I counted the petals on the flowers – five per flower. I glanced up and she was staring at me. Unblinking and still. She saw me peeking through my fingers at her.

'Get up and dance.'

I didn't answer and put my head down again. She came over and picked me up.

'Dance for five more minutes and you can go to the toilet.'

So, I did, and when five minutes had gone, she denied ever saying that. And so, it went on for hours.

Meanwhile, my little friend had gone home and muttered something to her mother about me playing with someone else. My own mother wasn't concerned as she assumed I was at my friend's house and had eaten lunch there as I had done dozens of times in the preceding weeks. No one started looking for me until around six o'clock when my dinner was about to be served.

Mum had called my friend's house and realised that no one had seen me since ten that morning. Not one to panic, she knocked on a few other friends' doors and then some neighbours', many of whom reported seeing me that morning but not since. Increasingly concerned, she went to my friend's house where she was grilled a bit more closely by both her own mother and mine. Eventually, she reluctantly told them about how we had met the girl and details of the house where she had taken us inside.

I don't remember how I heard Mum knock on the door. The music was still blaring, but I knew she had come for me, another knock and the doorbell rang, then a banging on the front window. My heart leapt and I bolted for the door, but she grabbed me and hissed at me to be quiet. It was at that moment that I knew she wasn't going to let me go. As melodramatic as it sounds, I knew then and I know now that this seventeen-year-old girl intended never to let me go.

The door again. I tried to shout but my mouth was bone dry and only a squeak came out. She grabbed my mouth and clamped her hand over it.

Mum was persistent.

The girl dragged me towards the door with her hand over my mouth. 'Don't you make a sound.'

It's hard now to describe that moment of pure fear. I've since read that in such moments the brain sometimes achieves a sort of higher clarity. I don't know if that was true here, but something in my mind clicked. I remember very distinctly thinking, *I might die now. If I don't get away from her, I might die now. If I was a superhero, I would fly out of here, I'd be so strong I could fight back. But I'm not and I might die now* and then *If I don't die now, then I'll become a superhero. I'll never feel like this again.*

All this thinking happened while she was opening the door. She had me in a virtual stranglehold, pushed up against the wall behind the door. My neck was hurting, and her fingers dug into my cheeks. Then I heard my mother's voice: 'Is Jenny here please? Her friend told me that she might be?'

'No, I did see her this morning, but she isn't here.'

Again, I knew then how far she was willing to go. As an adult now, and a parent myself, I can only imagine with horror what she was planning.

'Where was she when you saw her?'

'Just in the schoolyard. She was with the little blonde girl, playing ball.'

Mum was almost buying it; I heard her voice begin to fade a little and I knew if I didn't act now, I wouldn't see her again. I reached up with my hand and I grabbed the girl's little finger. I pulled it to the side as hard as I could and as her hand peeled away, I shouted one word: 'Mum.'

My mother pushed open the door and pushed the girl aside at the same time. She grabbed me and I remember nothing else. No harsh words and nothing more. Just relief as she carried me home and closed the door.

What you might find shocking is that nothing was ever done, as far as I am aware, to follow this up. I don't think my mother ever told my dad what had happened. I remember her running me a bath and checking me over, but physically I wasn't really hurt. A few bruises perhaps where she had grabbed me, and I was exhausted with red eyes, but I cleaned up OK and ate my dinner as if nothing had happened.

The next day, I went out to play again and I don't remember being frightened, or particularly avoiding the area where the girl lived. In later years, I asked Mum about the incident repeatedly. Her response was that I was fine and that I bounced back straight away. I came home, ate my dinner and asked to play outside again the next day. I had never told her exactly what had gone on in the house, and she had no answer for me when I asked her what she thought about the girl lying about me being there or what she may have been planning.

She told me that they thought less of the incident because it was a female who had been involved. She said that Dad, who was connected to everyone in the neighbourhood, including some of the crime families in Liverpool, would have certainly taken action and it didn't seem necessary. Essentially, I think she just assumed that I'd been playing with the girl, and she had lied because she had kept me for too long. The truth was beyond her imagination, so I think she probably dismissed it.

Not long after that a 'for sale' sign appeared at the girl's house. I saw her once or twice after school started but she never looked me in the eye, and I was with people when it happened. The house was sold before Christmas and the family left the neighbourhood.

Looking back, this was as close to a light bulb moment as I ever got. Reflecting on the incident now, young as I was, I think that was absolutely the point that made me pick a side and is one strong reason why I never became a career criminal. Even now, I hate to talk about the incident as it sounds so melodramatic, but I knew in my heart that that girl was full of hate and spite and had no empathy or remorse. She meant me real, probably fatal, harm and I have never forgotten what that felt like.

Compared to some of the awful crimes we read about, what happened to me was very minor. I have never really been overtly haunted by it and I don't ponder or dwell on these events as an adult. However, I now often think that what happened on that sunny day in Liverpool when I was a little girl almost certainly meant that I would grow up to be someone who tries to help other people. My path to security hasn't been straightforward, but, in the end, it's what my job is about, and I think my fate was decided on that afternoon in my childhood when I saw what some people are capable of.

After the kidnapping, and some increasingly nasty incidents with local bullies, Mum encouraged me to hang out with my extended family – especially two of my older male cousins and their friends – rather than only with the other kids in the neighbourhood. This was partly out of necessity, due to the shifts she worked, and partly because she wanted me to be more streetwise and not wander into a stranger's house because they offered me some juice.

My cousins, Jack and Adam, were as different in stature and temperament as you could imagine. Jack, the eldest, would have been just about fifteen and was jovial and restless in nature. Adam was a couple of years younger, annoyingly clever and quiet and intense. They were friends as well as brothers, and for the most part looked after themselves very well with limited input from their parents who both worked shifts.

Mum hoped that the boys would teach me to be more careful when I was out and about. They lived just about near enough for me to go and stay fairly often, and they had lots of friends with younger siblings I would enjoy hanging out with. They would look after me and she expected that I would be less vulnerable in a larger group, so I was put on the bus and sent to their house on a regular basis.

I would often stay over for a couple of nights at weekends and during the school holidays. The boys would meet me at the bus stop, let me hang out with them and look after me, taking me with them on their adventures, including their main hobby of what has come to be known as 'urban exploration' or the exploration of abandoned and restricted buildings.

At this time around Liverpool there were lots of empty buildings from the prosperous years of the city's past. Many once grand and beautiful sites, some now restored and in use once again, were abandoned and desolate during the 1970s and '80s.

We visited empty banks and abandoned psychiatric hospitals and houses that were nothing but shells of what they once had been. Decrepit factories and abandoned shopping centres, disused offices and blocked-up tunnels, as well as many parks, bowling greens, community halls and school buildings. If it was empty, it was fair game.

Tagging along behind them, I thought all of this was normal. I knew my friends didn't do this as much as me, but plenty of them did similar things, and even today when I mention my childhood urban exploration when giving keynotes, many people come up to me and tell me they did the same thing as kids. It seemed harmless enough at the time, especially considering I had chums who never went to school much and whose parents didn't even feed them most of the time. What I was up to with the boys was nothing compared to some of the stuff many people I knew were getting up to to try to survive and occupy themselves at that time.

For the most part the boys were sensible and certainly looked out for me. This had been the case one weekend in late summer. I'd stayed the night before and was playing in the garden by myself when I saw the two of them sitting at the outside table and chatting conspiratorially. I wandered up and asked them what they were doing.

They said I should get ready for the bus back home but I got a bit whiney and asked if I could stay another night and they gave in and said they were just going to hang around the arcades and fairground for a while with their mates that night, and that I could tag along if I wasn't a nuisance.

Ooh, the fair, I thought, *what fun this is going to be, a visit to the fair! At night!* Then something occurred to me. I ran down to Jack.

'Jack, Jack, can we go to the zoo as well? Please?'

'Closed Jen, it will be late, remember.'

'Let's go anyway,' I said. 'Let's jump over the fence and go and see the animals.'

This might sound strange, but it wasn't such a stretch.

I'd seen them climb fences many times to avoid paying to get in. They had 'bunked in' to any number of destinations and events that we had attended and passed me over the walls or fences or gates if I had been with them. I'd already been to various circuses and village fetes, music gigs and gatherings without anyone ever paying and I only realised later that when they told me it was a 'free concert' they were probably lying and that purchasing a ticket was the normal thing to do.

It was no real surprise that I wanted to visit the zoo because I was quietly, but rather annoyingly, obsessed with lions. I had visited the site just weeks previously with my parents and had spent an extended period observing the lion enclosure. I had been particularly taken with the large male and had talked about the visit, and especially the lions, ever since, consuming books, films and television programmes about big cats whenever I could.

And so it came to pass that a couple of hours later I found myself being passed over a flimsy wooden fence into a tatty-looking, litter-ridden flower bed somewhere in the grounds of Southport Zoo. Remarkable to consider now, but the site seemed to have no security whatsoever. There were no apparent cameras, alarms or guards at all as far as I can remember.

We really did just climb over the fence and drop down directly into the zoo grounds, my little red sandals sinking into the flower bed as I watched the boys drink from cans of cider and wander down a side path and out of sight, glancing back at me only briefly as they disappeared.

Young as I was, I don't remember being anxious, instead feeling the now familiar exhilaration that accompanies any infiltration task or covert mission into a site. There is a jittery nervous energy that comes not just from the fact that you are in a forbidden place and liable to be caught and stopped at any point, but from the new perspective any illicit entry gives.

When you have gained access to somewhere you are not supposed to be, you are forced to see things differently, to listen and observe more attentively. Of necessity you are more alert, and things that normally don't matter or even apply in the light of day absolutely do apply and matter in the murky reality of covert entry. You have to discipline your imagination and control your fear, improvise, when necessary, make decisions on your feet and continuously adapt to changing circumstances and environmental factors while also staying alert to being detected and caught yourself.

While that night in the zoo was in many ways a harmless childish jaunt, it is the first time I really remember being inside a facility without permission. The heightened sense of purpose and urgency, all of my senses sharpened and body and mind on a sort of high alert, is something that has never left me, even now after forty years doing the job and breaking into hundreds of different sites.

For me then, and ever since, it is the focus required on a job that is so intoxicating, the need to block out distractions and single-mindedly pursue a goal. Every infiltration is a unique challenge, a puzzle to solve, a set of obstacles to overcome. But normal rules don't apply: you are operating apart from every-one else and moral and ethical lines are blurred.

I felt it strongly that first time in the zoo, standing on my own and taking in my surroundings, that there was a separation from normal life and routine, a freedom to act outside the rules and an excitement that comes with danger that you chose for yourself. Only a few weeks before I had been half-paralysed with fear and helplessness in the neighbour's house; by contrast, this sense of control, of choice, however reckless, was potent and very welcome.

I took a moment to get my bearings, looking around and let-ting my eyes grow accustomed to the fading evening light and thinking about what I had to do next. The lion, always referred to as 'Caesar' in my mind, was a full-grown African male and was kept, along with two lionesses, in a cage made of what looked like very flimsy chicken wire at the centre of the site. The place was not large and its simple layout was familiar to me, with the smaller cages at the back of the site and the large glass chimp enclosure somewhere behind me near the front entrance.

I knew roughly where I was headed and set off down a little path towards the centrepiece of the facility. I reached into my pocket and grabbed my torch, a red plastic *Sesame Street* toy which gave almost no light at all. I shook it a bit, the flimsy components rattling on the inside, and a faint light flickered on as I padded slowly towards the centre of the zoo where Caesar's cage was located. After only a couple of minutes I could see the cage directly in front of me, exactly as I remembered it from the family visit. By this time my eyes had grown accustomed to the fading light, and I could make out a couple of dark objects lying on the floor of the enclosure.

I fumbled with the torch, pointing its beam in the direc-tion of the cage, but it was barely bright enough to illuminate the flower beds that had been planted just outside the wire. I walked closer and ducked under the ornamental wooden fence that formed the last barrier between the viewing public and the cage itself, trying not to stand on the plants in the flower beds as I got closer to the wire.

Grasping the wire with my left hand, I pressed my face against the wire and poked the torch a few inches through a gap. Squinting, I could just make out the shape of a couple of huge logs, tree trunks really, that had been placed in the centre of the cage. I pressed my face harder against the wire, my eyes scanning the far corners of the cage for any further evidence of its occupants. Empty. Disappointed, I shook the torch again and turned my head around to listen for Jack and Adam, but I couldn't hear them anymore. Resigned, I decided to go and find them. I took a step back, let go of the fence and turned my head back to take one final look in the cage.

There, just inches in front of my own face, was Caesar. He had crept up on me, silently stalked me from within his enclosure, his huge head and body now directly in front of me on the other side of the wire.

At that point, everything happened at once, I felt the heat of his body and smelt his chicken soup breath warm on my face as I let out a loud scream. Dropping the torch, I fell backwards as he stood on his hind legs and threw his entire bulk against the wire, which buckled forward with the force of the blow. With deafening growls and roars, Caesar clawed and bit at the fence in a frenzy, as I stumbled to my feet and screamed again. Jack and Adam appeared and grabbed me, pulling me out of the flower beds and under the fence, then dragging me to my feet and pulling me with them and running towards the entrance. They were laughing, and saying 'Oh shit. *Oh shit!*' through the gasping breaths.

The other occupants of the zoo followed Caesar's lead and a cacophony of noise enveloped us. We could hear the two lionesses adding to the roaring, chimps and monkeys whooping alarm calls, horses whinnying, the banging of many, many cage doors, what sounded like parrots screaming and a chorus of dogs barking from apparently every direction.

I don't remember climbing the fence, I was probably half flung over like before. I do remember Jack picking me up and carrying me on the other side as we crossed the road beyond, because my legs had turned half to jelly and I thought I might wee myself, and we needed to get out of there. From the entrance we turned right, ran across a couple more roads, climbed over a wall, down some steps, before finally dropping down onto the beachfront and pressing ourselves against the wall.

Things were never the same after that. I'd had a narrow escape of course, but once I was out of immediate danger I could only think of the experience in positive terms. I'd come close to being wiped out, to being killed and I'd got away with it. I'd seen my lion up close, and he hadn't caught me, and, importantly, I had given the cousins a night to remember.

We gradually caught our breath. The boys looked at me: 'You OK, Jens?'

I stared at them both and put my finger to my lips: 'Ssh! Listen . . .' I whispered. 'I can still hear him!'

Carried on the wind of the night air you could still hear the animals, especially Caesar, roaring in anger. A visceral sound designed to terrify and carry for miles if the conditions were right, and one that a caged animal likely doesn't feel motivated to make very often. Yet, on that still summer night in Southport the conditions allowed that roar to carry over the sounds of the fairground, across the shabby seaside town and onto the beach. Caesar, for once in his miserable captive life, really showed the power of what he might have been, had he not been confined in a chicken wire cage in a zoo. The noise was otherworldly, primal in its anger, and it went on for as long as we listened.

I grinned at Jack. 'That was brilliant. Can we do it again? Can I pee now?'

3

THE DAISY CHALLENGE

The sheer thrill of what had happened at the zoo never left me, and I became a nuisance asking to stay over at the cousins' more often and asking them if I could tag along. They tolerated me to a point, but I didn't go as often as I would have liked, and so learnt to improvise and create my own fun, looking to regain the excitement of my encounter with the lion.

Not long after the zoo incident I'd been caught short while out playing alone. Desperate for a pee and some way from home, I'd decided to pop into a random house near the little car park I was playing in, to use the bathroom. The house wasn't entirely unknown to me; in fact, one of the kids I saw regularly playing out lived there, although I didn't know her name. The front door had been open and, rather than knocking, explaining the situation and asking permission to use the facilities, I simply crept in through the open front door, dashed up the stairs and went straight into the bathroom at the top. I locked the door and emptied my bladder as quickly as I could.

Just as I was about to open the door and leave, I heard footsteps coming up the stairs and walking past the bathroom. I waited and listened, holding my breath. I pressed my ear up to the door but couldn't hear anything, so I lay down and tried to look under the gap beneath the door, but I couldn't see anything. Eventually, I stood up again, quietly turned the door handle and carefully peered out.

To my right, on the landing only about two metres away from me, stood a man with his back to me. He must have been the father of the girl I had seen going in and out of the house. He was staring at a ceiling hatch, hands on hips and muttering quietly to himself. I pushed the door open further and crept out, padding down the stairs but accelerating all the way and dashed out of the still-open front door. I ran around the back of their house, which was on a corner, and away down the street, keeping going until I was at the wasteland at the bottom. I caught my breath and looked back behind me for the first time. Nothing. So, I just carried on with my day and never gave it a second thought.

I never told anyone about this first time, but held it deliciously secret inside my own memory. It was so funny to me that I could do that and nobody else knew. I remember telling baffled friends in school that I was 'already invisible' and giggling to myself because only I knew what I meant. Subsequently, I repeated the exercise many times, in dozens of houses in and around where I lived. Eventually, I couldn't resist telling my friends about my little hobby and daring them to do it too. Before too long there was a bunch of us at it, trying houses further afield, the 'needing a pee' line becoming a back-up of sorts in case we ever got caught.

After a while I decided we should add another element to the dare, and I invented the 'daisy challenge' to up the stakes a little.

The challenge consisted of picking a flower, often a daisy from the various scraps of tatty grass in the neighbourhood, or, and I am ashamed to say this, from someone's front garden, running into a house and leaving it on a pillow in one of the bedrooms. This added another element to the game, keeping score and competing for who had done the most, or how many we could try in one morning. I remember running into dozens of houses, and leaving flowers on pillows, in coffee mugs, on stairs, in toilet bowls and sometimes even in the pockets of clothing hanging on washing lines.

We were nothing if not prolific, and if you left your front door open, which surprisingly given the crime levels most people did, I would likely pay you a visit and leave you a flower. That was the daisy challenge, and it was addictive.

Now, before you judge me, remember that we were still only just about ten years old at this point, and we had a strict rule that you weren't allowed to steal anything at all. This was a red line for me, real burglary was rife at the time, and I saw the damage it could cause to someone's sense of security. My parents would have absolutely killed me if I had ever taken anything that didn't belong to me. You can't nick anything was the biggest rule, so I passed it on, and the challenge remained a strictly no-theft game. The thrill of sneaking unseen into people's houses, and the many, many times we almost got caught, gave me a feeling something close to what I had felt at the zoo. Sooner or later, though, the novelty was bound to wear off and almost inevitably I began to look for other ways to kill time and create excitement.

It was during the first summer of high school, when I was twelve, that my breaking-and-entering habit got more serious and I found myself on the lookout for a target building that we might try to sneak or climb into.

Like many teenagers, I was fascinated by the dark side of things, and had begun reading widely about the occult, listening to increasingly rebellious and heavy rock music, and was generally enamoured with all things gothic. On my daily journey to high school, I passed a local funeral parlour, housed in a striking building that had survived the Blitz. I was taken by its sombre façade and naively fascinated by the rituals that lay within. Over the course of a few months, my interest turned into mild fascination which got gradually stronger until eventually I decided I wanted to get inside and look around to see a body.

When I tell this story as part of a keynote, I always say it was a bit like the movie *Stand By Me*. When you are a kid, you *think* you want to see a body. The truth is that when this happens and you really do see one, it is not at all what you expect, and, as I was about to find out, you tend to change your mind.

I got a couple of my friends together and told them the plan. I had been observing the building for some time, and there was a series of metal roller service doors at the side of the building that were raised and closed as 'deliveries' were made and hearses left. Beyond the doors I had seen a sort of yard where there was an unloading area. I hadn't been able to see what lay beyond that, but I suspected the vehicles backed right up to an internal door as once the drivers got out, they seemed to vanish completely for a while and, despite my spending a lot of time watching from across the road, I'd never seen them loading or unloading anything. The loading area itself had many cupboards, bins and canisters lining the walls; it was cavernous and would provide lots of places to hide.

I explained my plan to the others, suggesting we wait nearby until it was getting dark, sneak in behind one of the delivery vans, then hide inside the loading area until the employees had all gone home. Then we would see if we could find where they kept the corpses inside the building, have a quick look and then raise one of the shutter doors just enough to roll under, and leave. It was a terrible plan and only one of my pals was at all interested in coming along.

The lack of enthusiasm from my friends was a tad disappointing, but I knew if I waited and asked my cousins, the boys would do it. Sure enough, after a while when Jack and Adam were staying at my house one weekend, I told them what I wanted to do, and they agreed, although Adam was more enthusiastic than Jack, who was fully grown by now and I think was mostly just looking out for me. The job was set for Saturday evening; we would keep lookout all afternoon and, if a delivery came, we would be in. We agreed to take a quick look, touch absolutely nothing, then quickly and quietly leave through the roller shutter doors. Jack was working later in a bar in Liverpool, so we would have to be quick and then he could catch the train into the city and do his shift at the bar.

We'd be half an hour tops, and it would liven up a Saturday night. Sorted.

It wasn't easy to keep a watch on the doors. The funeral parlour was on a residential street, and so we had to keep circling to keep an eye out for deliveries as there was no bus stop or bench nearby to linger on unnoticed. Eventually, at about four o'clock, we saw a black van turn the corner of the road and drive quickly up to the loading bay doors. It came to a halt and did a quick manoeuvre so it could back up through the shutters and into the loading bay. The doors lifted and the van backed up at some speed into the gloom beyond, he wasn't hanging around.

The doors started to lower, and we realised this was our chance, we ran over to the entrance and lined up on either side with our backs to the wall. Adam, myself and the one mate who had not chickened out of joining us lined up on one side and Jack pressed his back to the wall on the other. Jack peered into the bay and then nodded to us. We crept into the gloom.

There was no sign of the driver, but the van was backed up to what I could now see was a large double door that led into the interior of the building, fitting neatly into the space beyond. We could hear clanking and movement as they unloaded whatever was in the back of the van, but no one seemed to be speaking. Looking around I saw a large green skip and some garden chairs pushed up to the side of the wall, and I shuffled over and crouched down behind the skip with my friend. I'd lost Jack and Adam, but I had long ago learnt not to worry about either of them in situations like this. After a few minutes, the driver got back into the van, slammed the door, and drove out as the shutters raised with none of us being seen. A few seconds after that, Jack's face appeared around the side of the skip. 'Stay down,' he hissed, and padded away.

It was cold and uncomfortable behind the skip, and it seemed a very long time until we heard a low whistle, and I poked my head over the top. Jack and Adam were on the other side of the bay, beginning to stand up in between a pile of black bin bags. I grinned and gave them a thumbs up and was about to step out from behind the skip when the two interior doors suddenly crashed open and yellow light swamped the bay. I ducked back down and held my breath as two male employees walked into the bay, chatting about the day's football and heading to the pub for a pint.

They walked over to the bay doors and pushed a large button on the wall. The shutters raised again, and they clicked some switches on the wall, dimming the interior light beyond the double doors to a faint glow. Pressing the button again, the shutter reversed and began to close, and they ducked underneath and stood just beyond in the street until the doors clanged shut. We heard the jangling of keys, and the metallic rattling of what sounded like chains, before the noise stopped and their voices grew faint as they walked off towards the pub.

After a minute or two, Adam said: 'That's it, they've gone. The doors are open.'

I walked out from behind the skip, my chum just behind me, and joined my cousins standing in the middle of the bay, their faces illuminated by the dim light in the building beyond. 'They didn't just lock us in, did they, Jack?' I asked.

'Nope.'

'OK,' I said, looking directly at him, but he turned and followed Adam who was already through the doors and into the gloomy interior. I looked to my friend who shrugged and so we followed them inside.

There was a corridor with a couple of doors on either side, branching into an open office area at the end. It smelt strongly of pine disinfectant. Suddenly a wave of nerves hit me and seeing a bathroom sign on one of the doors up ahead, I bolted off and dived towards it. 'I'll only be a second,' I muttered as I went and lunged inside the tiny cubicle. I knelt on the floor and put my head over the bowl, but I didn't vomit. I sat back on the floor feeling dizzy and hot. My mouth was extremely dry, my legs were shaking, and it had all come over me so quickly. What the hell was wrong? It wasn't like me to bottle out like this. After a minute or so, I stood up and started to feel better. I splashed my face and opened the door. The three boys were all stood directly outside and were looking at me.

'I don't know,' I said. 'Thought I was going to throw up. This is not good, Jack; we shouldn't be here.'

'It was your idea.'

'Yes, well, it feels wrong.'

They smiled and disappeared around the corner at the end of the little corridor. I sighed and followed. It opened into a carpeted reception area with some armchairs and a wooden reception desk with artificial lilies on it, and a small coffee table next to the chairs. To the right there was a door signed 'Chapel of Rest'. Adam reached for the handle.

'*Don't!*' I said.

He didn't answer me and tried it anyway, but the handle wouldn't turn. Locked.

'Let's just go,' I whined and headed back out of the reception area. I decided that I'd leave anyway, on my own if necessary.

The whole thing felt disrespectful and wrong, and it felt like a burglary, which was never the intention. I started to think, perhaps for the first time with any great clarity, that should we be caught in the middle of doing this we would have no explanation for it. Also, I was worried about Jack. He was older now, no longer a juvenile; if he was caught, he would surely not just walk away. The potentially huge consequences had started to dawn on me. If we got caught it would be Jack that got the blame from the police and worse, from my dad, and it would be my fault.

'OK, Jens, we'll go,' I heard him say. 'I've got to get to work anyway.'

I sighed with relief and walked down the corridor, turning right at the little corner near the double doors. As I walked towards them, the boys ran past me and Adam stood in front of the doors, blocking the exit. 'But first, we have to do what we came for, Jen. We have to have a look in there.'

He gestured towards a door on the right of the corridor. I looked and there was a little brass sign that said 'Private. Mortuary Staff Only' screwed to the door. Ah.

'It'll be locked, like the other one,' I said.

'Try it.'

'You try it!'

'OK,' he said, and moved towards the door, but before I could bolt through the gap he had left in the double doors, I felt a firm grip on my shoulders.

'It was your idea, Jen,' Jack said. 'You're going in too.'

He had a point. I had put this little crew together, so there was no way I could back out of anything now. It was my idea and my responsibility. It was a hard lesson, but Jack was right. If I was going to put people into this type of situation, if I was going to ask people to take risks, then I had to own them myself. I couldn't back down now and let the others finish the job. If you were in, you were in all the way, especially if you were leading.

Adam grabbed the handle and looked up at me as he turned it. The door opened silently, and Jack pushed me and then my buddy into a darkened room. The place had an oily feel to it and the air was ripe with a strong chemical smell, what I could only place as nail varnish remover. It was cold and dark, and I skidded a little on the tiled floor as we went further in. Jack sniggered and I turned to pummel him and push his hands off my shoulder.

'You fucking idiot,' I said, but my voice died abruptly as I saw a table in the middle of the room, at about the same time as the boys saw it.

'Shit!' we said, virtually in unison.

The room was large, with tiled walls and high ceilings. There were steel pipes snaking up the walls, but no ornamental details or features, only a couple of barred windows set high up on the walls near the ceiling. Standing in the middle of the sloping floor, about two metres in front of us, was a rectangular metal table with something large and human shaped lying under a green canvas sheet, bars of light from the windows casting shadows over its bulk.

'It's supposed to be in a fridge,' my mate said. 'I've seen it on TV, it's not meant to be just lying there.'

We were quiet for a second and then I turned towards the door. Jack stopped me.

'A quick look, Jen. You can't just go. It was your idea. We are your crew tonight, it's your job.'

'It's not my job, you are not my crew. It's your crew, Jack; it's always been your crew. I'm not in charge, you are, I don't like it.'

But I knew he was right and despite my protests he steered me firmly closer to the table while Adam did the same to my friend who was also now apparently having second thoughts. We skidded a little as we got within touching distance of the table and I noticed that the floor sloped gently downwards. There was some guttering leading to a metal drain directly underneath the table, and I realised with horror that we were standing in what was basically a giant sink.

I stopped and folded my arms. Jack stopped pushing me, but he held on tight with his arms around my chest. My mate now seemed happy enough, perhaps overcome with ghoulish curiosity, so Adam let him go and stepped slowly away and moved towards the table at the centre of the room.

He looked at Jack and nodded and then, without a moment's hesitation, approached the table and pulled the sheet away in a single fluid movement, dropping it onto the floor.

Lying on the table was the body of a man in perhaps his late forties. He was completely naked, and his eyes were open, he had curly dark hair and his hands were in a stiff pose as if he was gripping the handles of a bike. There were black, green and purple bruises all over his body, and his knees were slightly bent, as if he had died perched on top of a bar stool.

We were quiet for a while, then I turned and buried my

face in Jack's chest, and Adam covered the guy up again, and I whined, 'OK. We are done. We've done it; let's go. Please, let's go.'

Jack's grip on me loosened to a hug and we all shuffled towards the door. He reached for the handle and pulled, but the door didn't open. He took his arms from around me and tried again. Nothing. He pulled and pushed with all his might, Adam running over to help but nothing. It was locked. Then, all I remember was shouting, screaming even, pandemonium for a couple of minutes while the realisation slowly dawned that we were stuck in this room.

'Adam, force the lock,' I said, but there was nothing we could have used to do it in the room. There were metal cupboards, but they were heavy-duty industrial models firmly closed and heavily padlocked. Jack looked up to the windows, but the room was huge, those windows were at least three metres high, and all barred.

I was at the cupboards, looking underneath to see if we could tip them over, ignore the locks and bust them open from the back to get at the contents and find something that might help. Jack was trying to climb up the bare walls and reach the bars on the window, while my little mate, on his first 'rodeo', was still desperately pulling at the door, but there was nothing we could use and nothing we could do.

We were stuck there for a couple of hours. Sitting in silence, pacing the room, climbing up to the windows, trying to open or stand on the cupboards, and pulling at the door repeatedly. It was no use; we were basically in a cell. A huge, sterile sink-shaped cell, with a naked dead guy. It was far from ideal.

Finally, Adam looked up. 'I need a lever; find me a lever.'

I looked at Adam, and then at Jack, and almost at the same time we had the same idea. Adam went over to the table and slid on his back underneath, the green sheet flapping as he passed under it. 'We need to unscrew these table legs and then I can lever the door open from underneath or force the bars on that window. Jack, you can stand on this table.'

'But what about the man?' I said.

'He can lie down over there.'

I suddenly felt hot again and the tears welled up, my legs went wobbly, and I folded down. My mate, though, was fine, and seemed to be enjoying himself. 'I'll lift him,' he said. 'We can lay him down over there, he won't get cold. Ha-ha.'

No one else laughed and I put my head between my legs. I heard the boys walk over and the sound of the sheet hitting the floor. One of them made a whimper and then there was a short nervous laugh. 'OK,' said Jack. 'For fuck's sake let's just do this . . .'

'No! Stop!' I interrupted them. 'Roll him onto the sheet.'

'Good idea, Jens. Use the sheet, tuck it under him, and then we can do a "shake the bed" thing and carry him down.'

They were hesitant, though, and were circling the table looking for the best way to do it, when I thought I heard something. 'Wait! Did you hear that?'

'What?'

And then we all heard it, the unmistakable sound of the shutter doors lifting in the bay beyond the corridor.

'They'll be coming to put him in a fridge,' my mate said with a note of slight hysteria in his voice. 'I told ya. Didn't I tell ya? I saw it on the telly, right; they don't leave these dead people on tables. There is like a big fridge, right, and it's got like sort of sliding drawers . . .' (he mimed a closing motion).

'Mate! Shut the fuck up right now!' said Jack in his most menacing voice, and the kid stopped mid-sentence but continued to mime a 'closing drawer' movement with both hands.

Jack beckoned us all over to the door. 'When that door opens, we have one chance. Scream, shout and wave your arms, dive straight for the shutters, and run. Head for the railway bridge. We've got one shot; I'll push him out of the way. Make noise. Ready?'

We all nodded.

Sure enough, after a couple of seconds we saw the handle on the door bend down and it opened, flooding the room with fluorescent light. The poor bloke must have had the worst fright as Jack pushed him flat against the wall, and we all started screaming as we ran past him, through the doors, and ducking under the loading bay shutters and out into the road.

The railway bridge was about five minutes away, and a quiet covered place. Me and my friend arrived first, with Adam following closely behind, and after a few seconds we heard Jack's footsteps running to join us. He came up to me and smiled, gasping: 'Great plan, Jen. I'm late for work!' He glanced at Adam and jogged off towards the train station and on into work. He was hours late for his shift but no doubt he would think of something.

My chum had got his breath back and looked at Adam. 'That was awesome,' he grinned, punching the air and trying to high five Adam who just looked at his hand. 'Can I come next time, mate?'

Adam looked at him without saying anything, and the kid grinned again before jogging off into the night.

I looked at Adam who was frowning at me. 'I get it. I won't ask him again.'

When we got home, we told Mum we had been at a friend's house and had lost track of time. She wasn't happy or particularly sold on the story, but she let it go, told us off for being so late and we went straight to bed.

I didn't sleep at first partly due to the excitement but mostly because I felt guilty for having brought my cousins and my friend on a job that had gone so badly wrong. We had managed to get away in the end, but it had been a stupid idea and the consequences of being caught were very serious, especially for Jack. Taking my mate along had also been a bad idea. He had never even been inside an abandoned building before, let alone one still in use and it wasn't as if it was a normal office or shop either. I had added an unknown entity to the crew and he had been, if not a liability exactly, rather less than helpful, enjoying the whole grisly experience far too much.

Lastly, and most importantly, Jack's words kept buzzing around my head: it was my idea, my job and my crew, and I nearly bailed on all of them. If I was going to bring people along with me, I had to take charge and show some leadership, even in the most stupid and fucked-up circumstances. At the very least I had to see it through until the end. I couldn't ask other people to do what I wasn't prepared to do myself. In the oddest of circumstances and for the stupidest of reasons, I'd failed my crew. I resolved not to let that happen again, even if it meant never attempting anything remotely similar in the future, but as I fell asleep, I already knew that there would almost certainly be a next time, preferably with a better exit plan in place.

I slept late into the next morning and when I woke up Adam had already left for home. Mum asked me to strip the linen from the spare bed so it could be washed. I found a white silk flower petal under Adam's pillow and put it in my jewellery box for safekeeping. I thought of the bloke on the table and once again felt guilty at the disrespect we had shown.

'Sorry, mate,' I said in my head, and then decided not to think too carefully about him ever again.

4

THE EIGHTH FLOOR

By the time I was fifteen we had moved from our old terraced house to an apartment on the fifth floor of a block of flats overlooking the River Mersey. My dad's health, never great, had faded dramatically, and he spent most days at home, enjoying watching the traffic come and go on the river, and doing the occasional driving job for weddings and funerals in the area.

I was a good student and spent many hours studying in my room and reading, in between working in various cafés, bars and shops to earn some cash. Never one to keep conventional working hours, I would often sit at my bedroom window through the night, working and enjoying the city skyline.

Not far from our flat, directly opposite my bedroom window, was a huge and ugly 1970s high-rise office building, about thirteen floors high. It was busy all day with government workers sitting at desks, having meetings, and generally walking about doing whatever administration tasks they were assigned. Dad had decent binoculars for the ships and I would sometimes use them to look into the building, watching the workers as they went about their day. I had a great view directly into the offices, and I soon got to recognise individual people whom I took to mentally naming.

There was one, 'Lonely Guy', who rarely moved from his desk. He ate his lunch at 11.45 every single day, from what looked like a children's lunch box of bright blue plastic. He left at exactly five o'clock every night and caught the number 81 bus to Aigburth from the bus stop outside the building about six minutes later. He didn't work on Wednesdays, and when he was away, people often gathered near his desk, sat on it even and chatted and laughed as a group. When he was there, though, he rarely got visitors and I almost never saw anyone interacting with him. I felt a bit sorry for him, and assumed he was some sort of weirdo or at least unpopular for some reason, creating a back story for him and his colleagues.

There were others. 'Bad Manager' was so named because I often saw her with hands on hips, apparently shouting at other people. I saw her most often, moving around on the tenth floor, easy to spot in brightly coloured cardigans and never standing still. I couldn't be certain, but I thought I'd seen more than one person making rude gestures behind her back as she walked away from them.

There was 'Cricket Man', 'Miss Model', 'Cocky Boss' and numerous others I only idly observed over time. My desk was at the window, so watching was easy and broke up my studies. In time, I took to keeping Dad's second-best binoculars on my desk, so I had them handy when I stopped working for a moment and could look up and watch what was going on over the road. I watched the tea ladies with trolleys looping around the corridors, and opening windows on the landings as they did their rounds. I watched the cleaners potter around after office hours, leaning out of the landing windows smoking, vacuuming, emptying bins. It was amusing for me to think that none of them realised they were being observed like this, and it became a daily distraction from my increasingly intense studies as my exam dates drew nearer.

It was also, as it turned out, good practice for many hours of surveillance later in life preparing for infiltration work. I would spend hours observing patterns of behaviour, relationships between employees and which rules and procedures were overlooked and by whom.

I'd been watching the place for months when one day Dad walked into my room with a cup of tea and saw me looking through his binoculars at the building beyond. 'Are you still spying on those people?' he asked as he passed me the drink. I confirmed that yes, I was in fact still spying on them, and I mentioned that it was a very busy place.

'Yup, except for that eighth floor,' he said. 'Always dark, always quiet.'

And then he left.

I grabbed the binoculars and looked at the building. He was right. It wasn't that I hadn't noticed it before, but it hadn't really registered with me. The eighth floor of the building, now I thought about it, *was* always quiet, and in fact, looking at it now, it was always dark as well. I swept the binoculars around; I could just about see into most of the upper floors quite well and could clearly make out people moving about the offices. The trees and houses in between our flat and the office block obscured the lower floors, but all the visible floors were bustling and busy, except for the eighth floor, which was in darkness now, and had some sort of covering over the windows.

I lowered the binoculars and sipped my tea. Weird.

Over the next couple of weeks I continued my spying, watching the eighth floor particularly, and more frequently, for long periods and at all hours of the day and night. I started to make a few notes, following the security guards doing the rounds at night, noting the times and the shifts. I'd watch them get out of the lift on the seventh floor at around midnight. They would do a circuit of the office space, look in and around a few desks and then go back to the corridor. They disappeared for a few minutes and then I would catch them doing the same round on floor nine and then all the rest in turn. Never visible on the eighth.

After a few weeks of observations, I was certain that the floor was not in use, and I found myself frequently speculating on what might be the reason. Although the windows were covered, and I couldn't really see inside, I was soon convinced that no one ever used that floor. No cleaners having a crafty fag out of the windows, no security patrol, and no staff. Why, I wondered, would the windows be covered when no other floor had the same thing? It seemed to be a dead space, a no-go zone, and I wanted to know why. After a while, I could stand the mystery no longer and I decided to find out, reasoning that the best way to do that would be to break into the building at night and take a look for myself.

I didn't consider for more than a moment that I could have simply called the council offices to try to find out. I presumed that they either wouldn't have told me or might think I was some sort of oddball and I'd get myself into trouble. It seemed more logical to me to just go and look. I think that even if this had happened years later and the internet had been available for this type of research, I probably would still have gone and found out in person. I think I was always going to go and look; by now it was a large part of the person I was turning out to be.

I went out for a walk to break up the study one Sunday after-noon, and I wandered down to the building and did a circuit of the perimeter. At the back of the building, hidden from the road, I sat down on a low wall in a small car park and stared at the building. There were some large glass doors with 'Staff Entrance' and a service hatch next to them. I went past and had a little look inside. I walked around to the front of the building and stood at the bus stop outside, turning so I could stare at the front entrance.

I could make out a desk, but after twenty minutes or so of waiting as mystified bus drivers shook their heads at me and drove past, I decided that there were no guards on duty that day. Later, though, back at my desk, through the binoculars I saw one doing his round at about nine o'clock. The lighting flashed on as he entered the different offices and did his checks, flashing off again a few minutes later as he left and moved to the next floor.

Eighth floor. No lights, no guard. Nothing.

Next day, as I was heading home from school, I thought that I would go and have a look around again later that night and maybe get in and see what I could see. 'Tonight's the night.'

I got caught up in homework after dinner, but I kept an eye on the building, which was emptying as usual. I noticed there were still a few people bustling around after hours. This happened now and again. Sometimes teams did stay later for work reasons presumably, or the occasional office party. I weighed it up in my mind and decided to try. Whatever the occasion was, people hanging around after hours and breaking the pattern seemed like it might create an opportunity for me. I decided to give it a go; I checked my watch and it was 9.30.

I went to my wardrobe and pulled on a jumper and some trainers and grabbed my rucksack. I told my dad I was going to meet my friend and that I would be staying at her place that night. He told me to ring when I got there safely, and I gave him a kiss and headed out. It took me five minutes to walk towards the building and stand at the bus stop facing the front door and look at the reception. I could clearly see a security guard sat at the front desk watching a small portable TV and reading a newspaper with his feet up on the desk. Otherwise, it was quiet.

Right there and then I knew this wouldn't be too difficult. I walked straight in through the front door and over to the lift. I shouted over to him: 'I'm here for the assessment, mate.' He didn't so much as look up. I stood in front of the lift and looked for a button with the number eight on it, but the numbers went from seven straight to nine! *The plot thickens,* I thought.

Rather than stand there for any amount of time looking, I glanced around to see if there were any stairs as they were likely to be quieter than the lifts anyway. To the right of the lift doors at the end of the corridor there was a door with a 'FIRE ESCAPE' sign on it, a likely suspect. I glanced back at the desk, but the guard hadn't changed his position and had his back to me, so I walked over and opened the door, and sure enough there were the stairs. I closed the door behind me softly and walked over; glancing up, I could see the stairs winding upwards higher and higher towards the top of the building.

I started to climb quickly up the stairs, passing floor after floor, each with a single door with the corresponding number painted in large red letters on the outside. I scooted past floors one to six, but on the seventh floor I paused and pushed open the door a crack and peered around. I needed a back-up plan in case of emergency and I just wanted to check what was behind the doors before I got to my destination. Through the door was a featureless narrow landing area with the two lift doors directly in front of me, while to the left were the landing windows that the tea ladies used to smoke out of and through which I watched the cleaners and guards walking around the building.

I glanced out for a second to the view beyond and could see my own block of flats through the glass. I could have walked over and looked for my own bedroom from those windows, as easily as I had been watching the workers in the building I was currently infiltrating.

I closed the door and took a deep breath. I walked up the next flight of stairs and found myself standing outside the door that led onto the eighth floor. Immediately it felt different, although the stairs were the same, the door leading to the lifts and giving access to the floor was different. Whereas the other floors had standard fire doors with the floor number on them and a glass viewing panel at the top, this door was heavy duty with a large 'NO ENTRY' sign at the top, and a lockable handle.

I paused, looking at the door, when suddenly somewhere higher up on the staircase I heard a door slam and a couple of voices chatting as footsteps echoed down the stairs in my direction. There was nowhere to hide so I gave the door a little push, expecting resistance, and prepared myself to sneak down to the next floor and hide just inside door seven outside the lifts.

To my surprise the door moved inwards slightly with the pressure of my hand. I gasped in disbelief and pulled the handle down, pushed a bit harder and the door opened wider letting out a creak and raining a scattering of rust onto my trainers and over the floor. It was dark beyond, but the voices were getting closer, maybe three floors above me and moving in my direction, so I sloped quietly through the gap and into the gloom, grabbing the handle on the inside of the door and pulling it back a bit so the door wouldn't swing shut with a slam.

On the other side I was in darkness, and the smell of damp and stale air hit me straight away, along with a considerable temperature drop. I didn't look around at first but crouched down behind the door holding the handle and waiting, listening for the two people I had heard above me to walk past. I waited for a minute or two but heard nothing more of them. Figuring they must have only been changing floors, I put a pencil from my bag into the gap at the bottom of the door, preventing it from closing entirely, and turned around.

Although it was very dark in there, the wait behind the door had accustomed my eyes to the darkness, and I could see I was standing in a landing area, like on the other floors but with no lifts. As with all the other floors there was a single large window, this time wide open, on the wall to my left, and another door to my right. It too was open revealing another, bigger space beyond.

I quickly approached the door and stepped inside and tripped up a couple of metal steps, like those you might see on a fire escape. They led to a metal walkway extending the length of the building to both my left and right leaving a gap measuring about a foot from the external wall all around. The room had no lights, but I could see impressive views of the surrounding skyline through many windows, with street lighting from out-side below casting quite a glow inside. There were no blinds on the windows, as I had thought, but I noticed they had a black film covering on them which was likely why I couldn't see inside from my vantage point in the bedroom.

The interior of the floor was made up of a block of wooden box-like structures, painted a grubby white, with small win-dows every few paces. From the walkway you could do a complete circuit of the building with the exterior walls on one side, and these temporary wooden office structures on the other in the centre of the floor. There were dark gaps on either side of the walkway, which was only a few paces wide; if you lost your footing, you would fall at least six feet down by my estimation onto what must have been the ceiling of the seventh floor. Now and again little pathways shot from the runway to the exterior of the wooden structures in front of the windows.

I walked quickly along a couple of them and peered through

several windows, but I couldn't make out what was inside. I kept going, following the circuit around the outside of the structure, and tried another little offshoot path that led to a door. I walked up hopefully but when I tried the handle it was locked, so I continued forwards on the walkway to the next corner and stopped again. The view was amazing, I could pick out the entire Liverpool skyline, the Liver Building, the cathedrals and the docks, the Radio City tower and even Anfield, Liverpool Football Club's home ground, a view you couldn't see from our flat – much to Dad's annoyance.

I went back a few paces and stood for a second looking through the covered windows at my own apartment block, clearly visible over the trees and houses in between. I counted down the floors from the roof and picked out my own room, in darkness, and almost directly opposite me over the tops of the houses. I hoped Dad wasn't watching the building right now, as he might see me in the corridors when I had to run down and would be interested to know what the hell I was up to.

As I kept going, the thought occurred to me that I was on the long-pondered eighth floor and that it really *was* a dummy floor, and I was about to uncover its secrets. I stopped in front of another door and gave it a small push. It didn't move, but I noticed it had a glass viewing panel at the top. Peering through on my tiptoes, I could see some small green lights flickering beyond it on an electric panel box on a wall, beyond which was a large black shape.

I squinted and tried to make out what I was looking at, and as I did so I became aware of a dripping noise not far from me, I looked up and a watery mucus-like substance landed on my face. A 'snotsicle', in the slang of urban explorers. You usually only find these dirty, rusty, slimy drippers in tunnels and sewers, or rather they find you. I retched and rubbed my face with my sleeve and then pushed out at the door harder and more quickly; this was weird and felt uncomfortable, and now, most importantly, it was also disgusting. It was losing its appeal.

The door stayed put and I decided to leave, but as I turned, I jerked to the left to avoid another snotsicle drip and grabbed the handle. The door opened outwards as I pulled it, and I had stepped back but, recovering my balance, I could now move forward into the interior of the room and onto a narrow metal walkway. The pale light from beyond the door didn't help me see very much, but I could hear more dripping and feel a distant, guttural hum within the room.

Standing still and taking care not to slip, I reached into my backpack and found my torch on its cord. Placing it around my neck, I switched it on and pointed it forwards. The torch illuminated a dozen or so huge metal cylinders, about eight metres in circumference and reaching all the way up to the ceiling, lined up in the interior of the vast space before me. I was looking at a series of giant tanks that seemed to be somehow suspended from the ceiling above me.

I reached out and touched the nearest one with the back of my hand. It was icy cold, so much so that at first, I thought it was hot and I had been burnt. I pulled my hand away quickly and it had stuck to the metal side a little, like when you lick an ice cube. I could see a mark where I had touched the tank and saw that everything was covered in a heavy layer of dust. I became conscious of the fact I was breathing heavily, and there was a metallic taste, somewhere between blood and battery acid, on the end of my tongue. I turned away from the tank towards the door and decided to get out of there.

Mystery solved. Sort of.

I went out through the door and padded around the walkway

back to the main door and out onto the landing. I walked over to the window and had a last quick look for our flat, warm and inviting. I stared hard, looking to see if I could see Dad's light on in his room or people moving about. I stood for a while picking out various neighbours and counting the floors before I heard the unmistakable sound of an elevator clanking and getting increasingly closer. A light appeared above the door of the service elevator and then fluorescent lights above me snapped and fizzed into life; after the murky gloom of the interior, it was painfully bright and it jarred me into action.

I poked my head out, listened for footsteps and when I heard nothing took a step outside, looking up and down the staircases as I walked slowly and then ran faster downwards. My heart was racing, and I was feeling uneasy, but when I got to the lobby the reception desk was empty and everything was quiet. I walked towards the door and pushed it, but it didn't open. Security must have now locked it from the inside, I assumed. I looked up and there was a little latch at the top with a bolt, allowing it to be opened. I stretched up to slide it open, but I couldn't reach.

I ran over to the desk and looked for something to stand on – a chair or stool would be perfect. The chair was massive, though, and on wheels and I couldn't see how I might get it out from behind the desk, which seemed to be enclosed on three sides. Panicking a little, I jumped over the top and frantically looked for something, anything, I could use. Seeing what I needed, I grabbed it and ran to the door, standing on top of it I reached up, undid the latch and pulled the doors open.

I heard the lift moving again and ran off quietly into the night and towards home, where I took the lift to our apartment and closed the front door behind me. I went quietly to my room, calling softly to Dad something about a change of plans. I grabbed the binoculars and looked over at the building and I could see two security guards moving from floor to floor and looking around the offices with an urgency I'd not seen before.

Too late, chaps, I thought, and I peeled off my snotsicle-stained clothes with some relief and snuggled into my pyjamas, settling in front of the window with a mug of milk to watch the building a while longer before I went to sleep. After some time the activity stopped, and I imagined them reporting no further incidents and settling back down in puzzlement. *They'll be more vigilant for a bit but will soon let it slip again,* I thought.

Grinning to myself, I raised the mug to everyone in the building over the way, knowing I wouldn't watch them as closely from now on. The novelty was over. Then the design on the cup briefly caught my eye. It was one of my brother's souvenirs, left behind at home after he left to work internationally as a medic and always waiting for him when he came back on periodic visits. It had a picture of the Liverpool FC logo on the side of it.

I wondered what the guard must have felt when he found his own mug, upside down on the floor outside of the entrance door. A mug that also bore an LFC badge, and that was just about tall enough to boost me the few inches needed to reach the latch, and just about strong enough to turn upside down and withstand my weight for a few seconds while I slipped the door open and ran away.

Of course, the contents of the tanks remain a mystery, but over the years I've asked some of the people I've met along the way for their thoughts and it seems likely that they were simply storage tanks for water, perhaps as a safety measure or back-up for some sort of emergency. More importantly, over the years I've learnt that every building, actually every *person*, has some sort of eighth floor, some mystery or part of themselves that they would prefer to keep secret. I've known offices with secret and forgotten rooms on long unused and abandoned floors. I've found shortcuts under and around London skyscrapers in the form of long-forgotten tunnels. I've discovered false walls in factories with entire rooms behind them, clearly occupied, and often under the noses of oblivious or ignorant staff.

Buildings hide secrets, every bit as much as their human occupants. I would encounter many 'eighth floors' in the years to come and uncover many secrets. Doing so was to become my job and it requires many skills. Planning and surveillance for sure, experience and confidence as well, but perhaps the most obvious quality in a successful social engineer is curiosity, the urge to dig deeper, look further and to question that which everyone else takes for granted.

Finding the tanks on the eighth floor led to as many questions as it did answers, but I was content with my night's work, my curiosity, at least for now, and in that setting, more or less satisfied. I hadn't found all the answers, but I had found the answer I was looking for that night, the answer I was focused upon, and in that I was happy.

After a while, I got tired and lay down to sleep. I remember thinking that I could have asked permission to see the building, but I probably wouldn't have got it. I reasoned that, if someone wasn't doing anything wrong, why did permission matter anyway? I decided at that moment, lying in my own bed at the age of fifteen, that I most likely wouldn't ask anyone's permission to do anything much, ever again. And, having completed my first office infiltration, I couldn't have realised how many more there would be in the future.

5

POCKET MONEY

By the time I was fourteen, I was working weekends at various shops and cafés in Liverpool, and the boys both had jobs in the city's bars and clubs. Jack was behind the bar and working with the security staff at a club in the city centre, and soon Adam was a feature at the same place, resetting the tables, fixing any electrical issues, serving drinks and helping with any trouble.

I'd call in and say hello when I finished my shifts and they'd serve me a drink from the bar, usually a rum and Coke. Heavy on the Coke, light on the rum. I sometimes stayed for a while, and occasionally changed clothes in the club and met friends later. We'd go out drinking in and around Liverpool, and I'd head home in the early hours of Sunday morning or stay at a friend's place. Despite my young age, this was far from unusual at the time, and although a couple of doormen might have wondered about our age, we knew most of them and no one was ever asked for ID or refused entry. We looked older than we were and getting into the clubs was generally down to looking confident and acting like you belonged there. Funnily enough, I was quite good at that.

By the time I was sixteen, we were regulars around the clubs and pubs in the city centre and the fact that we were under-age never crossed my mind. In any case, we could always pop back to the club and see the boys if we needed to, and they would always get us into one of their places if we ever had any problems.

One night, at around 2 a.m., I had approached Jack for taxi money to get home as I had spent all of my own cash. We had walked home many times, but I had high heels on and didn't fancy the long hike back in the early hours and freezing cold. Jack looked at me: 'Spent your wages already, Cuz?'

'Yes, Jack, it's not hard. I get bugger all.'

'I thought you never bought your own drinks anyway?' he said with a grin.

This was usually true; there was nearly always gangs of lads out on the town happy to buy me and my friends our drinks, and we knew the bar staff at lots of places as well. I could make the wages from my Saturday job go a very long way, and usually beg, blag or borrow the rest if necessary. That night though, I was out of luck, and out of funds. He slipped a tenner into my hand: 'Come and see me on Monday night, I might have a job for you.'

'My dad won't let me work in a bar, Jack; he'd know . . .'

'It isn't in the bar. Come in around eight, OK?' Then he wandered back into the club and left me to see myself home.

That Monday I got to the club at eight, wandered in and found him sitting at a table smoking and chatting with the other security guards and club staff. He got up and met me as I made my way across the room, took me over to the bar and got me a glass of Coke – no rum.

He told me that he needed 'messages' hand-delivered around the city some weekends and that his boss would pay me for picking them up and dropping them off. He said that they needed petty cash for the tills, and sometimes other stuff, to be passed on, and that they needed someone they could trust to do it. So, rather than just coming into town, spending all my wages on drinking with my mates, I could be making some money instead by just dropping cash off around the city.

I'd met his boss a few times and he seemed nice enough, but it sounded dodgy, and I said so. 'Well, it is a *bit* dodgy,' said Jack, blue eyes looking straight at me. 'I mean, none of the money is going through the books, you know.'

This I did know, although not really in any detail, except that literally everyone did it, and no one talked about it. Even the little bakery near home that I worked in as my first weekend job didn't always put orders through the regular channels, accepting only payment in cash, and never through the cash register. I had been told it was 'standard in business' and I knew when not to pursue a topic, so I had shut up and accepted it.

I told Jack I'd do it and asked if I could have a proper drink. 'One drink,' he said. 'Then take this up to the pyramid; Danny will meet you there.' He tapped a fat parcel about the size of a novel, wrapped in a carrier bag and sealed with surgical tape.

'Danny? Now?'

'You've met him. Has all the piercings.'

I recalled a scruffy young bloke with a handsome face, covered in tattoos and piercings. He played snooker at the club sometimes and was nice enough, although he was clearly stoned a lot of the time. 'Er, OK.'

He passed me a shot of Bacardi and told me to put the parcel into my bag. I poured the shot into my Coke and drank it down. 'Shall I come back and tell you I met him?'

'No, no, we'll know. Come back on Friday night and you'll get paid. Say hello to your mum and dad for me.'

So, I did it. I walked up to the pyramid, which was the name we gave to the tomb of William MacKenzie on Rodney Street, and there was Danny, who didn't recognise me or even notice me the first time I walked past. I crossed the road and walked back again giving him a quick glance just to be sure. Then he smiled and held out his hand, as one might to a toddler that had strayed away. 'You got me something from Jack?' he said.

'You Robbie?' I asked.

He smiled. 'I'm not, but you're Jenny.'

'Hiya, Danny.' I gave him the bag and he tucked it inside his jacket.

'See you next time.'

That was how it began. I went home and told Mum and Dad that Jack and Adam said 'hello' and then went back to the club on Friday and was given £20 and another package. I delivered it to a doorman at a pub across town, who was flirty with me and gave me vodka, then I went back to the pub where Jack was working that night. I picked up another packet from him, smaller this time, and delivered that up some stairs leading to a little flat above a hippy shop at the student end of town, before heading home on the last train with £60 in my pocket.

I left my waitress job in the café the next week without a second thought. I'd been doing eight till six for £11, which was ridiculous. I'd covered twenty-five tables with a steep flight of stairs between my tables and the kitchen, with only one thirty-minute break, all for a nasty, rude boss who knew damn well it was exploitation. *Sod that for a game of soldiers, I'll deliver cash instead,* I'd thought, and that was that.

I'd deliver messages as well as parcels most weekends for Jack and his boss, as well as working at a local corner shop and babysitting some nights for a neighbour. Sometimes I'd collect the glasses as well and serve the odd drink if the club or one of the associate pubs was very busy. I would hang on until the end of the night and into the next morning, drinking and chatting with friends or Jack's staff and the older crowd at the club, or at lock-ins nearby. There wasn't always money to be made, though, and some weeks I'd avoid them altogether, heading to the other end of town to socialise with school friends, going to the cinema or for a meal with a boyfriend, or attending seemingly endless family functions.

In the sweltering summer of 1989, a friend and I decided to attend the Glastonbury festival in the south-west of England. We had no tickets and not much money, but we had heard that there were many unofficial ways to get in and so we booked a coach to Bristol and planned on heading down there early on the day before the event started, not really knowing what would happen.

We had packed a small bag each, with just a few toiletries, clean underwear and not much else. We had no tent, no plan and about £10 between us; I planned to hustle the rest. I'd heard that the Hare Krishnas let people sleep in their area for nothing and that they would give you some food as well. Failing that, there were Christian groups mining the festival for followers, so that was also an option, as they were contractually obliged, so to speak, to not turn people away. We didn't plan on sleeping much anyway and I could find most things I needed by now with a wink and a story, and a few skills I had learnt along the way.

The night before we were due to leave, we met in the city and made our way to the usual haunts. Adam was working at the club and slipped us a couple of drinks. He smirked when I told him we were travelling light but was concerned when I said we had little money. 'Look, in an emergency you can always get money from a vending machine, OK?' he had said. 'Only in an emergency, Jen, as you are nicking it and it's risky. OK? Do you want to know how?'

Silly question.

He winked and pulled me to one side, telling me not to tell my mate or anyone else about the trick. He told me if I was really struggling, I should go and find a drinks vending machine, in the bus station or wherever, and then made me write down a sequence of numbers on a beer mat. 'Make sure there is no one around, Cuz,' he had said. 'The machine will give you a load of change when you do this. About a fiver, OK? Only use in an emergency.'

I'd nodded, but as soon as I saw a vending machine in the train station on the way home, I'd given it a try. Nothing. This was odd, as Adam was usually right about this type of thing and didn't generally give me bad advice. I'd shrugged it off, gone home, catching the coach early the next morning with my friend.

A couple of hours into the journey to Bristol, the coach stopped at a service station on the motorway. My friend and I jumped off for a pee and to stretch our legs and, on our way out, I noticed another machine in the foyer of the service station. We decided to spend big and grab a Coke each, we got the drinks and I decided, casually really, to punch in the numbers again and give Adam's scam another try.

At first nothing happened, but then I heard a metallic clunk deep within the mechanism of the machine and another can of Coke dropped out of the hatch. I turned to my friend and smiled. 'Free Coke, that's not bad . . .' I started to say, when the unmistakable clatter of many coins being pumped into the change hatch interrupted me. The machine started vomiting out 50 pence pieces, loads of them! I bent down and covered the little hole and started putting them into my pockets in a panic.

Once it was out of 50p pieces, a couple of dozen 10p pieces followed and then it sort of sighed and was silent.

'Holy shit!' said my mate, but I shushed her and stood up, looking around. No one seemed to have noticed, most of our fellow travellers seemed also to be heading to Glastonbury and thankfully didn't really seem to be the most observant bunch. Another can popped out, and then another two, all different flavours, as the machine went through some sort of maintenance cycle and tested its mechanisms out.

'Fucking hell, it needs to stop!' I said, looking around and seeing our fellow passengers getting back on the coach. I looked back in a panic, there were only so many cans we could get away with carrying, let alone explaining why the machine was going crackers, but it groaned again and stopped clunking, becoming completely quiet.

'OK,' I said. 'Let's go.'

Counting the change on the coach, the machine had given us just shy of £25 and five cans of drink, meaning heavier bags and lighter moods as we made our way to Bristol and grabbed a local bus towards the festival itself.

Within sight of the gates, I heard Irish accents and a pair of sunburnt hairy arms wrapped themselves around both our shoulders. 'You got tickets, girls?'

The owner of the arms was a tall lad with strawberry blond curls, already pink with sunburn, who had advanced a couple of steps ahead of his group of friends to talk to us. He was bare-chested and grinning. We giggled and told him that, no, we had absolutely no plan whatsoever, let alone tickets, although I was very conscious of all the change jangling in the rucksacks as we walked.

'Then follow me, ladies,' he snorted, lighting a cigarette and picking up the pace, as a few of his mates joined us and we walked down a wide lane towards the entrance of the festival. As we got closer, there was a huge gathering of people in front of the entrance turnstiles, with hassled-looking staff trying to be heard above the mayhem and punching holes in paper tickets with a metal gadget. Our chances of sneaking past somehow didn't look good, but Irish arms steered us past the melee and around to the left, keeping us walking, past the crowds and along a hedge at the side of the main site and fields. We were heading away and objected, but he was still laughing and sang out, 'Trust me, ladies, trust me.'

With no other plan to speak of and in good company, we kept walking until eventually the crowds thinned almost completely and the air got quieter. We were flanking the outer fields of the festival, near the back of the camping areas, and seemed far away from the action, but as the hedge line curled slowly around to the right, we could see the beginnings of a low fence and a small crowd of people sitting or standing on the grass in front of it. As we got closer, we could hear distant music and the sound of a crowd not too far away. I could see people handing money to a couple of young blokes who seemed to be hoisting them over the top of the fence and into the field beyond. 'We've only got a couple of quid,' I whispered, glancing at my mate.

'It won't matter,' said Irish.

When we got to the front of what passed for a queue, he spoke to the two skinny lads pushing people over the fence. 'How much, mate?'

'Just give us a couple of quid, lad,' said chief hoister, in the thickest Scouse accent I'd ever heard.

I knew then we would get in anyway, and Irish kissed us both on the cheek as he passed the boy some cash and was boosted over. Our turn.

'We've only got a couple of quid on us,' I said in my sweetest, most Liverpudlian voice.

'Scousers go for nothing, lovely,' he said, although he squeezed my bum as he lifted me over, and my mate's too. Oh well, we were in.

On the other side Irish and his mates had disappeared, but we followed a tiny trickle of people moving quickly across what seemed to be a backstage area with a few lorries and what looked like workmen hanging around and taking no notice of us at all. After a while we passed some portable toilets and piles of rubbish bags, and just a bit beyond slipped easily into the regular crowd of concert goers enjoying the festival. That year it was estimated that over 100,000 people were at the festival; with ticket sales of only 60,000 it was a considerable safety risk and the first year that an extensive police presence was used at the site.

I know I had a blast, but I don't remember much apart from seeing the Pixies and the Wonder Stuff play, eating 'hash fudge' and breaking into a tent in the peace field that had Buddhist posters and leaflets inside, so we had somewhere to sleep. Good times. Glastonbury became an annual pilgrimage and is worthy of note here because it tested my breaking-and-entering skills for a while, before security measures forced me to use actual social engineering as a means of entry.

After that first year I don't remember climbing over fences very much, but I do remember paying to scramble through tunnels, bursting out on the other side and into an orange tent then walking out of the zipped door and into the crowd. Another year, about five of us were hidden under piles of luggage and clothes in the back of a dilapidated van, trying not to giggle as we drove into a camping area and past the security guards.

Festival security kept getting better, though, and as the fences gradually got more difficult to climb, tunnel under or break through, it became inevitable that sooner or later we would have to try other means. One year we got as far as the public entrance and could see no obvious way in. I sat down and started to watch people coming and going into the site. I was with a small group of friends, and I told them to leave me alone and to give me a minute to focus and I would work out how to get in.

As is often the case, the answer is to watch the people, observe the movements, the lines of drift used by those who were permitted to be there and then find a way to use that to gain access. Before long I noticed that there was a group of people who were moving in and out of the site without being stopped by the entrance staff. They were all carrying black plastic garbage sacks and wearing high-visibility vests. Litter patrol. We walked back towards a nearby village and found a small shop we had passed on the way in, buying some black rubbish bags and a packet of children's colouring pens.

Returning to the site, we put all our stuff, rucksacks, jackets, etc., into the black bags. We drew on the back of our hands with some green ink to replicate the ink stamp that gave the legitimate litter patrol their access, blurring it slightly so the pattern didn't matter (a trick we used many times to get into nightclub VIP areas and concerts) and we strolled up to the entrance gate dragging the bags behind us. I looked the entrance guy straight in the eye, held up my trash bag and said: 'Litter patrol, mate. We're supposed to go and get our yellow vests?'

The guy waved us through without a second look and that was that. The next year we had our own yellow vests with us, and the same thing happened, we were waved in without incident because we looked the part and acted like we belonged there.

I tell the Glastonbury story a lot when I do corporate training and keynotes because it illustrates so many of the principles of social engineering. We were relying on the authority principle, the vests, to give us legitimacy. We were confident, had a plausible back story and some props to back it up, which is generally more than enough to convince a stressed and underpaid security guard who only needs a reason, any reason, to choose the easiest way through a given situation. Finally, and most importantly, it shows that I don't need to work on the locks, I need to work on the people. If someone, anyone, *can* bypass security, then it is only a question of time before it *is* bypassed. People get tired, distracted and stressed. They make errors of judgement, are riddled with prejudice and ideas about what a threat looks like. They are also subject to emotional ploys, bribery and/or coercion. I don't look at picking a lock, I look at the person whose job it is to keep the lock closed, then persuade them to open it.

I'd stayed on in school after my GCSEs to do A levels as I had done well. I had my sights on studying English Literature at university and had been accepted for the entrance exam into Oxford, although I later failed the entrance interview. I got a letter from them assuring me that they often 'did accept students from the maintained sector' but just not myself this time. If I was to get the grades required, which I did, then I could go the year after my exams. My chosen college was Worcester, because of Keats and the ducks, but I never went. I'd never have fitted into the culture there and may well have been tempted to roof surf my way through my degree rather than study much.

In the end, I went to York for a week but found it provincial and cloyingly quaint, so I ended up at home, attending the University of Liverpool, studying English Language and

Literature, and coincidentally walking past the usual clubs and pubs every time I had to attend a lecture or go to class.

I'd mostly stopped doing deliveries for Jack and his boss, although I popped in to say hello most weeks and still did the odd errand if they needed it. I'd also stopped partying so much at weekends and was hanging out a little more with my university mates. Adam, always very bright, was studying as well and had ambitions to become a civil engineer. Jack had got involved with various questionable people and was dating a series of pretty, but dopey, women, none of whom I particularly liked. We were growing apart.

The last delivery I did for Jack and his boss around the city had been different and had signalled the end of my sideline as a courier service for him and his boss. It had been a pick-up, rather than a drop-off, and I had once again met Danny, who was with another man and his girlfriend, waiting for me by St Luke's, also known as the 'bombed-out church', in the middle of Liverpool. He passed me a package and I was sure they walked off rather more quickly than normal. I unzipped my bag to put it inside and noticed it was heavier and bulkier than usual, making a series of metallic clanks as I dropped it into an inside pocket, next to my course textbooks.

I marched down to Jack's club and found him, as usual, sitting near the bar with the other staff. He jumped up to meet me and motioned for me to follow him into the cleaning area behind the bar. I opened the bag and held out the package for him to take, but he told me to wait while he pulled on a pair of yellow rubber gloves, and then took it from me. 'Nice one, Jack. Why do you need those?' I'd almost shouted. 'What about me? I've not been wearing gloves, have I? Am I running [I lowered my voice] guns now?'

'Shut up, Jen. It's not like that. Just give it over.'

I thrust it into his hand and flounced out of the room and over to the cash register behind the bar. A couple of customers were waiting to be served and, with Jack fumbling about in the anteroom, I served them both a pint, although I couldn't open the till. 'I'll bring your change over to the table,' I said.

When he eventually appeared he was all smiles. I held out my hand and looked at him. 'I'm not doing it anymore, that wasn't what I said I'd do.'

'It's OK. We have other people to do that anyway,' he replied.

'Fine. *Fine!* Trust all your little scallies with it, Jack, I don't care.' Hand still out, I pursed my lips at him. 'And those two blokes need change from a fiver for two pints of lager.'

'Do you want to work in here?' he asked.

'My dad won't let me, Jack. He'll find out, so no,' I said. 'Everything has to be legit anyway or uni will find out and I might get thrown out.'

He'd nodded and smiled, and I couldn't resist smiling back and hugging him. He always could win me over, but I wasn't picking up any more damn parcels for him and he knew it.

It was a while until I saw him again, but one evening after having a few drinks with my uni mates, I called into the club to say hello.

'Wanna make a ton of cash?' he asked.

Jack told me that they were doing a deal with a new club up the road who were selling tickets to their VIP opening event in two weeks' time. It was simple work. All I had to do was dress up nicely the week before and sell some tickets for the event in and around the city. For a tenner, the ticket got them entrance to the new club, a drink at the bar and access to the VIP lounge where various footballers and other cool and shiny people hung out. I got to keep £3 per ticket sold as commission.

It would involve banter. I would have to pop in and around the bars, approach people cold and get them excited about the new club and what it had to offer. I'd not seen inside the club and the last time I'd walked past I'd noticed that it looked a little run-down for a new nightclub, but then I wasn't into clubbing much anymore, and I didn't have to like it to sell the tickets.

Jack told me the tickets were limited and cash only and, dis-playing uncharacteristic protectiveness towards me, that one of the security boys would shadow me a little at first, just in case anyone got overfamiliar when I was flogging the tickets. He said that every ticket was numbered so we could keep track and that they were a minimum of £10 each; if I sold them for more, we could split the mark-up. I was to pick them up the following Friday night at around five, glad rags and war paint on, and see how many I could sell.

Jack gave me a roll of tickets and a bum bag with some change in it and told me to start at the bars around Matthew Street, avoiding the area around the actual club itself and its neighbours. With one of his gorillas in tow, I set off into the city to sell the tickets. While it was a bit nerve-racking at first, I'd never had a problem chatting to people and by the time I was talking to my fourth or fifth group of revellers I had my sales banter down to a fine art.

If the group was a gang of single lads, then I would tell them I'd mostly sold the rest of the tickets to groups of women. If the group was made up of women, I'd tell them that the football players would be in the VIP lounge. If I found a mixed group I'd talk about the atmosphere and the music, making up what-ever I thought would appeal to them based on their clothes and responses.

I mostly approached people either drinking outside the bars or near to the doors, avoiding the staff and never lingering too long. It took me a couple of hours to sell all my tickets, but by the time I got back to Jack's place at around 10pm I had managed to flog well over a hundred of them at at least £10 each.

The club was heaving, so we made our way upstairs and to the back to sort out the cash, the gorilla handing over a thick wad of banknotes to Jack for counting. Jack seemed surprised I had sold them all, but he counted out my money and laughed. 'Great job, Cuz!' He handed me a large wedge of cash and tipped my minder from the club's cut.

I stared at the money in my hand. There was just about £600, which I stuffed back into my bum bag, the gorilla refusing to take another tip from me. I went downstairs and got a drink from the bar, relaxing a little, what a great job! As I was leaving, Jack pulled me to one side. 'We'll do that again at some point, Jen. Just need to wait for events and such at the club.' I nodded; I was down for making that kind of easy cash any time!

'Just one thing, though,' he said. 'Don't go to the opening, OK? It would be a bit weird if you were there, looking at everyone going in, you know.' I nodded in agreement, although I was a bit puzzled, finished my drink and grabbed a taxi home.

Over the following week, I frittered away quite a bit of my earnings on clothes, books, jewellery and make-up. It was great to feel so rich, 'minted' as my friends put it, and by the following Saturday, the night of the new club's grand opening, I was ready to party. I met two of my friends in a pub near the train station in Liverpool and had bought the first two rounds of drinks. They were grateful but curious and so I swore them to secrecy and told them where I got the cash.

'We should go and see what it's like – it sounds brilliant!' the first said.

My other mate concurred. 'Yeah, let's go! You'll probably get in free after selling all those tickets for them. Come on, let's do it.'

I agreed, curiosity getting the better of me and reasoning that Jack would never know if I went for just one drink and laid low. We walked across the city, the streets busy with people enjoying the weekend nightlife. Liverpool has always been a big party city.

As we got close to the other club, I noticed many, many people milling around outside, some of whom I recognised from the previous week when I sold them their tickets. Instead of the relaxed party atmosphere I'd expected, there seemed to be tension in the air and a feeling of confusion. I could hear arguing coming from near the entrance doors, which were closed, unusual for a club at this hour on a Saturday. I could see several security staff in animated discussions with a group of lads I remembered flirting with for a while the week before, before selling them all tickets at £15 a pop. Something was wrong, and I turned back, walking around the corner and down a side alleyway, followed by my friends.

'There's a problem, I can tell,' I said. 'Go and see what's happening. I'm going to head back up to Jack's club.'

My mates rolled their eyes; the club where Jack worked was where we finished our nights out, not where we started, they didn't want to hang out there yet. 'Look, I can't stay, can I? They'll recognise me and whatever is going on I don't want to get the blame! Just find out what's happening, enjoy yourselves if you get in and come find me later? I'm going, though. Jack will kill me if he knows I came here when he said to leave it. OK? See you later.'

I turned and walked away from them, making my way across town and into Jack's club. He was busy and had some girls hanging around him, so I sat down in a corner and drank a couple of drinks on my own, exchanging the odd greeting with some of the staff and regulars I knew in the bar. Before long my two friends walked in and came over to find me. They looked around, checking Jack was at the bar, before turning to me and explaining, breathlessly, what they had found out.

The altercation at the doors of the new club was down to the fact that the people waiting to get in had tickets for a non-existent VIP event. The security staff were baffled and angry as hordes of punters arrived at their doors, presenting them with legitimate-looking tickets bearing the logo of the club and today's date for the party. Except no such event had been planned, and no one inside the club had any idea what was going on.

My friends had chatted to a couple of girls waiting to get in and expecting to see footballers *on the door*, never mind inside the place, and had heard another group of people angrily arguing with the increasingly agitated staff and insisting on being allowed through the doors to hear the opening set of a famous DJ. They had noticed the doormen pocketing the tickets and looking mystified while angry punters argued with them about false advertising and lies.

I felt sick to my stomach and went hot and cold at the same time. I looked over to Jack who was at the end of the bar talking to his boss and laughing, a girl's arms around his neck. That stare must have weighed quite a bit, because his eyes met mine across the bar and he waggled his eyebrows at me and beckoned me over. I told my friends I'd grab them a drink, got up and walked over, my mouth dry: 'Jack, I—'

'Jens, you know Celia, don't you?'

I could hardly look at his new companion and pursed my lips. Then, I opened my mouth to speak, but Jack interrupted. 'See how busy it is tonight, Jen? Lots of people have come up from the other side of town. There was some problem I think with that new club.' He looked me straight in the eye, 'You know the club I mean, don't you? It's the one I *fucking told you* to avoid!'

and he turned back to his boss and signalled the barman to bring me a drink.

I looked around but could see no one I had sold tickets to at the bar. This was fortunate because there may well have been problems if I was recognised by someone we had conned, which was of course why Jack had told me to avoid the club at the other end of town, a fact that might have been useful to know.

My friends had been joined at their table by a group of lads. I put three fingers up to the bartender, and picked the glasses up with both hands, taking them over to my friends and interrupting the conversation. They looked at me and mouthed, 'Are you OK?' across the table. I sighed, nodded, and sank the drink, mouthing back 'It's fine'. I rolled my eyes at Jack, before deciding to forget about it all for the rest of the night and avoid my cousin until he calmed down.

Jack never apologised for getting me into all of this and he was never on his own long enough for me to challenge him about it. He caught me glaring at him once, some weeks later and, reading my mind, smiled and said, 'You knew what you were doing.' I suppose at some level he was right, but it sat uncomfortably with me. I couldn't enjoy spending money that I'd earned dishonestly, and I wasn't proud of myself for doing such a good job of ripping people off, however minor the consequences, and the truth was that you could never really be sure what those consequences really were, or how far they reached. I didn't want to be one of the bad guys even if it meant having money, but I loved my cousin and felt vulnerable moving away from what he wanted me to do, from being part of the crew that I'd known for most of my life.

I reluctantly agreed to pulling the con a couple more times in nearby cities, but I didn't sell many tickets and felt wretched and ashamed of myself for doing it, and it wasn't long before I told the boys I was out and the con petered out altogether.

We didn't talk about it much, but I could tell that he thought I was being melodramatic, maybe to cover up the fact that I'd lost my nerve. Whereas for me it wasn't just the fact that I was ashamed of conning people, or that I disagreed with my cousin's view that the whole thing had been a harmless prank with no real victims. It was also that I'd lost respect for Jack. He had been my childhood hero and I loved him like a brother. I'd looked up to him and would have followed him anywhere. Dammit, I had followed him without question for years, but I knew I wasn't going to follow him blindly anymore.

We would work together again but I didn't trust him in the same way. Our paths were moving further apart, and we were never as close again.

6

PARROTS AND PEACOCKS

Jack had got to know many of the people on the Liverpool scene during his time in the clubs, and among them were some of the footballers from the clubs based in the city. At the time, they were among the few people in the area who had any real money, and they had the expensive cars, houses and lifestyle to prove it. They were obvious targets for criminals, and were sick of being robbed. Even so, a minority flaunted their wealth somewhat recklessly at a time of financial hardship for many others, earning them the local nickname of 'peacocks', with some emphasis on the second half of the word.

One day, Jack picked me up outside university and we drove to 'millionaires' row', a road of beautiful houses in an affluent area about forty minutes from the city centre. Jack parked his car in a huge drive next to a flashy sports car and a Jeep. Before we could ring the bell, a famous footballer, whom I had seen on TV many times, opened the front door and let us into the house. A pretty woman, who I assumed was the guy's wife, was on the phone in the kitchen, and seemed agitated when she saw Jack, relaxing a little as I followed behind. I cracked a small smile at her, but she didn't return it and turned away.

The guy showed us upstairs and into a large ensuite bathroom at the side of a ransacked master bedroom with a cream carpet covered in muddy footprints. There were clothes pouring out of drawers and make-up strewn across the floor, the wardrobe doors were wide open and shoe boxes and coat-hangers spilled out. *No wonder the wife is unhappy,* I thought, *being burgled is horrible.* My mum and dad had been robbed, along with almost everyone else in my street, a couple of times, and the impact went far beyond what was stolen. It was a real invasion of privacy and destroyed their peace of mind. I felt bad for them both.

In the bathroom, Jack chatted about alarms and was asking if the police had been called and might be arriving so we could get out of their way. Feeling useless, I decided to start jotting a few things down inside one of my university notebooks and followed them as they wandered about the house looking at other rooms, checking for more damage, and speculating as to who the culprits might be.

Outside, we had a walk around and something began to bother me. I just couldn't work out why the burglars had used the bathroom window as a point of entry, when there were many other easier ways in. I pointed this out to Jack and the footballer, and asked, 'Where did they leave? I mean, how did they get out again?'

'Through the back door from the kitchen, we think; it was open when we got back, as well as the sliding doors to the garden.'

On our way home we picked up Adam from college and I explained my thinking behind the break-in. In my opinion, they were probably amateurs; a bit of planning was evident, but it seemed mostly improvised, likely kids who weren't looking for anything in particular and had, thankfully, been disturbed. They'd left expensive perfume and jewellery in the bedroom, along with designer clothes and make-up, easily sold on and portable. They had climbed through that tiny window when everyone knows how to open sliding doors without proper locks from the outside, and they had left footprints, and likely fingerprints, everywhere. It all pointed to opportunistic, low life kids.

As for the footballer and his wife, I'd said, they could easily make themselves more secure. They needed to clean up the garden a bit and put the kids' toys and bikes into a locked shed with their gardening tools, so that these couldn't be used to force or improvise a way into the house. They needed better, stronger locks on those sliding doors, and they could afford, and so should immediately install, a decent alarm system throughout the house. It wasn't hard or especially costly to stop this happening to them again; it would just take a bit of thought and focus and we, of course, knew good lock and alarm guys.

I managed to talk myself into writing a little report for them, and a second visit was scheduled to discuss our findings a couple of weeks later. Surprisingly enough to me, they listened carefully as I went through the document and gave them a few recommendations. The wife seemed especially attentive, and seemed relieved to be talking to me, rather than Jack and the boys who might have seemed threatening at times. I, by contrast, appeared entirely approachable, looked very innocent and was not at all intimidating. She directed all her questions to me and agreed to buy an alarm system from our contact, while never looking at the boys, who clearly made her uncomfortable, even though we were all there to try and help. It wasn't a problem on this occasion, but judging whether someone is trustworthy, based on appearances is dangerous – Ted Bundy was handsome, polite and well dressed.

People expect a criminal to look, sound and act like a criminal, based on whatever their expectations of what that might be. The fact that I don't look dangerous, even now, is partly why I am successful at my job. No one ever thinks I could be up to no good because, for most people, I simply don't represent what they imagine a criminal to look like, even when I am simulating a robbery, breaking into a building, or digging for information in some way. Those expectations and opinions will be somewhat shaped by experience, but are also formed by personal and cultural prejudices, such as misogyny or regionalist and racist views, which are then reinforced by clichéd images and stereotypes in popular culture and the media.

For example, most people do not suspect a woman to be a criminal, especially a well-dressed, polite and now middle-aged woman. This makes them easy to con, just by reversing the stereotype, and is a considerable risk and real problem in terms of personal safety and security.

It is also a common belief that hackers are young men in black hoodies, leaning over laptops in basements and working with computers. If you search online for images of hackers these are the pictures you will find. However, the truth is that most security breaches involve people making mistakes or being manipulated, and the hacker behind that will be some sort of social engineer, many of whom are women, who don't really need technology to manipulate a target.

Equally dangerous is the belief held by many that they are able to spot a threat, or identify someone as a criminal, and are therefore at less of a risk than everybody else. It's misplaced confidence, a Dunning–Kruger effect* for their own security,

---

* The Dunning-Kruger effect, in psychology, is a cognitive bias whereby people with limited knowledge or competence in a given intellectual or social domain greatly overestimate their own knowledge or competence in that domain relative to objective criteria or to the performance of their peers or of people in general. https://www.britannica.com/science/Dunning-Kruger-effect

and it is why, for many a job, I am the person chosen to walk past security, follow a mark or dash around inside an office or a bank. I look normal and non-threatening, and I will still look like that even if I am in the process of dismantling your security systems or robbing you blind at your own request.

People think that criminals will behave suspiciously, or that they themselves are smart enough to spot a bogus approach when confronted with it. The truth is very different as the soaring statistics for scams of all kinds suggest. Scams, cons and fraud evolve quickly, are often personal in nature and reflect whatever is taking place in the wider world. Confidence that one is able to spot an approach is dangerous because the right script, especially if personalised and timely, and if delivered by someone who does not fit your idea of a criminal, will catch anyone, and I do mean anyone, out.

Sitting across from that footballer's wife, I realised that to her the boys probably didn't look all that different from how she imagined the people who had robbed her would look. This wasn't her fault and wasn't entirely unfounded, but on this occasion it worked in my favour because she was listening to me and I realised I could really help them. That felt good, I wanted them to be safe.

After speaking for a while, the footballer eventually stopped me and asked me a question: 'You say that everyone can get through the doors but they were locked from the inside. Maybe they couldn't get through them?'

'Honestly, anyone can open them,' I said. 'It's easy.'

'Go on then,' he said. Jack stood up as if to do it, but the footballer stopped him. 'Not you. Her,' he said, and Jack threw me a glance and sat back down.

Even though I was 99 per cent certain I knew how to do it, there was just that tiny bit of doubt at the back of my mind that nagged me. If I failed, I would look an idiot, and so would Jack who was sitting right behind me; he had trusted me to do this and so I needed to get it right. I put down my notes and walked over to the doors, slid them open and walked out onto the wooden decking beyond. The footballer walked up and slid them shut again, locking me out and engaging the lock on the handle inside. I could see Jack over his shoulder, anxious for once and watching me closely from his position on the sofa.

Here goes nothing.

I took hold of the handle and lifted the door upwards a tiny bit (as much as it would let me and I had the strength for, only a centimetre at most), before pulling down the handle and bumping the door to the side. They moved easily and gave a satisfying slam as they opened fully and hit the frame.*

The footballer and his wife gasped, Jack looked down to cover up his relief, and I tried to hide a happy grin. To their eyes, I would have simply opened the doors and I wasn't about to tell them the trick of how to do it. 'I've a knack,' I said. 'You need to get someone to refit these doors properly. We can help.' The rest was plain sailing.

Mr Footballer was very pleased and when I saw Jack again a week or two later, he slipped a white envelope into my hand. Fifty quid. 'A tip for working with Mr Footballer, his missus liked you a lot.' I felt very happy, not just with the cash but because I knew they had put the measures we'd suggested in place and that they would be safer as a result. That felt good. Much, much better than ripping people off. I wanted to do more of that.

---

* Most of the time when forcing doors from the outside, the various hacks and tricks are only possible because the doors are fitted incorrectly, which weakens the standard, already flimsy, locks they are supplied with. Gaps between the door and the frame are the exploitable factor allowing pressure or movement around the lock to facilitate access. Seriously, get your doors fitted correctly and tightly to the frame with non-standard, strong locks.

After that Mr Footballer recommended us to a few of his friends, fellow players and business contacts. We did several high-value domestic properties, and found the same or very similar security issues, issuing a short report with some suggestions on it, and selling a few alarms and new locks if required. After a while, I was doing a couple of visits a month on my own and reporting back to the boys if the customer needed quotes or information on the alarm systems.

There was one occasion when I had been given a time and address and had turned up a few minutes early to a large house in the middle of nowhere owned by yet another footballer. When I got there the place seemed deserted and, after trying a few times and getting no answer at the intercom on the gates, I pushed at them a little, lifting a flimsy latch and they swung open.*

I walked through and found myself in a neat, paved driveway with a modern-looking house in front of me, I knocked on the door and rang the doorbell a few times but there was no response. 'Hello! Hellooo! I'm here for the security thing. Hellooo!' I shouted, but I was met with silence, and with no car in the drive the place seemed empty.

I was annoyed. I had no car and had made my way here by bus and train, as well as a fifteen-minute walk from the station. I had the date and time right, so this was now going to be a wasted journey and, given who the owner was (an apparently obnoxious individual who played for a team I didn't support), I was grumpy as hell at the sheer waste of my time. I knocked loudly on the front door a couple more times.

Wondering what to do, I looked up at the building in front

---

* I'd like to emphasise again that security is most effective when it gets used! It's no use having locks, alarms, fences and gates if you don't use them. Honestly, it's a thing.

of me. It was very tall for a domestic property and from my vantage point in the drive I couldn't really see the higher levels, I wandered to the left and saw that it was possible to walk around the outside of the building and into the back garden. I reasoned that I could check the garden and exterior of the house and write that bit of the report up in advance of what would have to be a return visit.

Without too much further thought and with no attempt at concealment, as I had legitimate reason to be there, I walked around the side of the house. Clearly expensive, and not at all to my taste, it was a modern, wooden-clad design with lots of sharp angles and large windows lined with roller blinds that flanked the walls to my right as I walked towards the back of the building. Nosiness overcame me and I peered through a gap into a large living room with garishly patterned furniture. I shuddered, noting, not for the first or last time in my life, how money doesn't necessarily equate to good taste. I looked again and for a second I thought I saw something move inside the house, a flickering shape on the edge of my vision moving rapidly in the room beyond.

I pulled back instinctively and pressed up against the wall, expecting to hear a dog barking, perhaps, or someone open-ing the front door. I waited a second but heard nothing and reminded myself again I was *allowed* to be there, I'd been *asked* to come. I looked at my watch: it was ten minutes later than the appointment time.

I looked through the window again, hands shielding my eyes to peer through the little gap in the blinds. I couldn't see any-thing moving anymore, but I did notice a bundle of something on a coffee table next to one of the chairs. I squinted again and quickly realised it was a huge pile of money! – I was looking at a stack of banknotes about ten inches high, in a messy bundle on top of the table, a couple of grand easily. My opinion of this guy was not improving. What kind of rich idiot leaves a couple of grand on a side table in his ugly living room?

I pulled out my little notepad and wrote 'CASH??' and 'movement?' on a new page. I looked back inside and craned my neck to see if there was anything else of significance lying around, some gold bullion perhaps or a priceless emerald tiara? But I couldn't see much more, so I pottered around further to the rear and stood for a second with the building on my right and an extensive but dull garden in front of me, a grass lawn framed by a border of high leylandii trees. From a security point of view this was OK. You would see anyone moving across the lawn and the trees acted as a barrier but left no real cover for someone to hide. I made a note and a bit of a sketch.

I moved around to the other side of the building and came to a back door, probably to a utility room as it was clearly functional with a large viewing panel. I tried the handle. It was firmly locked, a good thing, and I made another note in my book. Then, inside the property I heard a phone ring, an answering machine kick into life and a youthful female voice leaving a message loud enough for me to hear. 'Hiya, it's Jane, give me a call about Friday please. I can't wait to see you.' Then, almost immediately another one: 'It's me, Fran. I miss you, let's meet up soon. I want to come over.'

I'd made my mind up about this guy by now and was ready to abandon the task. What with the women, the money and the no-show, I really didn't care if he did get burgled at this point and decided to leave.

I thought I would very quickly continue my circuit of the house and make a few more notes so the report had some substance, but I'd tell Jack the guy was a tosser when I saw him, and someone else could finish the job. I navigated some dustbins and walked up some steps onto a flagged patio area with some metal garden furniture outside of yet another pair of sliding glass French doors. *Ha!*

With no curtains or blinds covering them, I walked over and had a good look inside. I could see a large living room with newspapers and coffee cups strewn on a shaggy rug on a carpeted floor, next to a large fireplace. On the hearth in front of the fire was another pile of what looked like more banknotes. I stared hard, trying to see better, and then something flashed past on my peripheral vision. I was sure this time, there was something moving in that house.

Somewhere in a different room, the answering machine kicked in again with another female voice, although I couldn't hear the words now. I decided to leave and turned away, before realising I couldn't have said this part of the assessment was complete if I didn't at least try the handle of the doors. They looked new so hopefully they would be difficult for me to lift upwards and pull, as had worked so well on the first footballer's house. *OK, quick try of the door and then home,* I thought.

I put the pad and pen down on the floor and reached for the handle. Using the same trick as in the other house, I pulled up and moved the handle sharply towards the centre of the doors. Nothing, first test passed. Then the door made a little noise and seemed to drop an inch or two, settling into the rails. Oh dear, not that secure then, maybe it was worth just quickly trying one more thing.

I reached into my bag and got out a little screwdriver from a pencil case. Let's see if they stayed shut with a little light leverage then. I knelt and inserted the screwdriver into the rail at the bottom of the door, fiddling with it a little I reached up and grabbed the handle. Pushing the screwdriver upwards, I lifted the handle and the door wobbled but didn't open. I bent down to adjust it, but had already decided that this was well secured and would have to be really forced to get it open. *It is better than the last few places*, I thought, mentally giving him reluctant credit. As I straightened up outside the glazed doors, I glanced back inside the house and clearly saw the source of the movement.

Inside the room and flapping violently in drunken circuits around the room were several huge, brightly coloured parrots. Flashing green, red and blue plumage, they were fluttering in between the furniture and around each other. Catching sight of me at the window, they began to squawk and scream loudly, flying towards the glass doors and swerving upwards at the last second to prevent a collision with the glass. I almost fell back in fright and staggered to a standing position further back from the doors. As burglar alarms went this wasn't too bad.

OK. Assessment over, I thought, and made to leave, then the answering machine started off again and they increased the screeching in a deafening cacophony and taking more swoops towards the glass. Enough.

I ran around to the front of the house back the way I came, where I practically collided with a white sports car pulling into the drive, footballer at the wheel, gates closing. He smiled and motioned at me to hang on. Unimpressed and skittish by now, I took a deep breath and waited. *When you are ready, pal,* I thought. *Don't rush on my account.*

He parked the car at an angle and climbed out, giving me another grin as he walked over and stuck out his hand. He was very, very tall and, I couldn't help noticing, very good-looking. 'I'm sorry I'm late, darling. Traffic, traffic,' he said in a thick southern accent. 'You are the security fella, aren't you?'

I bristled a little at both 'darling' and 'fella'. 'Yes,' I said.

'Sorry, I looked around the outside when you weren't in. I think I frightened your parrots.' I shook his hand.

He immediately pivoted his grip to my wrist and held on to it really hard. 'Ow!' I said, squirming. 'Get off me!'

He pulled me right in to him until he was inches away from my face and wrapped his arms around me in a tight bear hug. 'Your name is?' he snarled, pushing against me and twisting my wrist harder.

'Jenny!' I spat. 'Jack sent me.' He let go, his face melting into a million-pounds-a-month smile.

'Apologies, sorry, had to check. Come in, come in,' and he opened the door and pressed the numbers 1234 into an alarm pad inside a long hallway. I followed him into a kitchen where I declined a coffee and looked around anxiously for the birds. The answering machine went off again somewhere else in the property as yet another female voice left a message.

'Sorry, sorry!' he said. 'That thing will go all day. Did I grab you hard? Don't know my own strength.'

I smiled, hiding gritted teeth. 'It's fine. They told me you were careful.'

He looked at me in a strange way for just a second.

'Are the birds OK? I saw them when I was checking around the back. I should look around,' I said.

'Yes, they are only in two rooms, so if you start upstairs I'll move them into the lounge for you. There's nothing to see in there anyway,' he said.

Apart from the three grand in loose tenners on the coffee table, I thought. *Idiot!*

Deciding to put distance between us for the visit, I headed upstairs as he suggested but got ready to grab something to knock him on the head with if he got even slightly close to me. Hopefully, there would be a vase or something handy I could

use if I needed to clobber him, but I felt extremely uncomfortable with the whole thing. *Another excellent opportunity from my
darling cousins,* I thought to myself, making a mental note to
tell Jack the guy was a pig and a weirdo and thanks a bunch for
putting me alone in an empty house with him.

I went upstairs and found myself on a landing, and then
noticed another flight of stairs leading to a third floor. I could
hear him opening doors and crooning, presumably to his birds,
on the ground floor, I shouted down: 'Er, am I OK to start at
the top, mate?'

'Yeah, yeah, just whatever you need, don't worry,' he said.

The top floor was open plan, the master bedroom, with
skylights on the ceiling and a neatly made large futon in the
centre of the space. There were two bedside tables with drawers either side and some cushions scattered around. It smelt of
expensive aftershave, but the air was stale and the lighting was
bright, reflected by a huge mirror on the back wall. I walked
further in and stood under the skylights. They were tightly shut
but only held by latches on the inside, easy to lever open from
the outside, although someone would have to climb onto that
roof to do it.

I stepped back and almost knocked the side table over. He
shouted up: 'Is Jack or someone coming as well? I thought there
would be . . . another person with you.'

'He should be here already,' I lied. 'Maybe he's caught in
traffic.' I hoped I sounded convincing; I was glad that he hadn't
followed me upstairs.

I turned to leave and then saw that the drawer on the side
table was an inch or two open. Curiosity gripped me and I
leaned over to have a look, but I couldn't see inside. I absolutely
knew that I shouldn't peek, it was private and unnecessary, and
a risk, but I was angry with the guy as well as being slightly

intrigued. I felt my wrist which was still throbbing from his earlier grip.

I reached over with my finger and pulled slightly. The drawer slid silently and smoothly open, as expensive furniture tends to do, and I peeked inside. There was a large bag of white powder, almost certainly cocaine, but in a quantity I'd never seen either in clubs or even on TV before. At least a teacupful and possibly more, there was also yet more cash and a box of condoms. *Urgh.*

I shut the drawer and walked over to the stairs before heading back again and carefully adjusting the drawer so it was just a couple of inches open as I had first seen it. I heard him walking up the stairs and I made my way to the landing. 'Everything OK? Have you seen everything you need, darlin'?'

Creep, I thought, as the bloody answering machine went off again. 'I'm going to have to come back, I think,' I said. 'I need the boys with me for some of this, but it's a good start.'

He nodded and flashed the grin at me again, 'No worries, babe.'

I headed down the next flight of stairs, with him following me quickly behind. I was, by now, moving a bit too quickly and it was obvious he had me a bit flustered. I felt he was creepy and weird, and now I knew he was a cokehead as well, or even a dealer and I knew how unpredictable that could be. I went straight to the front door and he reached up to open it. I thanked him and my eyes moved towards a little table under yet another mirror with more notes, a smaller pile this time, but still substantial. He followed my gaze.

'Oh, I should tip you . . .' he said and moved a bit closer.

'That's fine,' I said. 'Just pay Jack and all the boys when we are done. He's my cousin, you know, Jack.'

His demeanour changing instantly, he stepped backwards and folded his arms. 'Oh right, yeah. Will do, love. Do you need a cab? Sorry about that thing earlier, had no idea. I mean sorry about, y'know, grabbing you and such.'

'I'm fine, thanks,' I said, happy to see him suddenly scared. I walked through the door and stepped out onto his drive.

'You shouldn't leave all that cash lying about, mate,' I said. 'That's not, you know, safe.' He laughed a bit too hard and slammed the door shut.

As I walked back towards the train station, I couldn't help but think if I had been genuinely dishonest, I could easily have taken some of that cash. Many would have, but I just wasn't that person. Despite everything, I saw myself as fundamentally honest, or at least trying very hard to be fundamentally honest.

I gave Jack the full story when I saw him a few days later. He barely batted an eyelid when I told him about the coke and the cash, laughed at the birds and the answering machine, the briefest flash of anger moving across his face when I told him he had grabbed me. 'Did you like him?' he asked.

'What?! *No!* He is a creep, he's horrible.'

'Christine has shagged him,' he said, speaking of one of his exes.

'Well, I hope she has seen a doctor,' I replied. 'He seems to have shagged half of Liverpool judging by those stupid girls on the answering machine.'

When it came to writing the report, there wasn't a lot to say. I noted that the house itself was actually fairly secure: it had decent enough doors and locks, with access control and a good alarm system. There were a few small upgrades we could make, maybe reinforce the skylights, but in practical terms his physical security was about as good as money could buy for a domestic residence at the time. However, it wasn't his physical security that was the problem.

The truth was the real threat to his safety was himself. The cash left out so casually, the drugs barely concealed made him a prime target for robbery, while the never-ending parade of apparently casual girlfriends would ensure that these things were unlikely to be much of a secret. Then there was the sexism, the aggressiveness and the arrogance. These were qualities that made the possibility of him taking my advice, any advice in fact, unlikely, but that also pretty much guaranteed that he would have, if not enemies exactly, plenty of people who would not be troubled if he was to meet with misfortune.

My conundrum was how to say all of this in a professional report, bearing in mind that while he would be unlikely to act on my advice, he would almost certainly choose to be offended, which might have had a knock-on effect for future work. In the event, I wrote a scant report with a few vague references to placing his valuables in a safe, if he had one, or investing in one if he hadn't. I sent the report through anyway and stopped thinking about him.

A week or two later, one of the bar staff told me that he had been banned from the club and some other pubs after causing some fights and being generally obnoxious. He had also, apparently, lit a cigarette from a burning rolled-up £50 note through which he had just snorted cocaine, at the end of Jack's bar. A mistake. Drugs were generally tolerated if people were discreet, but this would have caused uproar. I was glad I wouldn't run into him again.

A few months later, I heard that he had been robbed at home, held at gunpoint, and was moving house. The burglars had slapped him around a bit, taken many valuables and, according to the radio, they had also let 'three beloved pets, exotic parakeets' loose, which had been rounded up by police and neighbours over the following few days. His 'fiancée' had apparently been with him at the time but was unavailable for

comment and traumatised by the incident. He was now trans-
ferring to a different club in the south. With alacrity.

The parrot-owning footballer was an extreme example of
someone who was, from a security perspective, their own
worst enemy. Even in those days before social media, his lack of
discretion, unsympathetic character and lifestyle choices made
him vulnerable on many counts, but most likely from what we
would refer to in the security world as insider threat.

Many businesses are breached by a member of their own
staff. The vast majority of these incidents are down to mistakes or gaps in internal security procedures or technology.
Carelessness such as a shared password, unpatched software,
a lost laptop, even a digital or physical shortcut taken, anything that exposes a vulnerability by default comes under
the category of accidental insider threat or mistake. While
unfortunate, vigilance and monitoring, by technical solutions,
alongside good internal communications mean that most of
the time organisations can learn from and correct such lapses.

Mistakes aside, there is another form of insider threat that
causes less frequent but often more serious problems, and that
is when the attack is malicious and deliberate. This type of
breach is potentially very damaging not only because an insider
has knowledge and access to systems and locations that an
external party won't have, but also in psychological terms. It
is a betrayal of trust and often instils paranoia, setting teams at
odds with each other and undermining loyalty. Motivations for
this sort of threat are varied, including bribery and coercion,
the revenge of a disgruntled employee, even as far as corporate
espionage and terrorism.

Regardless, good communication and respect are key to
preventing this type of breach, along with common sense and
technical defences. We should know our colleagues and do our

best to create a positive environment for everyone we work with, even if only at team or line manager level. People become unhappy or outgrow their work environment, and people do move on, but companies should do their best to ensure this is done professionally and with kindness, ensuring that access to sensitive information and systems is completely removed.

We also need to watch for differences in patterns of behaviour that might signal a change in attitude towards the organisation, and we should monitor how information is accessed and moved in and around the company. This can't be done through monitoring technology alone; it also requires a knowledge of staff and colleagues and a genuine interest in their well-being so that a disgruntled or coerced employee can be identified and helped before they present a risk to the company.

These are basic security steps, but the technical aspects are so much easier than the people-based measures. Fundamentally, almost every business and every individual has valuables they wish to protect, or at least things they would prefer to remain private. In some ways this leaves us all vulnerable, but we can reduce our insider threat, whatever form that takes, by exercising some personal discretion and through forming good relationships with other people.

Our footballer was careless with his valuables, an attitude perhaps reinforced, and partly justified by, his excellent physical security measures which would help keep external intruders away. However, he was also careless with his relationships, and continually introduced potential insider threats to his home.

Statistically at least, there was a likelihood that one or more of his many companions may have objected to their temporary and apparently disposable status, continually announced through the constant answering machine messages. Even supposing this wasn't an issue, if he treated others the way he had treated me, it was a fair assumption that people wouldn't always think of him fondly. Putting all of that aside, he had lots of unsecured cash, and presumably drugs in his home, and at least some of these companions might well have been aware of that. Motivations such as greed and revenge are obvious here, as well as the possibility of coercion, bribery and even publicity for others.

Ultimately, it was his attitude to the people he dealt with that was perhaps the biggest danger for the parrot guy. I never knew for sure, but if I were a betting woman I would put a lot of money on that robbery being informed by one or more of those answerphone ladies, perhaps even the 'fiancée' who was with him at the time. However, I was certain of one thing: it was once again, a very human problem.

7

DOORS AND DIARIES

I got my first solo physical infiltration job while I was still studying at the University of Liverpool and living at home with my
parents. A call came through one evening and Mum came and
got me from my room. 'It's work,' she said, smiling, and I got
up and went to the phone, expecting to hear Jack or Adam on
the other end asking me to do a shift in the bar. To my surprise,
a well-spoken, older male voice greeted me over the line.

'Hello Jenny. My name is Frank. We've not met but I know
your two cousins. I have a job I'd like to pay you to do, if you
can manage it.' I was surprised, but it wasn't so unusual that
I was overly suspicious and I'd check with the boys in person
the following day. I was also just about out of cash, my student grant and meagre savings rapidly disappearing with the
expenses and social life of a new term. I kept myself afloat with
some waitressing and occasional bar work for the boys, but it
was a struggle and I was intrigued by the very polite and formal
manner of the man at the end of the phone.

He told me that there was a government building, near the
waterfront in Liverpool, whose directors needed me to check
if their security was lacking. The early 1990s were a turbulent
period for public departments, and spending had been slashed,

especially in Liverpool. This meant that staffing had been cut to an absolute minimum and this included security measures and personnel. If I could show they needed help, they might be able to squeeze some additional budget for better measures in the future. It sounded plausible.

He explained that there was a specific target for the job: inside one of the desks there was a diary/address book belonging to a local councillor and politician who we'll call Mr Trilby. I was supposed to go in, take the diary as proof of entry, and post it to him before the coming weekend. This gave me just under a week to do the job. I had asked Frank a few questions, but he had assured me that all was well and that 'most of the management' had been informed about the 'security audit'.

'What about the guy with the diary? Mr Trilby? Is he informed?' I asked.

'No, no,' came the response. 'But that wouldn't work, would it?'

'OK then,' I said, lowering my voice as Mum bustled around making dinner. 'I'll ask the boys and we'll let you know.'

'Do you really need the boys on this one, Jenny?' he countered. 'Should be very quick and it won't be difficult. Security consists of two men covering three different buildings. I could do it myself if I was nearby.'

I thought for a second and agreed with him but added I would ask them anyway. The next day, on my way into university, I stopped by the club and spoke to the boys about the call and the job I'd been asked to do. Jack and Adam were fine with me doing it alone and showed little interest in the details. Importantly though, they had recognised the name the guy had given me over the phone and smirked when I said I had wondered about the owner being unaware.

'Frank's OK, Jen,' Jack said. 'Pays well and is legit. Well, sort of. And he knows Chris.'

This name put my mind at ease. Chris was another cousin, in a very senior and legitimate role. It wasn't as if we spoke to him very much, but if this Frank knew Chris then he was almost certainly law enforcement or in some related discipline. In Liverpool at the time most of us were not exactly fans of the establishment due to political unrest and social issues, but this did reassure me that the job was legitimate enough to be taken.

I let the boys know I would go for a poke around the next day and likely make the move one evening when the building was quieter. After that I'd call the bar and let them know all was OK, or pop in if I finished early enough. Any problems, and I would let them know as soon as I had a chance. They nodded in agreement, but I could tell they had paid almost no attention to my plans and were soon submerged in their work in the club, talking to the other staff and forgetting I was there. I really was on my own for this one.

After my university classes finished the next day, I made my way through the city and towards the river, coming to a stop across the road from the target building. I sat down at a bus stop conveniently more or less opposite the building and watched the comings and goings. The building was grey and gloomy in the murky afternoon light and people seemed to be leaving and entering quite freely. I crossed the road and walked around the building, noting a few entrances and gathering points for people. It was busy. I knew it was a government office, but it seemed that members of the public were also allowed inside certain areas, and people milled around at the front entrance smoking and looking at pieces of paper.

It was a good thing that this was the case. Public access would make it easy enough to wander around inside and, if challenged, claim I was late for some appointment and had got lost. I walked inside the front door and glanced around. There were various signs and notices in the lobby and a shabby front desk with some leaflets and pens on it, but there was no one there and so I walked over to the lifts.

The floor I needed, local government administration, was clearly marked next to the grimy buttons on the wall; my guy, Mr Trilby, worked in that department. I waited a while for the lift but I wasn't nervous. This was a public building and I had no intention of doing anything wrong on this visit, which was purely a reconnaissance.

When the lift reached my floor the doors opened revealing a few tables and chairs in a small waiting area, and a door to my left. There was no one about so I walked forwards a few steps left and took a look through the glass panels on the door. I could see a bustling office beyond, with people sitting at banks of desks and some enclosed rooms at the rear. Moving closer still, I could make out the guy I was looking for, easily recognisable from local newspapers and television, sitting at a large desk talking with two other people in one of the office rooms at the far end. I was certain it was him and that was surely his own desk. This was the right place and getting through the door wasn't going to be too difficult – it was a standard handle and latch by the looks of it.

They probably don't even lock it, I thought. *I'll just have to return when it's a bit quieter and have a gander. Done.*

I had stepped back slightly from the main office door when it swung open, and a young guy in a loud tie looked me up and down. 'Are you lost?' he said, smiling at me.

'No, actually,' I replied, smiling back, and stepping towards the lifts. 'I just wanted to speak with Mr Trilby. That's him in there isn't it?' I nodded, and he mirrored the action back.

'I'll leave it though for a bit, he looks busy.'

'Yes, well he's heading for the conference tomorrow, so he is a bit chocka,' the guy said.

'Conference?'

'The Labour Party conference?' he sighed, getting a bit impatient.

'Oh yeah, of course, of course,' I said. 'It'll wait.'

Back in the city, I bought a coffee and thought about how slack the security was. If someone had any malicious intentions, they could easily have got in and attacked him, and it wasn't as if he was universally popular – he was a politician after all. He was very exposed, especially considering how volatile everything had been politically lately in my city and beyond – no wonder they were testing the security. The job wouldn't be too hard, though; I could go back later when the building would be mostly empty and just go and grab his book.

After doing some university work, I made my way back to the building at around eight o'clock. I took the same lift as earlier in the day and got out into the corridor. As soon as I stepped out of the lift, I realised it was not going to happen that night. I could see he was still at his desk, writing away, and there were quite a few people in the office space beyond. I could have waited somewhere for him to leave, but I felt uneasy. I missed having the boys to ask for help in this situation. I missed their noise and laughter. I missed their advice. I decided to try again the next day and made my way home.

I returned the following evening a little later than before, arriving at around 8.30, and watched from the bus stop outside for about twenty minutes. When I didn't see any movement or signs of life, I crossed the road and walked unimpeded through the main entrance. As before, the front desk was unmanned, and the building was very quiet. I could hear the lifts moving somewhere high above me, so I decided to avoid them and took the stairs to the floor I needed. Cautious, I moved slowly into the corridor, I listened and looked around for signs of life, but the place was completely dead. Likely, the entire office was at that conference, or otherwise not staying too late tonight after the late finish the previous day.

I walked to the door and tried the handle. It was stiff but old and worn out, so I pulled hard and it opened without too much resistance, the flimsy locking latch yielding easily under pressure. Fix your locks, people.

Once inside the room I smelt tobacco smoke and takeaway fish and chips, which would be something of a red flag for me these days, as it meant the place was either very recently vacated or still occupied. Back then, I don't remember giving it much thought and I walked straight in and made for the office at the end of the room. The door was wedged open, and I went over to the desk. After a bit of shuffling around, I found a diary/address book in the top drawer. It was shabby and looked well used, and I wondered why he hadn't taken it with him to his conference. It seemed strange but I thought it was probably part of the test and I was glad I was almost done.

Grinning at the thought of telling the boys how easy it had been, I stashed the book in my bag and turned to leave, when the door to the lobby area opened and two security guards walked through. I don't know if they were on routine patrol, or whether they had heard something, but I panicked and ran out of the office and towards another set of doors at the opposite end of the room. The guards immediately ran across the office after me and I heard them shouting as I looked around another, dustier, corridor and made for a door with a fire exit evacuation plan taped to it.

Behind the door were more stairs, but these were concrete

and lit only with emergency lighting. I paused for a second and turned to run down the stairs, hoping to outrun the guards and burst out of a door on the ground floor before they could grab me. However, before I ran a thought occurred to me and I then pulled a move that has come to be something of a signature for me. Instead of diving down towards the lower floors and a quick exit, I ran upwards.

I don't remember considering hiding on the roof at this point although I did this often as my career progressed. I just assumed that the guards would probably think I would run down the stairs to try to get out of the building as quickly as possible. By this logic I supposed that I could go through a door on one of the floors above and hide from them there, while they ran downwards for a while, assuming I'd descended, until they realised their mistake. So I half-ran, half-tripped upwards to the floor above. The doors below banged and I stood out of sight against the building wall as they discussed where I might have gone.

'Can you see her?'

'No.'

They ran down a flight or two and so I ran as quietly as I could up a couple of flights, but they heard my footsteps and changed direction. 'She went up, get her!' one of them shouted, and they started to run after me. I was lucky in that neither of them was in particularly good shape and I was then physically fit and used to running. I had a good few flights on them when I saw the door at the top and realised I had nowhere else to run. It was clearly marked with a 'NO ENTRY TO ROOF' sign, but I tried the handle and it opened, the door flying out of my hand, caught by a vicious wind, sheets of icy driving rain immediately hitting my face. There was no way I was heading further up there, I had no idea if it was safe and it was dark and scary as well as being wild with the rain. They were about to catch me and I didn't want two fat security guards wrestling with me on that roof.

Now, one thing you learn if you have something you shouldn't have with you, and are going to be caught, is to dump the evidence. It's crime 101 and I knew that the only thing that could prove I had done anything wrong was my having that diary. In the last twenty seconds before a sweating guard laid his chubby hand on my arm, I took the diary and flung it up into the void and onto the roof before shouting out in a shaking voice.

'It's OK, it's OK. I'm not running away, I'm here. I've not done anything; you just gave me a fright.' They grabbed me firmly but not at all roughly and walked me down a flight and into the lift.

'What are you up to?' they asked.

I played it dumb. I looked like what I was. A student. I could see that neither of these two was going to be rough with me. They looked more amused and puzzled than anything else. 'I just was looking for Mr Trilby,' I said. 'Honest. I just want to speak with him before he gets to the conference.'

They exchanged glances and looked bewildered. Sitting me down in what looked like a little staff common room, they tried again. 'I'm calling the bizzies [police] if you don't tell the truth. Why are you in the office and what have you took? Are you a smackhead?'

I giggled a bit despite the situation. This was like being stopped by Laurel and Hardy. As long as they didn't follow through and call the police, which I doubted, I'd be fine. 'Oh! As if the bizzies would come and help you deal with a nineteen-year-old girl,' I said. 'I told you I haven't nicked anything, and I am obviously *not* a smackhead, am I?'

They looked at each other and I dropped the attitude.

'Honest to God. I am just a student. I'm from Walton. I just wanted to talk to him. You gave me a fright, so I ran. Sorry. I was only looking around. I am really sorry.' I started to cry a bit and one of them handed me a torn piece of some sort of hard paper tissue. 'Can I go? I need to get back home or my dad will kill me.'

They exchanged glances. I could see, through watery eyes, that they believed me. 'Look, mate. Empty the bag. It's just books and that. I just wanted to talk to him,' I sniffled.

'Oh, have it back,' the older one said. 'For fuck's sake, love. We could have battered you. He'll be back tomorrow or something, make an appointment. OK?'

'Yeah, go on girl,' the other one said, kindly. 'Have this back, I'm sure it is just your books. Get home out of this rain, OK? Where do you live again?'

'Walton. By the ground. Olney Street.'

'Ha! I bet you are a Blue, aren't you?'

I nodded, lying, and picked up the bag. 'Thanks, and I'm sorry. My dad will kill me, I'm so late.'

And with that, those two lovely guards let me go, holding open the door for me as I walked out of the building and into the rain. I walked away glumly until I was out of sight of the building, then straightened myself up to think. There was no way I wasn't going back for that diary. I sat on a bench a few blocks away. The rain was getting heavier now and despite the cold there was some thunder and lightning in the sky. After a while I got fed up and cold and grabbed a bus home. I had a cup of tea and toast with my parents and went to bed, but I couldn't sleep and ended up sitting up in bed and staring out of the window at the Liverpool skyline.

The building was just about visible alongside the more famous features of the city, and they were all being thrashed by the heavy rain. The book was on the roof. It would be soaked. Maybe it was ruined, and I wouldn't get paid, even if I went back and got it somehow. I pictured the boys' faces when I told them I'd failed. They would likely laugh at me, and I would lose confidence in doing any job on my own. It would suck.

Without really processing much more about it, I got dressed again and told my dad I was going back to uni to stay with a friend. I kissed him and told him I'd call when I got to her digs safely and I went out into the rain, catching a train into the city and walking back towards the building I'd left not two hours before. The building was in darkness now, and I was soaked to the bone, but through the rain I could still see a faint light through the glass entrance doors. It was worth a try.

I crossed the road and took a closer look through the doors without pushing them, as even these guards would surely have locked them by now. The lobby was deserted, as it had been every time before. I had butterflies in my stomach. The security guards had been lovely, but if they caught me a second time, they might be more determined to get an answer from me, maybe actually call the police. While I had initially accepted Frank's story about the whole thing being author-ised, I realised I wasn't sure how this would fly with the local plod. In that moment of doubt, I also knew that I doubted Frank and his entire story. I didn't really know what side he was on and, like the footballer's wife, had trusted someone for no real reason other than the fact that he sounded legitimate and knew the boys. However, the boys weren't always fully legitimate themselves. I hadn't checked in with my cousin Chris because although he would be as straight and above board as it was possible to be, that was exactly why the rest of us avoided talking to him unless it was absolutely necessary. He would have asked too many questions, always disapproved of anything we did, and most certainly would have told my dad what I had been asked to do and he would have stopped me doing the job outright.

Tired, soaked and increasingly doubtful, I was debating whether to return at first light and hope some early starter would let me tailgate into the building behind them, when, suddenly, but very clearly, I saw one half of the doors blow open a little in the wind and wobble on its hinges.

It wasn't locked.

My wet feet left puddles on the floor of the lobby, through the doors and up the stairs as I made my way directly for the roof. The door opened easily, and the book was there, soggy and dishevelled, but there. I picked it up and put it carefully in my backpack, then made my way down the stairs and out of the building with no further incidents.

At my friend's digs, I left it drying on a radiator overnight and posted it from the university post office before my first lecture that morning. Not long afterwards a cheque landed at my parents' place. I gleefully cashed it and went out for some celebratory drinks with a bunch of friends, telling them I had finally been paid for some shifts I'd done in the bar.

The owner of the diary turned out not to be a good person. I kept an ear out for mentions of him in the news for a couple of years after the job, always scared that he would somehow refer to the theft in an interview on policing or something, but to my knowledge he never did and was removed from office just a couple of years later for a variety of reasons making him unfit for office. When I heard he had gone, I finally relaxed about the job and decided that in future I would trust Frank, whom I had eventually checked out with Cousin Chris, and who had shown faith in my ability to get the task done by myself.

That first solo job gave me a sense of confidence in the work that wasn't always to be trusted. It had been so easy, and the security guards were naive, so unprepared and underpaid to deal with someone determined to get in. It was a defining moment, because it made me think that anyone, really, could have done it, including people with violent or purely malicious intentions. While I had done lots of similar jobs with the boys, it was this one that I remember as my first paid 'rodeo'.

I decided I'd take more jobs like this if they came in and keep as many of the details as possible to myself. I could do without the hassle of my cousins, or anyone else, having opinions on how I did the jobs. I didn't need judgement and would ask for advice or help if I needed it. Beyond that, I was happy to carry on with plan A, which was to finish my degree, get a decent job somewhere and make enough money to buy my own place. If being a burglar of sorts sometimes would help to fund that, fine; as long as I was comfortable with the client, and no one got hurt or lost anything, I decided it was OK. If I had permission to do it and was getting paid, the con was on. I would use whatever I had, but I wasn't going to shout about it anytime soon and I thought of it as a useful way of supplementing my income and making some connections.

As the years went by, I went from university to starting my career, doing office jobs and bits of other work. I was smart enough and a hard worker and I progressed from graduate positions to management in a relatively short space of time. Alongside my legitimate career, jobs from Frank and others continued to come in and for the most part I accepted them, enjoying the extra cash and keeping very quiet about it all. I would certainly have been fired from my regular positions if I had told any company about my other work, and the workplace was rife with politics and dramas of its own. I'd had to stop working in the bar at weekends because no firm allowed its workers to earn a second income, but they were never going to know about the 'security' work unless I told them.

Before long the novelty faded and my clandestine income, and how I made it, became just another part of my life. I carried on working, accepting jobs and building my legitimate career at the same time, never talking about it to my colleagues or friends, although I always wondered whether some of them had an idea there was more to me than I let on.

I calculate now that at conservative estimate, the number of buildings I have in some way infiltrated is in the hundreds, most of them with the full permission of the owners. It was many, many years before I advertised my services, or even really articulated properly what I am able to do, but the work kept coming and was varied, and while the vast majority of these jobs were not remarkable, some of them stand out because of the location, events or people I met on the way.

There was the time when I and a small crew I had put together were asked to test the security of a large funfair in the south of England, and I had to hide inside a ghost train while security guards with dogs looked for me. I was asked to play poker in a hotel in Northern Ireland in order to give feedback on 'tells' to a friend of a client. I'd studied body language for years, applying my knowledge to negotiations, and to help me read people better on my infiltration jobs. Years later I'd use it during corporate investigations into deception or internal issues and during various surveillance tasks.

I once investigated a guy suspected of selling company information to a competitor and was rooting around his office late at night, when he suddenly returned and I had to bolt out of his office and make a run for it. I had found upskirt pictures, presumably of female colleagues, in his desk, along with numerous keys hidden in various locations around his office and maps of the building and general area pinned on the walls of his office, but concealed by standard photographs and training certificates. I had to run down corridors and out of a fire escape as he chased me, shouting threats and expletives that echoed around the factory walls.

In Belgium I had successfully completed a job inside a CEO's office, before discovering that the door had locked shut and trapped me inside. To escape I'd climbed out of the window and edged around the outside of the building on a wide window ledge, only to see what was either a second security team, or actual burglars, rifling through papers and picking locks inside another office. I left undetected as teams of police poured into the building, presumably to arrest the real criminals inside. When I got back, I had breakfast with a colleague immediately afterwards and continued with a normal business day as if nothing unusual had happened.

I'd exposed theft at a firm in Asia, resulting in four of their employees immediately fleeing the country and prompting a corporate scandal unprecedented in their company history that made the news all over Asia. I'd analysed criminal interrogations in many contexts and countries, assisting law enforcement and private security in many cases, some of which were mind-boggling in their seriousness, and the heartbreak and human cost they had caused.

Occasionally, I employed small teams on a job-by-job basis. They had helped me infiltrate everything from banks to theatres, theme parks to nuclear power plants, factories and the offices and mansions of the super-wealthy and famous. While there was an increasing need for technical hacking on the job, it wasn't something I pursued myself, and I had many an occasion when pure cheek and quick thinking unlocked a site for me and the team. Often just doing our research and working with the shortcuts and culture that already existed in a client's premises would be enough for us to find a way in.

One factory we worked on required creative thinking. The security team had just spent a fortune on perimeter defence and their manager told me that he knew my reputation but doubted I'd get past. 'It's cost two million quid, Jen. That fence is rock solid. The only way you'll ever get past is if someone leaves a door open for you!' He'd laughed over a gin and tonic and a pie in his local. 'Good luck, and I'll see you for the debrief on Friday.'

We'd uncovered a couple of potentially useful things during our reconnaissance, and I'd discussed how we might use them with my team. Firstly, we had found from an open job specification that employees on the site were covered by an auto-repair insurance policy. This meant that little issues with their company vehicles, like a replacement headlight or flat tyre, would be covered by the firm and repaired on site by local mechanics while they carried on with their working day at the offices inside. We'd also noticed that several older fleet cars were permanently parked up at the rear of the car park, seemingly unused near the brand-new exterior fence.

Extensive research had shown that the employees themselves were a solemn bunch who seemed to be very rules-driven and respectful of hierarchy. I assumed that this would equate to an obedient and risk-averse working culture, and a plan had formed in my head. With only their head of security fully aware of the timing, we made our way to the site shortly before five o'clock on the day of the test in a small white van with a magnetic sign we had had made for us saying: 'JR Auto Repair – Windscreens, Tyres and Repairs – we come to you!'

My confederate pulled up and handed a 'job sheet' to one of

the guards. 'Here to look at a vehicle for a reported cracked windscreen,' he said, giving the registration number. The guard went back into the hut and tapped at a computer; he came back. 'Yeah. I've not got a visit down today, but it's in the back of the car park, on the right, mate,' he said and raised the barrier. 'When the right guy gets back in tomorrow, I'll let him know you've had a look.'

'OK,' we replied and drove through, making our way to the scruffy car at the rear of the site.

The night before we had crept up to the site on foot and looked at the fleet car parked about three metres behind the fence. We had aimed a few pebbles at the windscreen in an attempt to crack the glass, but throwing through the fence had proved difficult and, in fits of giggles, we had aborted. My friend had dug a pellet gun out of his car and returned at first light that morning. He reported back that the car looked like it hadn't been moved for weeks, along with several other cars in a similar state, parked and seemingly forgotten by everyone on site. It had been partly boxed in by a few other vehicles and was covered in bird mess and leaves. After several attempts with the pellet gun, he had managed to hit home on the windscreen and had made a decent chip in the glass but hadn't managed to shatter it. It was enough.

We drove to the car and while he got out and looked around, I stayed in the passenger seat. After much shaking of the head and making notes on a clipboard, he got back into the van and slowly made his way back to the security gate. As we passed the edge of the factory building, he stopped near a back door and I got out and went over to some large rubbish bins and pallets near a door. I crouched behind them and watched as he returned back to the security barrier which lifted and let him leave.

We later found that the guards had called the HR guy in charge of the fleet, but had told them we had already left. The guy had promised to follow this up, but to our knowledge never did, and later said he had presumed it had all been taken care of, as usual, by the auto repair contractors.

A few staff had started to leave through the door to my right as their shift finished. I was nicely hidden by the bins and pallets, and waited for a quiet moment, before reaching into my bag and quickly tacking an A4 piece of paper to the door. We had printed it the night before at our hotel and written the following upon it: 'Please DO NOT close this door! Thank you!'

We'd scrawled a vague signature beneath it.

A couple more people came out, chatting and removing ear defenders, letting the door close behind them and oblivious to me still crouching, well hidden behind the bins. However, before too long a guy in a suit came through the door looking at his phone and dawdling a little. He stopped, reading something on a text and then glanced up at the door to make sure it closed behind him. I couldn't see exactly what happened next from my vantage point, but he seemed to hesitate briefly and then push it back open and walk inside. After that, more people come through the door, although now I could hear them before I saw them, and I'd stopped hearing the gentle plunk noise as it closed behind them. I waited some more and gradually the flow of people slowed down and eventually stopped as the car park emptied.

I stood up cautiously and moved from my hiding spot behind the bins. Looking at the door I could see it had been wedged open by a paper towel. *Obey the rules or be damned,* I thought, and I walked into the site and finished the job.

Apart from a fraught few minutes waiting for the security guards to patrol so I could duck under the barrier and leave, there was nothing unusual to report. On the Friday, in front of the security guy and his team, I explained in simple terms what had happened, showing them some bits and pieces I'd picked up from the factory and office interior and handing them the now-scruffy sign I'd pinned on the door.

They were attentive and responsive clients and as far as I know made good efforts to harden off the gaps we had found in their site and procedures. I couldn't help but feel sorry for the security guy, though. As I described how I got in and handed him the sign, he put his head in his hands and looked at his colleague. 'Two million quid, Brian,' he had muttered, forlornly. 'Two *million* quid.'

As the years passed the jobs ebbed and flowed as life events took over. I got married, Dad died and then children came. I did a few social engineering jobs when I was pregnant, easy office infiltrations mostly, and I found that if no one had stopped me before they positively fell over themselves to help me when I had my baby bumps.

I'd never been completely content with corporate life and working in the manufacturing industry was precarious at best. I was increasingly using my negotiation skills to settle industrial disputes or make deals to outsource processes and product lines to the Far East, which made sense commercially but led to local upheaval and difficulties nearer to home. I'd put away some savings and decided to take a career break and think about what I really wanted to do.

Eventually, I decided to become an independent consultant and trainer, using some of the skills from my alternative career as well as a more conventional curriculum.

I focused on teaching non-verbal communications, negotiation skills and persuasion and influence courses, heavily editing my stories so they had commercial appeal and wouldn't alarm my delegates. I also taught contract law and business subjects and was never short of work.

The flexibility of choosing my own contracts also gave me time to continue with my security and social engineering work, which was always what I most enjoyed as well as paying the most generously. I still wasn't confident with being open in public about what I did, but I often used stories and redacted case studies from my security work in my other training. I gave examples of how I'd used the principles of influence to resolve disputes while working undercover and taught my negotiation groups to recognise when someone was being evasive through their body language and facial expressions. They always wanted more of the security stories and I occasionally told them a bit more over dinner or drinks, omitting sensitive details and being careful not to name clients or tell them too much about the real nature of the work I did.

Tentatively, I began occasionally speaking directly to certain clients about the other services I could provide. I wasn't yet a part of the security industry, or even well known in the wider industry, but the work kept on coming and before too long I started to wonder if I could start my own firm specialising in very niche, people-based security, physical infiltrations and investigation skills. I was gradually gaining the confidence to go fully public and announce to the world that I was, in fact, a social engineer, 'a burglar for hire'.

8

THE DEVIL ON THE ROOF

Although a lot of physical infiltration jobs are interesting because of the context, or a problem or a location, just as many are very routine and go entirely to plan. Over the years there have been countless straightforward infiltrations, and I've walked into many an office or building, maybe had a challenge from a staff member, but generally not that much of real note happens.

We get into the site, do our thing and leave. Report a few security issues to the team, present our findings and move on to the next job, destroying our reports and evidence as part of the confidentiality agreement I have with the clients. Sometimes, when things go well, I almost feel cheated that all the meticulous preparation is not required and we never need to use the many hours of tactical and strategic planning, research and pretexts we have put in prior to the job.

For example, there was a time when we had elaborately planned our approach, organised back-up plans and stories and had a B-team on standby to move in if the gang and I were stopped. In the event, the target, a large shopping complex just outside central London, was wide open and I walked into the office space unchallenged, found what I needed and left without incident. The debrief was quick and straightforward and the team and I couldn't help but feel a sense of anticlimax and disappointment in the job, because we had expected to have to use much more artifice and skill.

Often, after a couple of unremarkable jobs, I went back to working on my own, simplifying everything and dispensing with a crew, relying only on a client signature for the infiltration and some back-up from my office. One such job became remarkable for other reasons, and it happened in London at the centre of the corporate world in Canary Wharf.

I always think of Canary Wharf as a huge corporate theme park. It's full of new high-rise office buildings with bars and hotels dotted around to support the staff from the many businesses based there. In 1996 in the South Quay area, an IRA bomb exploded killing two people. It is now a site that is generally covered well by defensive technology and staff, with good operational procedures and resources put into its security. This made the entire site an excellent candidate for a physical test, just to make certain that all the investment and precautions couldn't be bypassed by any human element.

I was asked to get into a client office in one of the main buildings, on one of the higher floors. Our surveillance had shown excellent security at the front of the building. With cameras everywhere, security guards taking names, admission through electronic gates only after the issuing of passes as a named visitor, it should have been challenging. However, if the gates of the castle are well guarded then we look for other methods of entry and after not much digging we found a possible way in.

It was a warm summer afternoon when I made my move. Dressed in a nondescript black shirt and trousers, I put on a yellow high-visibility vest and, carrying a clipboard, made my way to the rear of the building and sat down in a staff smoking area hidden away from the bustle of the main lobby.

Before too long, several staff came out for their coffee break and smiled at me, gossiping about their supervisors and discussing plans for the weekend. I noticed that most of them were in the uniform of a coffee franchise that was situated inside the building. It's a fatal flaw of many security programmes that while the actual employees of the firm may well receive awareness training and have technical and physical precautions in place to keep them safe, often contractors and franchises, also allowed into the site, do not. The cleaners, gardeners and maintenance staff rarely receive any help, and it leaves the castle, as it were, vulnerable. After all, why bother with raising the drawbridge if the maid can walk in through an open side door?

I got chatting to a couple of women close by, commenting on their nails and talking about how it had been a tough week and I, like them, was also looking forward to the weekend. I was, I mentioned, going to go in, do my health and safety inspection and then go and have some drinks with the girls. As they got up to leave, I took a few steps in the opposite direction, but then seemed to change my mind and followed them towards the staff door up ahead. 'Easier this way,' I said, rolling my eyes, and they laughed in agreement as I followed them through the door and into the building. They waved a cheerful goodbye and disappeared down a corridor, while I made my way forwards, glancing around for some stairs.

I wasn't looking forward to that part of the job. The office I needed was over twenty floors up and that meant two flights of stairs per floor. My legs would be like jelly by the time I got there and, not being especially fit or lithe, I would definitely have to pause in my ascent. However, most lifts have cameras inside them, and although the head of security for the client and some of the more general security team for the building knew I would be doing the job that day, I didn't need the rest of the security team or some general member of staff catching me on CCTV and asking questions. So the stairs it had to be.

I found the flight easily enough and ascended a couple of floors. I paused for a breath and saw double doors in the stairwell instead of the single one I'd noticed on the other floors. It was only a couple of metres ahead of me so I went over and listened at it, wondering if it was some sort of maintenance space or, worse, the security office, often situated in an area beneath the main offices. I could hear some noise, like the clanking of plates and then the door flew open, forcing me to step aside and a lady pushing a trolley with coffee pots and water came through.

'Are you looking for the supply lift, love?' she said, without registering surprise on her face.

'No, no,' I said. 'I know it's just through here, right?'

'Yes,' she said. 'Be careful now, there is water on the floor. Don't slip!'

I thanked her and popped through the doors, thinking what an amazing cover a high-vis vest is. It was rare that anyone ever stopped me or asked any questions if I wore one. A classic authority ploy that works almost every time. I was grateful that it had worked again and mentally crossed my fingers that the supply lift was camera-free.

In contrast to the walnut-panelled, highly polished public lifts at the front of the building, the lift used by the maintenance, catering and cleaning staff was small, scruffy and dimly lit. These lifts are often used so that these teams can move quicker around the building while doing their jobs, and also, or so it seemed, so that they would be out of sight of the executives and their visitors in the fancier versions out front.

They were common enough in many of the corporate offices I had seen, which often also even had different restrooms for this type of staff member, small, functional and hidden away from view. I'd even been in some buildings with hidden supply tunnels and secret corridors that were used for this type of in-house maintenance. If you look carefully, you'll find them in lots of large buildings; it's how your coffee gets to your meeting while it is still hot and how your cleaner moves around. We should appreciate the people using them much more.

As she had mentioned, the floor in the little lift was wet, a small puddle pooling in the corner of the tiny compartment. I stood holding the door open without entering and looked around for cameras. There was nothing obvious, but there was a suspicious-looking glass-covered hole at the top of the floor buttons, which I could just about see if I poked my head inside. If it was a camera, it would see me if I stepped fully inside, but it was angled away from the door, so I was likely OK so far. I reached into my rucksack and took out a white sticky label and, just as a precaution, reached inside with my hand and covered it up.

Stepping inside, I took a proper look at the buttons. Unhelpfully they were not all clearly marked for the floor numbers, much of the writing upon them being worn away by years of use. I did a quick calculation and punched a button with a fuzzy number '2' on it, the second digit no longer visible. It was either the floor I needed or one or two above. It would do. The lift moved quickly, and I was grateful that it didn't stop to collect anyone else, arriving at my selected floor speedily. The doors opened and I stepped out into a tiny space with a little door to my left. Here goes.

Only when I walked through the door and into the corridor

beyond did I realise that I had managed to land on the exact floor I was after. Things were going well so far, and I went straight into the plan and the pretext I had for the job.

The door leading from the stairwell to the office space beyond was locked with an electronic keypad and I didn't have the combination. I googled the brand on my phone and saw that it usually had a four-digit code to unlock it, set by the client. I googled the factory setting for the pad: 1,2,3,4. Unfortunately, many people buy these types of keypads and don't ever change them from their factory settings. It was worth a try: 1,2,3,4. Nothing. Wrong code.

I looked carefully at the metal buttons, to see any signs of wear and tear. If any are shinier than the others that generally points to many fingers rubbing off dirt. It wasn't obvious, but I thought that the 2 and the 0 were shinier than the others. I tried 2,0,0,1.

No.

2,0,0,2.

No.

2,0,2,0.

A beeping noise and the door opened.

I took the clipboard out of the bag and walked through into the office beyond, consciously projecting that I was here for a purpose and not trying to hide or hesitate. A few faces looked up from desks and keyboards, but only briefly. I looked official and it wasn't their problem. No one interfered.

I stopped at a bank of desks with two people working on laptops at either end. I kneeled under the empty spaces and wrote some numbers down on the clipboard. Moving on to the next one, I did the same and when I got to the guy at the end of the row, I said a polite excuse me and added: 'Just checking the cable ports. Sorry to bother you, won't be a second.'

He smiled, preoccupied, and carried on with his work.

'Thanks,' I said and moved up a row.

As I carried on 'checking the cable ports', I managed to make my way around most of the open office space, before seeing the closed rooms at the end of the floor. This was where the management lived, so important they got their own personal cell. Part of my remit was to send an email from inside at least one of them. I knocked on a door. A woman's voice responded and I stepped into her office. 'Hiya. You had an issue with the cable? I'm here to just double-check the port.'

She looked confused. 'Slow connection? Logged you out?' I continued, looking at a list of imaginary complaints I'd printed out the day before. 'I'm just doing a basic check; the guys will come up later and look closer for you. I'll only be a second.'

She nodded and got back to typing away. I bent down and unplugged the cable to her monitor. 'What?!' she exclaimed. 'You just cut me off!'

'Oh God, sorry!' I said. 'Yeah, you've got a connection issue for sure. I'll report it.' I plugged the cable back in and her monitor came back.

'Ah. There you go!' I said. She smiled, but was clearly irritated, I pulled the cable again.

'It's gone again! I'm really busy!' she said in a controlled but angry tone. I plugged it back in.

'OK,' I said. 'Let's just register this fault and I'll leave you alone. I'll make sure the tech guys give you priority. Can you just send an email from your computer and they will do the remote checks now . . .?' She looked at me and started to object.

'. . . Or you'll probably lose your connectivity altogether in a minute and maybe your documents. I mean, I think so. I'm not technical.'

She sighed and opened her email. I stood behind her. 'No.

No,' I said. 'Just go to www.faultrecoveryjrjr.com, please.' She typed in the web address I'd given her, clacking hard on her keyboard and clearly annoyed. 'Just fill in the form and they'll be up shortly,' I said, watching her enter her ID number, password and email details into the spoofed form we had set up online.

'Sorry again.' I smiled as I left. 'Save those documents and they'll be up shortly.' I closed the door with a respectfully slow hand and moved to the next office. It was empty.

I turned on the computer, glancing up at the door frequently as I worked. A login screen appeared with the ID already typed in but no password. I looked around for somewhere it might be written down, under the keyboard, in the drawers. Tucked away at the back of the top drawer was a promising-looking little pad. I was about to look through it when the door opened, and a young woman looked in.

'Hi!' she said, looking right at me. 'Would you like a cuppa? I'm making one. Have you got all you need?'

'I have,' I said, smiling back. 'Milk, no sugar please.'

'We have herbal if you'd prefer?' She saw my expression. 'Builder's tea it is. John will be back by close of play if you need to look in his office as well?'

'I do,' I nodded and added, 'thanks babe, what's your name?'

'Cass,' she said and left to make me my cuppa.

I looked at the screen again. PASSWORD.

I flicked through the book but nothing obvious came up. Cass came in with my tea, in a china mug with their corporate branding. 'Thanks, Cass. This one is really knackered,' I said. 'I bet he moans about it all the time.'

She laughed and nodded. 'The password he gave us isn't working, though . . .' I said, letting it hang in the air.

'Try "HOTSPUR123",' she said immediately. 'That's his usual. He'll be glad to get it fixed.'

'Smashing,' I replied, watching her leave.

I tried 'HOTSPUR123' but it didn't work.

'HOTSPUR1234' and the screen opened to a desktop full of documents and open programs. I clicked email and, drinking my tea, sent myself and the client a quick email to verify the test was complete. I finished it with 'and you owe me a pint'. I drained the mug and put it inside my rucksack, then got ready to leave. That would do. I carefully logged him out and stood up to leave.

It was only then I noticed a change in the energy outside the door. The clicking and chatting, phones ringing and general bustle had quietened down. When the atmosphere changes like this it usually means something has happened, time to go. I stood at the door and looked through the window. It seemed the same as before if a little subdued. Then a fire alarm went off and the woman from the previous office stuck her head out and shouted, 'Test. Don't worry.'

Ah. I stepped out of the office, nodded at her and walked steadily over to the door to the stairs. 'The lift is that way,' she shouted, and I turned and smiled.

'Thanks.'

She suddenly looked at me a bit strangely. 'Are you based here?'

'Not all the time,' I replied, keeping walking. 'In the other sites as well. Thanks again.'

I opened the door and punched the button for the lift. She had smelt a rat, time to go. The lift came, but I had a feeling security would be waiting for me. It was fine. I'd done the test, but I'd prefer not to be caught at all. It looked unprofessional. I decided to go upwards and see if I could hang about for a while and maybe swap to the supply lift again. They'd see me in this lift if they were looking for someone, so the game was likely up anyway. I'd just try to avoid security for a while, wait until the hullabaloo had died down and then exit via the same staff entrance I'd used before. It was worth a shot. Just for the hell of it.

I pushed the top button and got out onto a floor with the same little corridor and layout as the one I'd just been on with the office. The door to the supply lift was in the same place so I made my way over and pushed it open. No lock on this one. This time though the door didn't show me another lift but another tiny flight of stairs with a fire door at the top of it. The roof. Excellent, although it would almost certainly be alarmed if I went through, it would be a good place to sit and wait for a while as the excitement died down and security would assume I had left.

The corridor was almost pitch dark, and I climbed the stairs slowly and sat down on the top. It was good to relax a while and I felt happy with how the job had gone down. I was sitting on the damp stairs, my backside feeling numb against the cold concrete and scrolling through my phone when I felt a gentle breeze against the back of my head. I shot onto my feet and stood up. The door to the roof was open and swinging gently on its hinges. The breeze was coming through, and I reached out to push it a little more and the smell of fresh air accompanied a streak of daylight peeking through the gap and into the gloomy space below.

I had to be careful; if it was open it likely meant someone was already up there, maybe part of the fire drill. I walked through the door and up a short flight of stairs, sticking my head up first and glancing over the top which was level with the surface of the roof. It was a vast space, framed by a little fence all the way around. There was a raised brick structure in the middle and lots of vents, what I presumed to be air-conditioning fans and a few fire hoses here and there. It looked deserted. I walked further up, listening carefully, but all I could hear was the wind blowing so I took a few more steps.

The view was amazing, I could see the river and London beyond. I took a few cautious steps and circled the structure in the middle just in case some worker or janitor was up there, but I was in luck, it was empty. I checked one more time for cameras before walking over to the railing and looking out over the river. It was glorious and a good place to wait for some time while any alarms raised at my office exploits below died down.

It would take a while to search the building, if that was what they had decided to do, but I figured they likely wouldn't bother and would make it known that a test was expected that day. Additionally, each floor belonged to a different firm, and once security realised I was gone they would probably search the lifts and stairs, maybe see me on the cameras and, well, even if they did come up and find me here, the job was over and a call to the client would clarify it was a security test.

I stood a while taking in the view and then reached into my bag for a cigarette. I put it to my lips and flicked my lighter, but the wind kept blowing out the flame. I tried again and was about to give up when I heard a click behind me and jumped in surprise as I realised there was someone standing there. With a Zippo. 'Light?'

It was a small dark-haired man in a suit, standing directly behind me and holding his lighter, which he put to my cigarette and looked me in the eye. In surprise I let the cigarette light and then looked at him.

'Bad for you,' he said. I nodded. I had meant to give up but, well, this wasn't really the time. I was trying to work out who he was and, more importantly, where he could have come from so quickly and quietly while I was up there, when he folded his arms and leaned against the railing next to me.

'You know, Jenny,' he said in slow measured tones, 'you really need to decide right now whether or not you are on the side of the angels.'

I looked straight ahead. Who was this? How did he know me? And what in hell did he mean by that?!

I leaned on the railing and thought for a second about what to say, but nothing came to mind, better to be quiet and let him carry on. I took a drag from the cigarette and blew the smoke directly in front of me. He stood up and took a few steps. I waited and when nothing further came, I turned around to ask him whether he was part of the security team and what he meant. To my shock, he was gone. It must only have been a few seconds but there was no sign of him. At all.

I glanced frantically around the roof. Nothing. I dropped the cigarette and ran to the little sunken part where the stairs were. Nothing. I ran quickly full circle around the brick struc-ture thinking I'd missed a door, but it was solid and there was no sign. Oh my God, did he jump?

I went back over to the railings, my heart pounding and looked over a bit further at the place we had both stood. If you had been inclined to jump you would not have fallen all the way down. There was a large, paved area, the top of the next floor, that was wider than this top roof (the building graduated a little towards the top) so a jump would have landed you a floor down but no further. Nothing. I circled around the entire railing looking for him with increasing puzzlement and some alarm, but I thought better of shouting out. What was going on?

Out of there now.

I grabbed my bag and made for the door. I ran down the stairs and straight into the corridor with the main lift. Making for the end, I found the main stairwell and proceeded to descend forty floors at the fastest speed I could manage, my knees screaming at me for the last few floors. Bursting through the doors to the supply lift on the lower floor, my thoughts raced as I walked out through the staff entrance, chucked the hi-vis into a bin, and made for Canary Wharf rail station as fast as I could. Only when I was sitting on the moving train did I stop for breath and take a moment to think about who this could be.

If he hadn't known my name, I would have assumed he was some executive taking a few moments of quiet, but he knew who I was! And what about that weird question? I mean I knew what he meant. In my work, you could be tempted to take jobs for personal gain, be a real criminal, but I gave that up long before I'd started my security business and always checked very thoroughly who the client was and whether they were on the right side, 'the side of the angels' as he had put it. Well, almost always. I suppose there were times when I might have been more careful, there had been the occasional job that perhaps I should have questioned more. I hated the fact that I had my doubts.

I thought about what he looked like. A beautiful and expensive grey suit, dark hair and eyes but I really hadn't got a good look at his face. That lighter was engraved with some sort of lettering, a monogram maybe, but I couldn't be sure. The shock he gave me had confused me and I was frustrated at myself for not remembering much about him. After many hours pondering, I decided he must have been a member of the security team, or one of a handful of executives who knew I was going to be in the building that day. Maybe he had seen me on CCTV and followed me up there to spook me out. Mission accomplished. I'd ask the team on the debrief – he would likely be there.

On the day of the debrief I half expected him to be in the room, but he was nowhere to be seen. I presented my findings, including the mug, to the security team, who sighed wearily at the ease with which I had gained access to the offices and computers. The meeting finished with them taking away action points on training and better security for the offices and supply lifts. I shook my contact's hand and asked him to stay behind for a one-to-one. I told him about the encounter, a detail I had left out of my official story, and asked him who the guy was.

'He must be one of your team, I think. Right?'

But the contact was as mystified as I was. He told me that occasionally the odd employee did go up to the roof, but it was a sackable offence from building management as it was obviously dangerous. Additionally, my description didn't fit anyone on the team or anyone he could think of that might have known I was in the building on that day.

'It's a mystery, Jen,' he said, and smiled. 'Good job he didn't try and throw you off!'

In the absence of a better explanation, I tried many times to find him on social media, obsessively googling the names of the firms who shared the building and looking at their corporate pages, but I never did. Eventually, I decided to forget about it and genuinely wondered if I'd imagined the whole thing. Until I met him again.

This time I was at a conference in Sweden. It was a couple of years later and I had started giving keynotes on social engin-eering for large corporate events around the world to educate people on the one hand and to finally move away from rooftops and hiding in cupboards on the other. I'd sneaked away to smoke somewhere hidden – the habit being frowned upon in Sweden – and had found a dark alleyway near the restaurant on the resort to take a moment of quiet before retiring. This time I hadn't even had a chance to find my lighter when I saw him at the top of the alley about five metres in front of me.

'You never have a light when you need one, do you?'

I recognised his voice immediately and looked at him.

'Where did you disappear to on the roof? I've been trying to find you online, what is your name?' I said without any preamble.

'Did you decide?'

I gave him a look and asked again. 'There's no need for the bloody dramatics, did you run for the stairs? You gave me a shock! I thought you had jumped over!'

He laughed and waggled his eyebrows. 'You'll work it out, Jen,' he said, and sauntered away down the alley.

Arsehole, I thought and decided that to pursue him would be pathetic. I let him go and looked out for him at the conference dinner but didn't see him there. Later, talking with a friend, I told her I'd seen him again, but had decided he was caught up in the drama and I was not going to think about it anymore. 'Your guess is as good as mine as to who he is,' I said.

'Fine,' she said. 'I reckon though if you see him again, he'll probably kill you. Ha, ha!'

'Oh, very funny,' I retorted, but from that moment I labelled him 'the devil on the roof' because I am pretty sure she is right.

9

RABBITS

By the time I felt I could admit in public that I broke into buildings for a living, the job had acquired a name. 'Social engineering', loosely defined as the practice of obtaining information and access to what should be secure or private through the manipulation of people, had started to be a trend. It was closely allied with the cyber security industry although I wondered, just before my first public talk in front of a technical cyber audience, whether these computer nerds would understand, much less give a toss, about what I did for a living.

It had come about because another more technical speaker had pulled out of a cyber security conference in London and they were looking for a speaker to fill a thirty-minute slot on the agenda. The audience consisted of tech journalists, ethical hackers and computer/cyber professionals and I was to be the last talk before lunch. I had been speaking in public for years on various topics, mostly to do with the dark arts of high-level soft skills. I'd spoken at events and conferences on topics such as lie detection, body language, influence and persuasion, negotiation and more, but I'd always shied away from publicly talking about what I do.

The guy before me had a technical topic to cover, and it was slow going for him to cover his points. He had slides with lots of text and statistics on them and he read them all out verbatim and then commented on each discussion point. There had been seven speakers before him and people were getting tired and distracted, tapping phones and yawning. The smell of lunch was wafting through the doors and some people were already shuffling past the tables and sneaking out of the theatre. This was going to be a tough crowd.

I glanced at my watch; we were running ten minutes over. One of the organisers inched over to me, a pretty American woman. She whispered loudly in my ear that they would need me to shorten my session to fifteen minutes. This was shaping up to be an awful job. I was annoyed that they would ask me to chop my talk down, but I could see it was needed and after all my topic about working with humans to prevent cons, while also telling some stories of how I actually pulled some cons, was likely of zero interest to this technical crowd. I figured I would get no work from this, make no interesting business connections, and probably never see any of them ever again. I decided I didn't care what they thought of me, so I agreed to shorten it to fifteen minutes. All killer, no filler.

I was wrong about the techies, who have utterly embraced both the wider concept of social engineering and me person-ally, and the rudeness, well, that was just shortness of time. For all they knew I was another speaker who simply read out their slides. I should have known better, after all most of my job involves reading people and reading the room. The guy finished and walked off stage to a smattering of applause; I walked on to a polite but uninterested and similarly small clap and looked out.

There are people who saw me do that first talk that I am still in touch with and who have become friends. They tell me they remember it a bit like a slap in the face. It was arrogant and aggressive, but I was angry, and I thought I would never be back, much less make an impact, so I gave it to them with both barrels and woke everyone up before lunch.

In fifteen minutes, I explained what I did and why all the technical defences they put in place probably wouldn't work as a defence against it. Social engineering relies on people being subject to manipulation, whether it be bribery, coercion, flattery, greed, emotional appeals or any one of the hundred other weaknesses that 'flesh is heir to'. Everyone can be got at, but many people believe that they can't.

People make mistakes and companies leave gaps in their security and/or operational procedures; if there is even one person involved in keeping an organisation secure then you have the weakest link in the chain right there in front of you. I often say that people are like locks, closed down until you find the key. You just look for the lever, the secret sauce, the one piece of information that opens them up and then, well, it's open season. At that point, even good security measures will struggle to stop a determined attacker. No anti-malware or virus detectors, no padlocks or fences, no burglar alarms or bio-technology is beyond the hack. That's what I told them on that morning in London, and they liked it, because they knew it was true.

If I am hired to do a social engineering job these days, it is likely to be as part of a penetration test team or 'red team' activity. The technical part of the team, the white-hat ethical hackers, will attack a computer network, looking for loopholes in code, gaps in the technical fence, and ways to get into the system and demonstrate what damage might be done if they were their malicious equivalent. Then they work with the client's technical teams to patch the vulnerabilities to make it harder for a criminal hacker to go down the same route and hack them for real.

Very often all this has been done and paid for long before anyone thinks to call me, or someone like me, to demonstrate the art of the possible where people are concerned and test the human element within their organisation. This is despite the fact that, in truth, most cyberattacks (as many as 90 per cent, depending on which study you consult) originate from human error or manipulation. Ignoring the human side of the equation is not an option; within that area there are different specialisms and methodologies, and I like to work in a certain way.

Jobs start with physical and online reconnaissance. I'm old school. I like to personally observe the people and location if possible. I check out who goes into the site and at what time. How do they gain access? What do they wear? Are they hurried or casual? Focused or relaxed?

I like to watch for at least a couple of days, at different times of the day and night, of the week and of the month. I watch how security patrols operate, when they change shifts and how alert, or not, they are. I note the companies that deliver to the site and the people that move around unchecked and unnoticed, often cleaners or maintenance staff and catering personnel. I look for natural lines of drift across a site. All the shortcuts and secret entrances that the staff use to move around more quickly, to meet or avoid each other and bypass rules.

People don't realise that companies are full of potential hackers because their own staff will often choose convenience over regulations, authority and safety. If you watch a group of staff for long enough, you'll observe how they go about doing this and you needn't reinvent the wheel yourself if you are trying to break in.

I've used countless 'secret' smoking shelters and meet-up

points as routes into buildings. I've climbed through gaps in fences used, but hidden, by company directors to move quickly from one site to the next. I've hidden inside hollow bushes in gardens, in covered corners of car parks, stood under fire escapes and under makeshift shelters on top of roofs, all because I've watched employees do the same to avoid being spotted. Everyone is a potential hacker, especially if inconvenienced or wanting to avoid being caught. Often, we just copy that.

We will also be doing some online reconnaissance as well. This uses open-source intelligence (OSINT) to gather details on a target company, or person, from the internet. The public don't realise how much information is available about individuals legally and usually for free or cheaply online. For example, the UK electoral roll will give you details of someone's current and former place of residence alongside all those who share or have shared the address, as well as their approximate ages. Government sites will give details of employment, criminal records and births, marriages and deaths. This information is easily found, and generally free to obtain, and this is without even understanding how to use a search engine effectively or scrape social media for details.

It is truly mind-blowing how much data can be obtained on practically everyone through these types of tools, and social engineers use them to paint a picture of a target company or person to help when they tailor their approach later on.

By way of an example, let me talk you through one such case of a woman I investigated as part of a client brief some years ago. The client had given consent for me to try to find out as much as possible about the target, whom I label 'Marge' when I present to an audience. Marge was one of five directors of the company I was working for; she knew I was coming for her and had given permission for me to research her and find out whatever I could. Like most people, she seemed to be a nice enough person with no apparent dirt to be dug. I left my cynicism behind me and assumed this to be the case. However, that didn't mean that the information on the net about Marge wasn't useful; it would absolutely help me trick my way into her organisation.

I found her address and age from an online telephone directory, and I had a look at her house using an online street map. It was a nice place in a quiet little quintessential English village, with a pub, a corner shop, a veterinarian practice, and that was about it. I plotted all of this out on my 'crazy wall' and drew up the connections between the information I was finding. A crazy wall, sometimes known as a murder wall, is something you will have seen dozens of times if you have ever watched police procedural films or television shows. It's a way of organising information about a target in one visual location. It can look messy but it's what I use to connect the details and find my way in.

I often start with a photograph of my main subject or person in the middle and then details of their place of work, residence, family, associates, movements and journeys and connect the pieces of information where appropriate using lines or pieces of red string. There are many digital ways of doing this as well, but for me, there is nothing like looking at a physical crazy wall with all the information on it to give me the fullest picture possible of my subject.

In Marge's case I had her address and information about her house, and now I started to fill in details of her family and associates, her friends and colleagues. To do this I went to social media and looked to fill any gaps. Aware she may be investigated, Marge had locked down her social media accounts to prying eyes, although I could still see they existed and, as she was using her real name and picture as an avatar, it was easy to be sure I was looking at the right person. Looking a little deeper, I could see friends and family commenting on a profile picture on a social media site. It was a picture of her with a fiftieth birthday cake and it confirmed her date of birth, her siblings, close friends and, most importantly, her children.

Her son, let's call him Bart, had clicked 'like' on her picture. His own account was not locked down and neither was his girlfriend's. I could find lots of information about him online and see where he lived and worked from professional networking sites. I could see pictures of him going back at least eight years, many of which were of him and Marge and a large dog. Knowing he had not long moved into his small flat in London with his girlfriend, I figured that the dog had been the family pet when he had lived with Marge. I couldn't confirm this, so it went on the crazy wall next to a large question mark in my assumptions list. From Marge's own professional networking sites I noticed that she spoke Spanish, was heavily involved in mentoring young women to be in her industry, and was an occasional keynote speaker at industry conferences. Also, she was head of Human Resources at her firm.

I now had all I needed to dismantle Marge and gain access to company data, information and anything else I wanted from her company. The organisation had asked me to try to get Marge to click on a bogus link in an email. Enticing people to do this is one of the most common ways hackers access company information, as the seemingly innocent link contains code that is activated when clicked, allowing the criminal access to company systems. Alternatively, that clicked link or open attachment might send the recipient to a malicious website that collects their data and login information so that the criminal can gain access to their device and any networks it is using. So-called phishing emails are rife, and clicking on suspicious links is a very bad idea. The general advice is to never click on a link, or open an attachment in an email, unless you are certain that you know who the sender is. This in itself is tricky as there are a myriad of ways to make a bogus email 'sender' look legitimate.

The type of phishing I do is known as 'spear-phishing' because, as in the case of Marge, my emails are specifically tailored to catch a particular target. Some general phishing scams send out thousands, even hundreds of thousands, of emails with basic information in them, hoping to play the percentages and catch a couple of people out. These are always going to be moderately successful as statistically they will happen to catch someone at the wrong time, or in the frame of mind to slip up or fall for the scam and click the link or open the attachment.

With full client permission we have sent emails pretending to be headhunters with documents labelled 'non-disclosure agreement' attached. We tell the mark via a phone call or vish (voice phish) that someone they knew well had recently left the company and recommended them for a job with a great salary and package. Even if they are happy in their position, curiosity takes over and they nearly always open the NDA so they can find out about the job, but more importantly, so I can tell them who recommended them.

We told one firm that their favourite bar, a watering hole near to their site, was unexpectedly shutting down that day and asked for a donation to a Just Giving collection for the friendly bar owner many of them knew well. When they turned up that night to wish him goodbye, they found him hale and hearty with no intention of closing, in on the scam and ready to give them their donations back. Every single one of them that had clicked on those links had exposed their organisation to potential malicious software and given access to their systems.

Never, ever click on those types of links. The email had all the red flags I warn people about every day. It was familiar and emotional, asked for money in an urgent timeframe and gave a call to action for the recipient. One phone call to the bar could have confirmed it was a scam. One forward to the organisation's technical security team would have stopped it, but no one reported it because we got their emotions high, so their logic went down. Fish in a barrel.

Another time we managed to get 257 of 300 employees furiously clicking on a link and calling a bogus helpline number when we told them, at 4.15 on a Friday afternoon, that caffeine was banned within the building as of eight o'clock the following Monday morning. So ferocious and immediate was the response that we stopped collecting angry voicemails when we hit fifty replies and had to get the head of HR and the CEO to calm everyone down and tell them it had been a test. Don't mess with people's coffee.

We use many ways to get people to take the bait, but the most important thing is to ensure it is a learning curve for everyone and, for me, generally has a humorous element to the scam so that people don't feel bad. There have been recent examples of companies testing their teams by telling people they had a bonus that was never real, or warning of punishment for some imagined violation. This generally does not generate an element of trust among the teams and between security staff and general workers; it is, in my opinion, ill-advised.

While I can't say that we have always succeeded in being kind in our scams, we do try not to bully people en masse – apart from anything else the effect doesn't last as long. Threatening to take coffee from people kept them chuckling and talking about the attempt for a long time; removing someone's income would be memorable but hardly conducive to good staff relations. We at least try to keep it within the realms of goodwill, unless the target in question is clearly malicious themselves. Then, the gloves are off.

In Marge's case we wanted to use the information we had gathered on her to get her to fall for an email scam and click a monitoring link that mimicked the sort a cybercriminal might use to get into the wider network of the company. As she was the HR director, if her system was breached it would potentially reveal much personal information on all of the staff, along with proprietary information from the firm and whatever personal details might be potentially usable for blackmail purposes. We would stop short of extortion or harm; a criminal would not be so magnanimous.

The first email we sent her purported to be from the veterinary practice in her village. We had no idea if she used this particular company, but it was likely from the proximity to her home and the fact that she had, at least at some point, owned the dog in Bart's pictures.

Dear Mrs Simpson,

We are writing to you concerning the attached invoice in connection with the treatment of your animal.
    This invoice is for immediate payment as it is overdue. Payment details below.
    Thank you.

Veterinarian.

She took a few minutes to open the attachment after she received the email. We watched as the tracking software we had embedded in the email counted her clicks on the document, each one a potential security breach if the email had been sent by an attacker, rather than by us as part of the test. When it failed to open as she expected she hit it again, seven times in total, before the tracker stopped pinging and we assumed she gave up. We hit her again immediately with another phishing email.

Some of her social media posts had confirmed her date of birth, which serendipitously was the following week, so this time our fake email pretended to be the pub in her village with an offer to help her celebrate.

Dear Mrs Simpson,

Happy Birthday! We are so glad you have chosen to celebrate with us and can't wait to welcome you for your birthday dinner.

Please confirm on the link below whether you have booked six people for 7pm or seven people for 6pm as we think there may be two conflicting bookings.

Don't forget to click on the voucher below and claim your free bottle of prosecco in the name of your booking party.

See you next week!

Local Pub

She clicked on the voucher straight away, another hit, and then on the link to the booking, and another, before presumably giving up and perhaps phoning the place. I had assumed that she would think someone was holding a surprise meal for her birthday and that she wouldn't be able to resist trying to find out who had made the arrangements or why she, as the recipient, was being informed of the 'surprise'.

Learning to spot phishing emails isn't always easy but there were a few red flags that might have alerted her that it wasn't real. First of all, the email itself was unexpected and out of context (as far as we know she hadn't chosen to celebrate her birthday at the pub), but she clicked on the links anyway, perhaps out of curiosity or a desire to correct the mistake, both common human tendencies exploited by scammers.

Secondly, while many of these communications sound plausible and may contain details or information that sound genuine, and personal, it's always advisable to hover over the address and check the origin of the sender email for clues to the legitimacy of the sender. While this isn't always an obvious tell, we sent this from a Hotmail account (678pub@hotmail.com) which a real business would be unlikely to use, and that might have raised her suspicions. Thirdly, the email offered her the prosecco, and asked her to click on a link. The promise of reward, however big or small, coupled with a call to action like this, is suspicious and unless you are certain of the legitimacy of the sender, you should not be tempted and should check carefully before you click or accept your gift.

Finally, if in doubt, don't reply, click on links or open any attachments but rather call the organisation directly (from a number you find independently of the suspicious communication) and confirm that the business the email came from is actually the real sender.

We were asked to try different approaches with Marge, and we included clues within all of them that they might be fake. However, awareness training to help people spot red flags in scam approaches is a relatively new concept and the familiarity in the emails, that she knew the pub and her birth date was right, was likely a deciding factor in her falling for these approaches. After leaving her alone for a while to ponder and perhaps correct the errors in the first email or indeed to plan her birthday meal at the pub, we soon followed up with more approaches. We sent emails that used flattery as the hook, offering speaking slots at women's networking events, HR conferences and training workshops. She clicked on most of these spear-phish emails because in spite of some obvious errors they were, nonetheless, specifically tailored to her profile and designed to appeal to her individual interests and associations, unlike the more generic phishing emails that may be more clearly a scam and are often spotted more easily. Additionally, the ideal situation is that the target *does* spot that the approach is fake and reports it to their security team. A good conclusion for such a test is that people see the issues, investigate further and are able to share the lessons from the approach with their colleagues, helping to prevent a real attack. However, this wasn't what happened with Marge and it remains the case that the more specific the information about the target is, the more likely they are to ignore any red flags and pursue the pattern laid out by the approach, regardless of the danger.

If you are reading this thinking you would never fall for something like this then you are wrong. We all can. Even I can. The right script and the right/wrong time, depending on how you look at it, will catch us all. It's just a question of dangling the bait and waiting for the fish to bite.

We helped her. The internal security team now had her attention and full backing for further training and development in this area. A lovely woman, I took her a bottle of prosecco, to replace the one she wasn't getting from the pub, and handed it to her after the debrief, apologising profusely for being so mean and wishing her well. She was happy to be protected and their entire team has likely been much safer and better informed ever since.

Not everyone is so happy when they see what we have done, though. I remember well a similar scenario when another female director, Susan, sitting in a boardroom, had listened to my findings and looked sceptical at the end. 'This is all very well, Jenny,' she had said, in a voice that wasn't used to being argued with. 'But really are we supposed to be paranoid now? I mean we could all be hit by buses tomorrow.'

She carried on addressing the room of her fellow board members. 'Look, the research was good, of course, but I'm struggling to see how it's that deep, really. How it could be used?' She looked back at me. 'No offence, Jen. But we've all done a little digging on our exes or whatever. I mean you found out my daughter's rabbit was called "Patch", but anyone could have found that on her social media. I just think we need to keep things in perspective.'

She looked back at me with just a hint of smugness.

'None taken.'

'Excuse me?'

'I've decided not to take offence,' I said flatly and finished my section up without further explanation. We were done. It was up to them to decide whether to act on what we had found, and I had another job the next morning. Some people don't get it, don't understand the potential application of personal information by malicious individuals. Not that it mattered – I'd done my job and it was up to them now. I called it a day and packed up to leave.

I was waiting for a taxi in the reception about ten minutes later and she appeared out of the lift. 'Jenny.'

'Oh! Hello, Susan,' I replied. 'What can I do for you?'

'I just wanted to let you know I wasn't trying to undermine you in there.'

'Er, OK.' I rolled my eyes.

'I just don't see how you could use the stuff you found to get to people. I mean, I don't care about what you found out. It's not important. I won't be recommending we invest more in this type of security awareness. I'm sorry.'

I smiled, sighing inwardly, and looked at her. Sometimes, despite my best efforts the devil in me takes over, and I decided that this might be a teachable moment for her. After all, if she didn't take this seriously, then her people wouldn't be protected, and I'd found some worrying gaps in their systems.

My taxi arrived and stopped outside the revolving glass door in front of reception. 'Susan. What would I have had to find that would have unsettled you? What would have made you act on my advice and implement the security I recommended?'

She smirked. 'You would have had to find something out about me that no one else knows. Then I would know you had done a thorough job and might, and I only say *might*, listen. But you didn't.'

'I did.'

'Really?' she said, folding her arms and leaning back on one leg, the pointed toe of one heeled shoe lifting in the air. In that moment she reminded me of every bully I've ever known. Confident in their position on the surface, but selfish and insecure underneath and often ignorant or impervious of how their own actions might impact the life and safety of other people.

'I assume you would like to know what it was,' I continued. She nodded, pushing her cheek outwards with her tongue.

'I'll whisper,' I said and stood back, letting her come to me.

'Go on, then. Hit me with it.'

I waved at my taxi driver and picked up my bag, leaning over to her and putting my mouth near her left shoulder. 'I saw you kill Patch. You nasty cow. You watch how you speak to me in future, or I'll fucking dismantle you.' I leaned back and looked her straight in the eye. I smiled sweetly and walked through the doors and into the taxi, catching just a glimpse of her open mouth through the glass doors as the car pulled away.

I chuckled to myself as my lift headed towards the airport. Susan had been a piece of work; we'd found reams of gossip about her online, numerous reports that she bullied and undermined staff, especially women working for her. She was also having a rather brittle affair with a colleague and seemed to lack empathy or awareness for anyone but herself. I suspected that she was referring to the affair when she pushed me to tell her our findings, but we nearly always found evidence of affairs and peccadilloes when we looked into a company and its people, and unless it directly threatened the security of the firm we steered clear of any comment or interference. The rabbit incident though was more intimate, more telling and shocking enough to throw her, which is why I mentioned it.

Her house hadn't been far from the pub I was staying at, and I'd taken a walk past one summer evening, just out of curiosity, when we found out about the affair. I'd taken a vantage point on a road nearby and I could clearly see her pottering about her garden and having a conversation with someone on her phone. I walked back to the pub and fetched my binoculars from my room; on my return, I stood back from the kerb and took a closer look. She was standing outside now, talking to someone seated at a garden table. It was the colleague with whom she was having the affair and they both had drinks in hand and were rather animated. A few minutes passed and then he stood up abruptly and left. I had the impression they had

had an argument. She followed him inside, but soon emerged again into the garden, picking up her drink from the wooden garden table and draining it in one, before roughly slamming down her glass.

Then I'd seen the rabbit, a small black and white ball of fluff, lollop over towards her as she stood hand on hip. In one swift motion, she moved her leg and elegantly, but firmly, aimed a hard kick at the poor thing. It was launched a couple of feet into the air and landed on the floor near the garden table. It didn't get up again. I'd gasped in horror and tried to get a view of it while simultaneously and frantically scrolling through my phone for inspiration to help it. Nothing came to mind, I had no one I knew nearby and was myself too far away to run down and help the poor creature. I seriously considered calling the police, or Susan herself if I could find the number, but I could tell it was already too late.

I looked back through the binoculars and she was standing, hands on hips, looking at the bundle of fur lying motionless on the floor. Then she went into the house leaving the back door open. A few minutes passed before she emerged again from the house, bent down over the furry body and scooped it into a black rubbish bag, which she then dumped into the waste bin outside the kitchen, before slamming the door and turning off the light.

I felt sick to my stomach, but what could I do? There was no real way to address this or even prove to anyone else what she had done and what it revealed about her character. It had irked me to feel so useless, so when the opportunity had arisen to do so I had enjoyed freaking her out.

I had also decided, however, that now I knew she was a potentially violent psychopath I wouldn't get further involved in the company. Despite this, and unlike our usual practice,

I did hand the sealed files we had on all of them over to their security team and HR directors. There was nothing major in any of them really, no more than you would find in most people's past if you dug hard enough, but Susan's was a big file. We had made sure to meticulously print and document every single comment and complaint about her that we had found online. If they were hearsay, unfair or unsubstantiated then her innocence would surely shine through and she would have nothing to fear. If, on the other hand, she was a violent bully, then the ensuing investigation would also surely find that out as well.

It was up to them now to take it further, but I was sure she would be more careful about hurting her pets from now on. I raised a sentimental drink to that little rabbit on my flight later that night. 'Cheers, Patch,' I said to myself. 'Let's hope they ruin the bitch.'

I O

MR BIG

Sometimes, when I tell people the Marge story or others like it, I detect a certain amount of smugness in the audience or listeners. It generally comes from people who don't use social media and think that this somehow makes them safe, or at least safer, from social engineering. This isn't really the case, and to prove it I tell them the story of Mr Big.

The Mr Big case came into me from the security team of a large UK business. They told me that they were having trouble getting further security funding from their MD and that he was a difficult man to persuade. They had decided that the best way to persuade him to give them some more money for the security improvements and hardening of operations that they needed was to hack him. They had stated that he was something of a technical dinosaur, and they thought that doing this in person would be more effective than doing it online.

They had hinted that perhaps even he might fall victim to the type of psychology and persuasion tactics a people hacker might use, and he had told them: 'Yes, whatever, do your worst.' And so they hired me to do exactly that, to prove to Mr Big that he was vulnerable, and then ask him for more money for their security budget while he was still reeling from the attack. Good plan.

I liked the look of the job as soon as it came in. The security guys were informed and smart enough not to tell me how to do the job, which is always helpful. I mean, the number of times I get called to do some work and the client *tells* me the best way to go about it. It drives me mad for a few reasons, not least of which is that it invalidates the entire point of the penetration test as far as I'm concerned. I mean, they wouldn't tell a real criminal or burglar how to break into their business, would they? Or how about telling me that I can't use certain exits or entrances, or that different members of staff are 'off-limits' for some reason, so I can't use any research on them to get past, because yes, that is *exactly* what happens in the criminal world, isn't it? The bad guys operate within specific boundaries given to them by their marks and targets!

For this job, however, the team had done the right thing and left the method and tactics to me and hadn't interfered too much. They had told me that Mr Big didn't consider security, and especially social engineering prevention, to be that big a deal for his businesses, but that if I could get to him personally then he would likely change his mind. They gave me four requirements and told me that short of doing any actual harm, physical or otherwise, to people or property, I could knock myself out trying to accomplish them. This was looking good. The four objectives were:

1. Find out his diary movements
2. Get him to talk about his private life
3. Get into his office and send them an email to prove access to his laptop
4. Get into his phone and send them a text to prove access to his phone.

I told them I expected to have this done within twenty-eight days of the contract being signed and rubbed my hands together in expectation of an easy job.

I started where I always do these days, online, and I had a quick look at his profile there. Mr Big was an interesting character and although he had a ferocious reputation, I really liked him from a distance. He was clearly a serial womaniser, drank, smoked and gambled, but he made no apologies for his lifestyle and seemed to otherwise treat his employees, ex-wives and associates well. I later got to know him a little. Speaking with a thick Yorkshire accent, he is rich and quite charismatic, often sarcastic and conservative in outlook, and had a reputation for being a total bastard if crossed. I couldn't wait to con him.

Almost immediately it became clear that he was not going to be the easiest of people to research. One issue is that when someone is well known, the amount of information about them online is huge, but not necessarily of much use. Sifting through the lies and misinformation about them becomes a time-consuming, thankless and often unproductive job. I once had to try to track and vish (voice phishing – scam phone call) a very bad person who had changed their name some years before to that of a famous sports personality. This made it nearly impossible to uncover real information about them and I struggled for a couple of weeks trying to track down much of use. I did eventually, but it took a lot of effort, some old-fashioned surveillance, and some serious contacts to get me close enough to them to make an effective approach.

Anyway, Mr Big was a public figure and so I could find a lot of press articles and opinion about him, but what was becoming clear was that he didn't seem to use social media, a fact later confirmed when I met him, and he asked me: 'What even is the twitters?'

This was challenging because I couldn't really get close to him personally unless I could find out more and, despite the reams of business articles about him, I was no closer to the real person underneath the public profile. I wanted to find some weak spots and vulnerabilities, some passions or fears I could use to get through, and he, wisely, didn't reveal very much about himself in interviews or online.

There was no Facebook profile, nothing on Twitter, nothing on Instagram, only a very limited professional profile, clearly not written by him, on LinkedIn. Damn it. In desperation, I threw a few names into other platforms and some specific research tools and what did come up, to my surprise, was that his scarily efficient secretary, let's call her Edna, was very active on Pinterest. She seemed to be a knitting enthusiast, with a special interest in crafting very detailed knitted cupcakes. It's a thing, and she was all over it.

This was not the best way in, but it was something. Maybe we could use the crafting connection to soften Edna up some-how, but I doubted it. The truth was Edna was terrifying. Mr Big hadn't got to the top of his game without picking his people well, and Edna absolutely epitomised the type of gatekeeping Rottweiler secretary that a powerful person in business should have. She was in her late fifties, single, extremely polite and efficient, clearly adored her boss and was super-loyal to him.

Like a cross between a wife and a big sister, she knew Mr Big better than he knew himself and would ruthlessly organise his diary, his contacts and everything else for him. If you wanted to speak with Mr Big you had to get past Edna. I had tried a couple of speculative phone calls just to test the waters. She had been polite but had got me off the phone very quickly, pointing us to standard responses, written communications or various other people and departments in the firm for all our enquiries. I wanted an Edna in my life, she was awesome, but I had more or less dismissed her as a way in.

Gatekeepers like Edna are often the target for social engineers as they hold the keys to the kingdom in terms of information. They tend to have access to all the important details within the business, because often people like Mr Big can't, or won't, remember every important date, name or password they need to run their many different businesses and busy lives.

For a person like Mr Big, the Ednas of this world are a life-line. Mr Big didn't need to be online because Edna was. She had all his login details, passwords, his physical keys and alarm codes. She knew where he was at any time, could sign off his credit cards and buy his family gifts if he forgot. Secretaries, personal assistants and admin managers often know more, and have as broad an access to, company information and secrets as the directors and managers of companies themselves, and they are often much more switched on.

Over the years, I have learnt that these gatekeepers could be difficult to crack, despite often being targeted by social engin-eers. Their whole job is to run things efficiently, and, to some extent, prevent people gaining access to their boss or client. Consequently, they are suspicious of approaches without solid proof of intent and assume that most people are trying to take advantage of their principal, which is, of course, absolutely true. The day I get myself an Edna is the day I will finally con-sider myself to be a successful grown-up.

What is also true, however, is that once you crack a gate-keeper the floodgates tend to open. Get past one of these people and you not only gain access to their boss but also to all the influence and power that person holds. Gatekeepers are as human as the next person, and the job is to find out what it is that really motivates them and also anything that makes them doubt themselves and others. I feel bad about writing this down – I don't want to inform any bad person as to how to get to somebody – but the truth is that all loyalty contains flaws.

When someone knows someone well, they also tend to understand that person's weaknesses and go into a sort of protective mode. If you can convince the gatekeeper that doing something will protect the principal or is for his or her own good; if you can persuade them that they are the only person who can prevent the principal being fooled, humiliated or hurt, then that gatekeeper will protect them as a general rule. For a gatekeeper, it will be more effective to bring out that protective instinct rather than try to move them from a more personal angle a lot of the time. My plan was to engage Edna and get her on our side by persuading her that Mr Big was in danger of some sort of mistake or humiliation that he couldn't see. If I could convince her to act in his defence, then I might be able to get her to do some of the work for me. The question was, how?

With nothing much to go on for Mr Big online, I cast the net a bit wider. These days even if you are a ghost online, you can still be tracked down one way or another, it just takes a bit longer and requires the use of more sinister tactics. In order for me to construct our approach, with not much else to go on, it was time for me to go back to basics. If I couldn't get to him directly I would get to those close to him and find a way in through them. The amount of free information online about all of us can be shocking. So let's go to his friends and family.

I created my crazy wall taping up photos and sticky notes of what we had so far. Edna and her knitting formed a solid but unimpressive branch to the top left and I started to fill in information on his family and friends on the right. He was on his fourth marriage and shared his residence with the current Mrs Big, and there were a few children and stepchildren scattered about various previous and current addresses. I could see his eldest daughter posting away on social media, and a picture began to emerge of Mr Big's extended family. He even had a couple of grandchildren I could see, and they went up on the wall as well. It was late one Sunday night when I stepped back, picked up a glass of wine and took another look at the cluster of photographs and people on my Mr Big crazy wall. I glanced at it sort of casually, so it wouldn't see me looking and have time to hide its secrets, and I suddenly saw it out of the corner of my eye, there it was. I knew how to get to Mr Big.

It is awful sometimes to think like a criminal. To know vulnerability when I see it and to immediately know how it could be exploited. Sometimes it is so clear how a bad person would get to someone that I feel sick when I spot it and know I will use it, but to protect a client you have to know where the pressure point is. Whether it is finding the dodgy deals or the affairs, the debts or the addictions, the secrets that human beings would prefer to keep private; or whether it's finding the things that they love and would protect and using that; we all have our weaknesses. It is just a question of finding them to use them against us.

While Mr Big had certainly had his fair share of scandals, both in business and personally, it was something much more personal that I knew I could use. In the absence of social media posts, I had gone back to basics and found what I could, including the legally required documents for all his business interests and directorships. Among his companies and investments, his shareholdings and his board positions there was one thing that really stood out. Mr Big and his wife were non-executive directors of a small charity raising money for and awareness of a particular illness prevalent in babies and children. When I looked at those pictures of his grandchildren it was suddenly very clear that one of them was afflicted with a serious illness. Ah.

Now, before you judge me here, remember we are hardening his safety and that of his family and businesses at the specific request of the target and his associates. We always stop short of doing any harm and have no wish or intention to hurt anyone or anything. I am a security professional, by trade and by passion, and I am very much in the business of protecting people who are vulnerable to malicious manipulation. It's hard sometimes for people to understand that to do this you have to be able to look at a situation as if you *actually are* a malicious individual, to see what needs to be fixed and protected. The way we used this information was short of what a criminal might be prepared to do, but nonetheless it demonstrates how a tiny piece of that crazy wall jigsaw might bring the entire house of cards crashing down.

Armed with this new information, getting to Mr Big was now going to be easy. A quick trip to the charity website and I found photos of him and his wife at various gala dinners and events, promoting the cause. Their events page showed that the next fundraiser was to be held the following month in an exclusive London hotel, and that tickets were still on sale. *Bingo*.

I put together a short email and sent it off to the charity, making a small donation to the cause and booking a couple of tickets to the London event. My pretext was that I was a reporter for a new online magazine that bridged the gap between large corporate entities and their chosen charities. We wanted to cover the story behind the cause and to interview the people who inspired the corporate backing. I told them we were happy to grab the power couple at the event, so they wouldn't be put to much trouble, and would mention them in a small piece we were putting together about the efficacy of different types of fundraising and whether glossy functions still had a place in the fundraising space.

Our magazine already had a website, which to the careful eye might have seemed a bit hastily cobbled together, but if you were looking at it you had clicked on the link in the email, and it was already too late. For our purposes the link wasn't malicious, of course, but it did track who clicked on it. Effectively, if Mr Big or the charity clicked on the link in the email we sent them, we could count them as having been successfully phished and would have access, in theory, to their entire system. They did click the link, of course, many, many times in some cases, but I had to get into his office as well, so there was to be an attack on multiple levels, using different means.

At the time, I was working with a keen but rather awkward young assistant. A psychology graduate, he was desperate to get into the business but rather less keen on the long hours and hard work it took to do the job thoroughly. We nicknamed him 'Watson' and I took him with me to London and sent him a hired suit to change into. In the bar of our own considerably less swanky hotel than the one we were about to visit, I took him through the pretext and his role on the job.

We were to let everyone have a few drinks and say hello before dinner, asking just a couple of generic questions about the charity. We were to be very polite and respectful, showing gradually increasing interest in the cause, and the couple, as the night drew on. We were not to get drunk, but a couple of drinks were fine. It was important to have only surface level conversation with everyone else, and to avoid being memorable or lingering near any staff or cameras. We would stick to the cover story. Crucially, if I got talking to Mr Big at some point, Watson was to stand behind him at an angle that meant he could see any pin number he might use to access his phone.

We drained our drinks, toasted the mark and walked out into the London night. We grabbed a taxi to the venue, a large hotel in Mayfair, and shuffled in alongside the various guests. We were not, I noted, mentally raising my eyebrow, asked for our invitations or ID on the way in and we made our way to the bar to order drinks and see if we could spot our mark.

I saw Mr and Mrs Big almost immediately at the centre of the crowd. I noticed how tall he was, and that he had an easy charisma I wasn't expecting. He was completely relaxed and was chatting away to a group of people with Mrs Big next to him. They appeared to be gracious and amusing hosts, putting everyone at ease. I popped over and introduced myself briefly to Mrs No.4, smiled and gave her a business card. I asked her when it would be OK to ask her a couple of very quick questions about the event and mentioned we had spoken to Edna (we hadn't) but wouldn't take up much of her time.

This approach needed careful handling – they all do, to be honest, in one way or another, but especially here. I have spoken in the past about needing to create an atmosphere of trust and familiarity to get people to relax and start to speak with you. You don't have long to do this when you approach someone, and the vital thing is that you in no way appear to be a threat. Being a woman gives me some advantage in this as most people are less threatened by that, but it is also because I make sure I blend into the background if I need to and am not especially memorable-looking in any way.

A colleague I worked with once on an absolutely terrifying criminal case sent me to deliver a message to a go-between, based on the fact that I looked both innocent and ordinary at the same time. He told our wider team that 'no one would ever think for even a moment that Jen was anything dodgy', and by that logic I could get closer for longer than many of my more striking colleagues.

When people I have worked with in the past see my current profile, they sometimes message me about my other life and ask me if I was ever up to this stuff while working alongside them, even though they realise from details and dates in interviews I have given that I must have been. One former colleague even sent me a rather ominous text message asking for a quiet chat about my security career, rather grumpy that I had kept the details from her. She questioned me via text: 'You are basically a safe-cracker now? When did you learn that?' and was largely incredulous that the entire time she knew me, worked and travelled with me, I was essentially up to no good, doing all of this and failing to inform her. She was certain she would have known or that I would have told her but also demanded to know more details about my exploits as an old friend and colleague.

What people fail to understand is that it has only relatively recently become acceptable to admit to what I do as a career. Even now, what I do needs extensive explanations outside of the security–cyber community in order to make sure people don't misunderstand me and think I am a straight-up criminal. I've met police and military who had no idea a job like mine existed, especially in the civilian world. So it is not as if I could have admitted to random work colleagues that, in my spare time and on business trips, I was sneaking out and talking my way into nearby premises, or doing surveillance for clients, or making secret detours on the way back to the office.

How could I have explained to my work mates that after saying goodnight and heading off to my room, I had headed back out into some strange city, climbed a fire escape and broken into an office, much less actually been paid for the effort, which was always against every company staff policy I worked for. A lot of the time, even my own family had no idea what was going on. It was safer for them not to know, not to worry. My husband usually knew something about what was happening – a location, my team and when to expect me back. It was all he ever really wanted to know; he simply puts it out of his mind until then.

One Friday night before we had the children, we were out for a few drinks in a local pub. Time had passed quickly, as it does in these situations, and we had run out of cash. For some reason the card machines in the pub had stopped working so a trip through the night to the cashpoint beckoned. I decided to go and, as he was only a few sips into his pint, my husband stayed at the bar. A few friends expressed some surprise that he was letting me venture out alone, at night, to fetch cash. It was one of the few times he has ever really given away how he feels about the job because he replied, 'She wanders around at night on her own all the time – she'll be fine.'

Another time we were drinking in what turned out to be a rough bikers' pub in Liverpool. He spotted a friend of ours and left me sitting on my own in an entirely different part of the bar surrounded by tattooed biker types. Our friend asked him if everything would be OK, and I am reliably informed my husband's answer was, 'Yes, she is in a good mood tonight, she won't hurt them.'

Anyway, back to Mrs No.4 in the big hotel in London. Dropping Edna's name immediately established a degree of credibility and familiarity. The first thing Mrs Big hears will stick in her mind for a couple of reasons, not least due to a cognitive bias called the 'primacy effect' which is the tendency for us to focus on the first thing someone says to us. Everything she hears after that has less impact. For good measure and to make her feel more in control, I give her the upper hand and hesitate over the name, fumble it and give her the chance to correct me, so I can be super-grateful.

'Hello, Mrs Big, my name is Soandso and I wondered if you could give me a few words very quickly for our online charity magazine? I spoke to Ed . . . Ed . . . Edith, I think, in your husband's office . . .'

'Edna?'

'. . . Ah yes, that's it – Edna – to ask permission first, but I'm not sure she was too happy with me! I think she thought we might need longer than just a sentence for the mag, so as it's so quick, I thought I'd be cheeky and just ask you now. Sorry if it's too much, but what is it about *this* cause that makes it so special to you and your husband . . .?'

There is so much to unpack here to do with scoping a target. Good preparation for an approach, especially one done in person, needs careful thought and the words, the exact words, really matter.

Firstly, I show deference by calling her 'Mrs Big'; I don't use her first name until she gives me permission, being super-polite and deferential. When we first approach people we don't have long to make a first impression, most people know that. I think the statistic often touted is that after the first thirty seconds people have made their mind up about a new person they have met, formed an opinion about them and applied numerous subconscious labels.

This is of course true, but easily reversed in most cases if you know how to manipulate someone's opinions. However, in the case of Mrs Big, I wanted her to feel the following about me when she noticed me:

1. Not at all threatening either professionally or personally
2. In need of a small favour, which she was able to easily give, in return for a disproportionately useful reciprocal reward (coverage in a magazine)
3. Empathetic towards me as someone who was something of a fish out of water at her posh charity event and really wanted to get out of there as soon as possible.

She was so lovely, answering my questions, grabbing Mr Big away from a group he was holding court with and generally being very gracious. I asked a few questions and Watson appeared dutifully over Mr Big's shoulder to observe if he punched any passcode, as we would have then referred to it, into his phone. After a while the conversation was winding down, but he still hadn't looked at his phone – at that time phones were not yet as ubiquitous and smart as they are now.

We needed that number. I excused myself briefly and called our office, telling them to try his number a few times so we could get him to take a call. I nipped to the bathroom and by the time I got back to the group, Watson was failing to keep the conversation going, and Mr Big was rattling his phone in his hand and complaining about the coverage in the venue. I raised my eyebrows to No.4, thanked her for her time and followed Mr Big out of the venue.

With Watson in tow, I gave Mr Big a quick wave as we passed him, grabbed a cab and watched him stare quizzically at his phone for a few more minutes before shaking his head and dashing back inside the hotel.

'I got most of his passcode,' said Watson.

'Most of it?'

'Yeah. Missed the end, I think; he turned away.'

'It happens. What did you get?'

'I got 195 . . . and then missed anything else.'

Jesus. 'It's six,' I said. 'It's 1956. His birth year, I'll put money on it.'

And I was right. For goodness' sake, people, stop using your birthday as a pin number. I know it's easy to remember, but it is also so easy to guess. *Stop it!* While I'm here can you also not use '1,2,3,4', '1,1,1,1' or similar.

The next morning, we caught a train back to Liverpool and I waited until around two o'clock to make the call that would trigger the next part of the plan. I called Mrs Big and told her that it was great meeting her and Mr Big the night before, and we just loved the story behind the charity. I also mentioned that, unfortunately, the recording of our interview from the night before was pretty much unusable due to background noise at the venue. I told her that now I had met her though, I'd be happy to do a bigger piece on the charity and put them on the cover. I'd need about an hour with them both and to take some pictures in a corporate setting. The real problem was the timescales though, as my editor was pushing me for it all by the end of the week. If we came to them, did it sound like something we could manage?

Although nothing is ever certain, I knew this was a tough one to resist as it used at least four different pressure points to get her to agree.

First of all, I'm throwing myself on her mercy and appealing to her good nature. This is hard enough in itself to resist, but there is also research to show that she would be more likely to help me with the request because she had already helped me out once before. The research by psychologist Robert Cialdini suggests that when we help someone with a little thing we effectively categorise them in our minds as 'someone I help', so when they ask for the next, bigger favour, it's very likely they will agree. It's known as the 'foot-in-the-door' technique and is often used in sales.

Next, I'm playing to her and, more importantly his, ego. I'm flattering them both with the promise of a bigger reward based on how impressed I was by their sparkling interview. So much so that they were going to be on the cover. If you add in the free publicity, philanthropic elements and the fact that I am not giving them much time to think, it's a pretty potent scam. The fact that it was not going to be us asking for the favour, but No.4, sealed the deal.

'He'll see you in his office on Thursday morning,' she said. 'Leave it with me.'

Edna sent an intern to collect us from reception. We could hear the power couple chatting in low voices behind a polished dark wood door as we waited for them in Edna's office. Watson was not doing so well. His coffee made waves in his cup and spilt over into the saucer. I frowned and raised my eyebrows to Edna. She twitched a hint of a smile back; I turned and spoke to Watson.

'Mate, were you born in a barn? *Deal* with the saucer!' I said.

He gave me a desperate sideways glance and before he could answer I spoke to the room in general. 'Honestly, *I'm* the one whose hand should be shaking after dropping that box on it.'

Watson was panicking and looked at me in bewilderment. I made a mental note to give him a code word so that in future he would know when to *go with the scam, follow my lead*. I turned to Edna: 'I dropped a big box of ink on my hand last night, I know it sounds daft but I am awful for hoarding bits and bobs. I make my own cards. I mean it's fine, there's no mark or anything like . . .' I let my voice fade out.

Edna lit up like a Christmas tree: 'I know what you mean. I

have tons of fabrics at home. Boxes of wool. I knit myself as a hobby, can't resist!'

'Ooh, it's the detail that counts, isn't it?' I went on. 'I'm useless at knitting but I find the cards so relaxing.'

'It *is* relaxing. It *is*!' she almost shouted.

Now I have Edna.

Her phone buzzed and she waved us to go in, smiling and winking at me now like an old friend. She had gone from road-block to enabler in one conversation. I sent her a homemade card (from Etsy) after we had reported back to say thank you. I like to think she appreciated it, and wasn't too cross, but I wouldn't count on it.

Mr Big's office was nice enough, with a large oval conference table in the middle of the room and some decent audiovisual equipment. Mrs No.4 came over to me and gave me a warm handshake, telling us we could set up our equipment on the table. Mr Big came in through another door at the rear of the room and gave me a broad smile.

'I've just been out to check my car,' he said, grinning. 'Scouser in the room and all that.'

I laughed politely, while privately feeling simultaneously smug and annoyed at the jibe, any ounce of guilt I may have felt at conning them disappearing immediately.

Watson clattered the equipment around while I made polite conversation and made a point of scanning the room for good angles to photograph. This gave me ample opportunity to wander over to his desk where I could see his computer was unlocked and his phone lying on the desk.

'I think we should shoot it with the desk behind you,' I said, as if I had a clue about photography. 'Watson, what do you think?'

At this point Watson came into his own and began to rattle

off quite an impressive, and I suspected rehearsed, monologue about lighting and positioning. It was perfect, because I could exchange knowing 'he's keen but a bit of a geek' glances with the power couple, which helped deepen a sense of rapport.

'OK, we won't keep you too long,' I said. 'Let's do the photos first while we all look fresh. Do you two want to go and straighten your tie, check your teeth?'

'I'll organise some coffee,' said Mrs B, and I smiled gratefully and asked for decaff. This is emphatically *not* what I would normally choose (death before decaff) but it often takes people longer to find it than normal coffee, so I threw it into the mix in case it bought us more time.

We worked quickly once we were alone. Watson started grabbing our equipment and stuffed it, clanking, into the bags, doing his best to obscure the tiny window into Edna's office as he worked. I dashed over to the desk and shuffled the mouse around. A dizzying display of family photographs appeared, moving jerkily around his screen, but when I clicked the screensaver disappeared and his computer was open, not password protected. I found his email and quickly sent the security team the code word we'd agreed to prove it was me in his office – DISMAY.

It was enough to prove our point and we were ready to leave. Watson pushed open the rear door and glanced around, it led to a hall area with stairs leading both up to the next floor and down to the ground floor. Perfect.

He left through the door, and it banged loudly. I hesitated. I told him to wait and went back to the door leading to Edna. I pushed a chair under the handle and went back to the desk. Opening the first drawer, then the second, I looked for his phone. Nothing. I glanced around again and noticed his suit jacket draped over the chair. It was worth checking the pockets; although most people would take their phone with them everywhere, he was less attached to his devices than most. I reached into the breast pocket, expensive silk lining brushing my hand, and there inside was a phone. I knew almost instantly that this wasn't the one he had used on the night of the dinner, which was a much bigger, more recent model. Likely he had both a personal and a business line. I went over to the door and opened it, bobbing my eyebrows to Edna on her desk phone. She put the mouthpiece to her shoulder.

'Edna, we are just going to swap the power packs out on the kit,' I garbled quickly. 'This one is knackered. Just going to clear the floor a bit for the shot as well, won't take a second. We'll be back up once we've picked up the new packs if that's OK. We've found the stairs, ignore the noise, cheers, thanks, cheers.'

She nodded impatiently, and I let the door close behind me. I pushed a couple of chairs up against it and looked at the screen on the phone. Walking to the rear door, I told Watson to go and throw the rest of the stuff in the car and leave the door at the bottom of the stairs open for me as I'd be down in two ticks. He left, slowly lumbering down the stairs with all the kit.

I looked at the phone again and smiled: 1,9,5,6. It flashed open and then blinked off. Blank. Shit, it was out of charge.

I could have left right then. The job was done and we had his phone pin, but I wanted to show I had got to him, I wanted to show off. I glanced around and saw a charging cable hanging out of a wall socket, I dived over and plugged the phone in. It buzzed and began charging, I'd have to wait a few seconds before I could use it.

I heard some voices in the office beyond. They were back and talking to Edna, who was probably explaining about the power packs and the chairs. I watched the little black and white battery icon flash into life. I'd need a few more minutes to get the charge, so I wandered to the window and made frantic gestures to Edna, who nodded, pursing her lips and looking impatient. I wouldn't have long to go.

Leave. Leave or get rumbled.

I tried the code again; the phone opened but the voices had stopped. I went to text and punched in my number; the handle of the door rattled gently. 'Just one second. Give me just a minute!' I shouted a little hysterically. I typed the message to myself from his phone: 'DISMAY (and your hubcaps).' Then I unplugged the phone, threw it onto his chair and bolted for the door.

I clattered down the stairs, about four flights, and found the door, propped open with a large tin pub ashtray. I looked around and saw Watson waiting anxiously for me in the car, engine running, about twenty metres away near a fire assembly point. Kicking the ashtray to one side, I ran to the car and jumped in.

'Drive, mate. We are done,' I said. Watson put the car into gear and slowly drove out of the car park and away from Mr Big's office. I pressed play on my car stereo and 'Have a Nice Day' by the Stereophonics started to play.

About two weeks after this job, Mr Big's security team emailed. They had been given some extra cash for their security budget and although the boss was 'a tad grumpy' at first, they had been to the office soon after I had sent the email and were on hand to explain what had happened to him as soon as I had scarpered, stopping him from calling the police.

Apparently, we had very much impressed the guy and, of all things, he wanted to take me for dinner in London for a chat. I reluctantly said yes, meaning to get out of it somehow nearer the time, but the day came around and I found myself sitting in a fabulously expensive restaurant in the middle of London, opposite Mr Big. Clearly a regular and a famous face, the waiters paid us lots of discreet attention, and he asked me what wine I would enjoy. I deferred to him saying I was a vegetarian and would order something to go with whatever the vegetarian option was that night.

Mr Big put down his menu and looked at me through expensive frameless glasses: 'Jenny. You are in one of the best restaurants in the world and someone else is paying. Take my advice, you should try the Wagyu beef.'

I smirked. I liked him a lot. He had charisma and was poking fun at me a little, which I deserved after rinsing him so thoroughly. I agreed to the beef with a little jitter. It had been a decade since I had eaten meat.

Over dinner we chatted about how I had got to him. He wanted to know the psychology behind the con and how we had tailored it specifically to him. He asked about his online presence and what needed to be done to protect himself, his family and employees from similar scams with malicious intent. He asked me lots of questions about my work and how I managed to get into such a niche and unusual area. He pointedly asked me what my parents thought about my work and whether they were proud of me. He also grilled me at some length as to whether I myself had ever been, or could ever be, socially engineered myself and how that might be done, laughing heartily at the examples and stories I told him.

He was great company, amusing and clever and I detected no trace of anger or resentment at what we had done. He congratulated me on a great job and promised me he would recommend us to his wider network.

'How was the beef?' he asked when we had finished eating.

'Bloody marvellous,' I replied truthfully, feeling extremely guilty at breaking my meat-free diet and knowing that I'd crossed the Rubicon and was back to being a carnivore.

He laughed. 'I got you back in the end, Jen,' he said. 'Vegetarianism RIP.'

11

PEST CONTROL

After a while, many jobs became almost too routine, offices and factories, all simple and standard infiltrations. I'd tailgate or sneak in and have a wander around. Leave a few USBs and business cards lying about and steal bits and pieces to present with customary ceremony at the debriefing session with the board. It was fun, but my boredom threshold shows how just about anything can become mundane if you do it frequently enough.

When the job to socially engineer the CEO of a tech company I'll call 'ElegantTech' came in, I wasn't hopeful that it would be very exciting. The client gave me a standard remit, and everything was very straightforward. We were supposed to research the CEO and the board of directors and find out what we could about them, then present it back to them framed, as usual, as to how the information could be weaponised against the company.

We had made numerous vishing calls to all and sundry in the organisation and while they hadn't been the easiest targets, they were pretty much rinsed after a month of the team going for them. We had sent emails with discounts for bars and restaurants, others telling them to switch the company Wi-Fi with malicious links and attachments, and had offered them everything from free pizza to fake parking tickets to ensure that practically their entire team had fallen for one of our scams. So far, so good.

The CEO, though, wasn't so easy. The security team had asked that we get into her phone and access something to prove we had it, to demonstrate the 'art of the possible'.

She was an elegant and extremely switched-on Indian woman. She never had her phone or her designer handbag very far from her manicured hands. The more I watched her, the more stumped I felt about how to get that phone physically out of her hands and into my own. Once I had the phone, my tech colleagues had shown me how to quickly 'backdoor' it so we could monitor it benignly for a while before her security could take over and end the con. It wasn't going to be easy to do; we had to grab it, do a few things with the SIM card and internal workings, then get it back to her quickly and without her knowing it, to complete the mission. As always, we were not allowed to go too far in terms of tactics and would stop short of spying on her, so we would never actually become the bad guys but rather demonstrate benignly what malicious people might think to do.

I had racked my brain as to how we were supposed to get hold of it. My mind kept coming back to just stealing the handbag, although it seemed vulgar – I prefer something more elegant if possible. I applied my mind for a while and eventually the answer presented itself, partly out of desperation and partly, I think, because I was bored of doing things quietly and thought I might show off, add a little theatre.

I was in my office thinking of how to get to her and the same phrase kept coming back to me: 'When will she *have* to drop her bag?' I was drawing a blank, so I decided to ring her office and try to find out some details about her movements in the coming weeks, hoping for some inspiration. I decided to pretend to be a somewhat clueless assistant and see if I could get a conversation going with someone that might give me an idea about how to get to her.

I tried her office directly first.

'Hi, it's Phoenix Publicity returning a call from this number. Is that ElegantTech?'

'Sorry, I don't know what that's about,' her assistant replied.

'Yeah, right. The whole thing is a bit disorganised, eh?' I carried on, trying a vaguely Scottish accent. 'It's probably something to do with the event next week I'd imagine? Who might be the best person to speak to about that?'

'Do you mean the conference?' came the response. I could run with that.

'Yeah, the conference, that's it. We aren't supposed to call it the conference though, I think. It has some other name. Sorry, I'm not sure, I'm new here. Anyway, can you put me through to your events department please, the call must have come from them, and thanks so much, sorry to be so bloody dizzy. Oops, now I swore, sorry, sorry . . .'

The assistant laughed. 'I'll put you on to Jodi, she works in marketing, and she is dealing with the Leadership Summit, I believe that's what we are calling it, next week. If she doesn't know herself, she can put you on to someone who does.'

I thanked her, apologising for my haplessness and asked for the direct line for Jodi, 'just in case'. She gave me the number with a chuckle, no doubt thinking it was extremely likely I would cut myself off the call or forget something else. I sounded completely disorganised and, like most people would, she took pity on me and tried to help me as much as she could. Then she told me to stop apologising and put me through to the marketing department where Jodi picked up.

It's important to tailor your persona to the mark/target of a con both in terms of the script you use and the character you present to them. The same approach won't work on everyone and adapting your script as well as the way you present yourself and your story is a form of tactical adaptation that can be the difference between successfully mining someone for information, or being caught out. You look to the person you are interacting with and how best to engage them, while also reading the context of the situation, seeing the exchange from their perspective and offering them an easy way to help you and so they can get on with whatever it is they happen to be prioritising at that moment.

Jodi sounded young, frazzled and cheerful. One of those clever, creative types whom companies employ to make them look cool. Marketing, I felt, probably suited her. I also felt that she would be happy to chat briefly, but would panic if I gave her too many details or actions so close to their big event.

I dropped the dizziness and switched to direct mode, figuring that she would grant a simple request if she could just to get me off the phone and get on with her busy day.

'Hi Jodi, look it's Simone here from the media bit,' I mumbled quickly, making the Scottish accent a little thicker and thinking on my feet. 'Kirsty put me on to you just very, very quickly because she wasn't sure if we could just bag a couple of spare places at the summit for Charlie and Simon from the US office? She said you'd know. Sorry to bother you, you must be crazy busy.'

Jodi didn't hesitate, bless her efficient little cotton socks. 'Sure, sure. Just make sure Ryan knows the numbers so they have a place on the list and are counted in the lunch numbers, all staff are welcome. Tell us allergies please.'

I thanked her and was getting off the phone, a plan forming

in my mind when she stopped, her tone changed and for a second I thought we were well and truly busted. Then she said, in a very serious voice: 'They aren't fucking vegan or something, are they? Make *sure* you let us know if they are, or they'll have no food and cause a huge fuss, it's a total pain in the arse.'

I laughed and said: 'As far as I know they are carnivorous, very much so, eat anything, but yes, I'll check. Cheers, Jodi, bye bye.'

I smiled, hung up and put the kettle on: a leadership summit, a lunch, a list of employees. This was the opportunity we needed, and I was starting to form a plan of how we could get Ms Elegant to drop her bag . . .

A few further calls revealed that, of course, the CEO was going to be there at the summit; she was, in fact, one of the speakers, and the entire thing was to be broadcast live to the company across the world via the internet. The company wanted the event to be funky and upbeat. No boring conference formats for them, they had decided to have a series of TED Talk-style presentations on a centre stage at a venue not far from their Midlands office. Ms Elegant was going to be the last talk before lunch and all employees could attend.

I had two accomplices in my crew on the day: Rudi, a petite Indian woman who looked much younger than her twenty-two years, and Justin, a tall and very good-looking twenty-eight-year-old guy, who, when not helping me out, was usually to be found surfing or doing some other extreme sport. Neither of them was especially comfortable in their corporate clothes, but they were convincing as colleagues from the USA as long as nobody looked too closely. The plan was to sign into the conference, collect our lanyards and sit among the crowd. We had practised, with much laughter, our American accents the night before and I had told them to try not to talk much as it was elaborate and would get them caught.

We had called and actually got several names on the list. Two of these were total fabrications but close to those of actual employees, I was using one that bore no resemblance to any actual employee name we could find, and then we gave two real names of their colleagues from America. While it might have been easier simply to choose five names of colleagues from overseas, tiering the deception like this was useful on a number of fronts. It's important to remember that our primary role is always to test security measures and procedures. Having some real, some close and some fake names broadens the scope of the test. At some point the company staff might, for example, query or block the entirely fabricated names, but still let the people impersonating their colleagues through simply because those names checked out. If one of the close names was questioned but they accepted a mixed up, misread or mispronounced explanation, then that was a different type of procedural error and different training would be required to stop it happening in reality at some later date. Additionally, if we were all using real colleague names and one of us was busted, then all three of us would be caught by association. Using different forms of fake names gave us another very slim modicum of protection.

However, on the day, as is often the case in social engineering, it really didn't matter because nobody – *nobody* – checked anything at all. Not the names, not the list, not the lanyards, not who we were, nothing. We literally waltzed in, grabbed our badges and melted into the conference crowd. This annoys me sometimes, when all our weeks and months of research and planning are no longer necessary at all because people just don't even care about security. Particularly in the early days this happened a lot. Nowadays people are becoming more aware, down to terrorism as much as anything, and the days of zero security checks are for the most part, thankfully, in the past.

We mingled with the crowd, pretending to talk on our phones and with our names/lanyards turned back to front to deter people from speaking with us. Mingling is easy, as is being anonymous, if you don't stray too much from your natural character or try too hard. The trick, I've always found, is to believe you belong in that room, in that office, in that bank. If you don't believe it yourself, you won't have sufficient presence to convince anyone else.

Gaining this confidence isn't easy and I strongly advise people wanting to become social engineers to spend as much time as possible in as many different social and public situations to gain what might be termed life experience. Essentially, it means that the first time you are called upon to infiltrate an office, it isn't the first office you have ever seen. Get about as much as you can. Mingle. Meet people. Practise talking to people and showing interest in them, get them to open up a little with only the intention of understanding them better. This is generally easier if you are a woman than if you are a man as there is less chance that someone will find you threatening or feel that you are hitting on them. Less, but not zero chance, so be careful.

We wandered around the reception area until some hidden speaker announced the summit was to about to start. Walking into the main theatre we could see the stage, which was very minimal, no lectern or podium, and surrounded by state-of-the-art video screens.

The chairperson was a young, fashionable TV presenter, and she introduced the other company speakers who got up to do their talks. I noted an entrance and an exit route on either side of the stage, but nothing else in the way of adornments meant that when our gal came out to speak, she likely wouldn't bring that handbag. It would look sloppy on the floor, and she wouldn't have a podium to hide it behind or a free hand to hold it. I was banking on it being left just out of sight, backstage.

Various managers came out and did their twelve minutes and we watched and communicated with each other via text. When the CEO came onto the stage, I texted the crew: 'Stand by.'

What I needed now was chaos and a reason to get her off that stage for long enough for me to dip out of sight, find that bag and grab her phone out of it. I would open the back and replace her SIM card, very briefly, with one of our own and a couple of other bits and pieces. It would take about three minutes. Then I would replace everything as normal, put back her phone and voila, we had access to her entire device, every email or text she received, every picture she took and every website she visited. We could show that we had access to her data and even though we wouldn't do anything with it, unlike a criminal, she would be effectively breached, or 'pwned' in hacker parlance, and our engagement would be over.

We needed a distraction that would cause sufficient disruption to give me time to do the switch but wouldn't prompt people to call any emergency services and waste their time. For this reason, we had decided against a fire alarm or any serious fabrication that might cause an actual evacuation. It had taken me a while to come up with the answer, but I knew it would do the job.

I waited until her talk was in full flow. She was impressive and the room was quiet, hanging on her every word. She wasn't the most entertaining speaker in the world, but she was confident in what she was saying and had excellent visuals to accompany her talk. It was a shame we were going to have to ruin it. I gave the signal, texting 'Plague' to my team.

The day before we had visited a pet shop and approached the live bait section of the store. We had found some large and pretty fierce-looking locusts that people buy to feed to pets such as lizards and frogs. On receiving my signal, Rudi and Justin reached into their bags and took out two plastic tubs which they opened to release exactly six locusts into the conference crowd sitting around them. Rudi dropped one locust onto the suit jacket of the guy seated in front of her, giving a loud gasp and tapping him on his shoulder. He was halfway through turning to look at her when he caught sight of the insect in his peripheral vision.

'*Shit!*' he proclaimed at full volume and stood upright, pulling off his jacket and treading on his neighbours' feet. The rest of the crowd turned around to see the cause of the disturbance, but then a woman a couple of rows further down spotted a second one on her shoe and screamed loudly, bolting out of her seat and staggering towards the aisle. Panic spread quickly as people pushed to leave, but although most people were noticeably confused by the situation, many stayed relatively calm and left only slowly.

I had let out a genuine shriek when I caught sight of one of the little buggers jumping down the centre aisle. They were mean-looking for sure but essentially harmless. Meanwhile, Justin was at the front of the hotel on the phone to their management and explaining that some students had pulled a trick in the hall as a publicity stunt and that the locusts were few and completely harmless. It wouldn't be long before people realised that there was no real danger and order would be restored. I had to act quickly.

I hurried to the front of the stage where I hid just behind the main black curtain and found the bag straight away where our CEO had placed it before going on stage. Pulling back into the gloom behind the curtain, I crouched down behind rows of stacked conference chairs, dug out her phone and following the instructions I'd been given by a technical contact began to do the swap. When you are nervous, your fine motor skills are shot to pieces, and I dropped it a couple of times before I managed to complete the job, hearing a satisfying click as I slipped her designer phone case back onto the handset and put the phone into the bag. I stood up and listened, hearing the CEO not far away on the stage, talking calmly to staff and asking, with no anger, but very clearly, if anyone had seen her bag. I admired her calmness and level attitude under the circumstances – sometimes you can really tell why someone is in charge.

The crackle of a speaker announced that the situation was under control and that people should return to their seats. Rudi had found the hotel security staff and initially admitted responsibility for the chaos, confessing to being behind the 'student prank'. She had found five of the locusts and replaced them in the tub in her bag, although she had told the hotel she had found them all. They were quizzing her right now in the office, but I wasn't concerned, she was very capable and actu-ally *was* still a student. Meanwhile, Justin had made his way to the hotel security office and passed on a letter from the security team explaining what we were doing and that we had their full permission to create the diversion (this is known in the busi-ness as a 'get-out-of-jail-free card'). The hotel guards would be calling the security team now who would be verifying the story, explaining it all as a corporate exercise and grudgingly instructing them to let us all go.

Standing in the dark behind the stage curtain, I could still hear the CEO, who by now was a little less calm and asking for security as her bag had been stolen. I moved towards the side of the stage and was about to drop the bag on the floor and walk away, and she'd find her phone as soon as someone thought to ring it within feet of where she stood.

Then there was a tap on my shoulder: 'Are you OK? Can I help you?' One of the audiovisual guys had seen me fumbling behind the curtain.

'Yeah,' I said. 'What the hell happened? My bag got moved and I saw it peeking out from behind the curtain just here. It was with this one.' I picked up her bag, held it aloft.

The AV guy smiled and turned to the CEO: 'Hey, miss. I think this might be your bag. Miss?'

She turned, a look of relief crossing her face as she reached for the bag and had a brief look inside. She said a quiet thank you to us both, her still-live microphone amplifying her words to the already almost full auditorium. 'Thank you so much, thank you.' And then, 'Well, ladies and gentlemen, we did promise you a lively conference!'

I left, heading towards the seating area, but kept going out through the back doors, through the hall of the hotel, on down the stairs and through the lobby into the street. I walked straight to a cab and was a mile away from the hotel within a couple of minutes. I imagined her restarting her speech, maybe having a joke with her staff, calming everyone down. She would handle the situation well.

I got texts from the crew confirming all of us had got away fine, including Rudi, and that the SIM swap had worked and the phone was, for all intents and purposes, hacked. I texted the head of security with the phrase 'A plague on your house!', declaring the assignment successful and complete to their security team and to the crew. I chuckled and tipped the surprised taxi driver a tenner. It had been a good day.

The CEO had been cool as a cucumber and I admired her greatly, but we could still get to her, and that made me proud of my crew and happy we had met our objectives. Moreover, it was yet another example of a non-technical hack. It was satisfying because as much as we had used cyber to research the company and inform our activities, the toughest nut to crack, our CEO, could only be got at by working with the humans. Even though the goal had been to hijack her phone, fundamentally we had to work with psychology, with emotion, with fear, to complete our task. The answer one way or another is always with the people; protecting them was not only the biggest challenge security faced, but also the best reason to work in the industry.

Back at the rendezvous point, my crew walked one by one into the bar, we high fived each other and ordered many drinks, saluting the one locust that never came back.

1 2

THE CAT AND THE CAKE

Burglars are very superstitious. Those that do it for real, as well as most other social engineers I know, keep to certain routines and rituals. I left a tiny silver octopus in a client's office once as a quirky but anonymous calling card. It was a random choice of object at the time, I'd found it last-minute in a market near the client's offices and decided to leave it in her desk as proof I had managed to get in. I'd called her the morning after the job and never forgot the gasp and then the laugh as I directed her to find it in her own drawer.

Of course, I had pictures and other evidence that showed where I had been on the infiltration, which we presented more formally to her and her team afterwards, but she had enjoyed the moment and now kept the object on her desk as a sort of lucky charm, reminding her not to let her security measures slip. I began taking the same octopus charms with me on my jobs and hiding one somewhere. Sometimes I reveal them to clients and sometimes I just leave one in some hidden corner for my own private amusement. The habit became something of a ritual and now I feel like I have to do it or the job will go wrong or be somehow cursed and incomplete.

I might label a job 'cursed' for several reasons. We could

213

initially fail to get past security and have to make unplanned return visits to the site. We could be spotted or stopped and have to abort the initial attempt and try again at a later date, which is costly both financially and in terms of my reputation. Sometimes, though, I label the job as cursed not just because things do not go exactly to plan, which is common whenever people are involved, but when something weird, dangerous or dramatic happens.

The nature of the work means that unexpected events often occur, but there is a special quality that has to exist for me to file a job under 'cursed'. There was the time I was trapped on a metal fire escape and a ferocious thunderstorm came from nowhere, lightning threatening to zap me before my colleague could get into the building and get me out from the inside. Another time, in Europe, we found a master key to an alarm system and switched it off, unlocking all the doors including those that kept the guard dogs in their kennels. We had got away, climbing the fence just in time, with three huge Rottweilers snapping at our heels. I labelled that job 'The Winter's Tale' after Shakespeare's famous stage direction 'Exit, pursued by a bear'. We laughed later, through gritted teeth, with the security team and their dog handlers, but the job was cursed, no question.

Even the most meticulous planning does not always make for a straightforward job. So many variables come into play when humans get involved that every infiltration is rife with unpredictable events that can spiral out of control. Improvisation is a key skill because I so often have to work with whatever happens around the job, even though it may not be directly related to it. I have to make decisions in the moment as to what might be important and what I can safely ignore. It is a fine line between staying focused and assessing the impact of peripheral variables, of surprises. Surprises curse jobs.

It is partly for this reason that I am quite strict with my crew on a job and have rules that must be followed to try to control as much of the environment as we can. For example, the crew is not generally allowed to eat or drink while we are on a job. This is because although we tend to spend a considerable amount of time in bathrooms regrouping, texting and hiding from staff, the last thing you need on a physical infiltration is to actually *need* the bathroom. This is a basic biological demand, as are hunger, thirst and the need to sleep, and it will absolutely take priority until the urge is met, at the potential expense of good judgement and focus.

I remember one occasion when I was hidden behind a large corporate display while a sales team had a meeting about the following day and the conference they were attending. My stomach began to rumble loudly as I had been there for the best part of the day and hadn't eaten anything since a scant bowl of hotel cereal early that morning. 'Was that your stomach, James?' a voice hissed at a colleague standing near the display.

'No, was it yours?' came the terse reply, when it was, in fact, mine – from behind their screens. Imagine if I'd been caught for something so stupid.

We take a few cereal bars with us on most jobs, just in case we need to stave off the hunger pangs and stop the tummy rumbling. I aim for a maximum of ninety minutes' contact time as a target on most jobs as any longer and people typically start to notice and engage with you. I also have found that taking some snack cheese is very useful, in case you meet a guard dog or need an excuse to be in a kitchen, which is often part of the brief.

'Please walk into our shared staffroom kitchen area and make and drink a hot beverage' is often a client contractual requirement and I've taken my time over many a cuppa in places I should not have been. People even help! I had one memorable occasion when the lovely security guard made me some tea while warning me earnestly to be careful of the boiling faucet. I made sure I spoke to him afterwards, so he didn't feel too bad about it. After all, I really do look and sound harmless. Poor bloke even gave me a few biscuits which broke one of my rules and could easily have led to a cursed job.

Thou shalt not eat anything at the client site, no matter how hungry thou art from hiding in cupboards etc. for hours.

Quite apart from the practical considerations of all of this, I am super-superstitious as every time I have eaten on a job something has gone wrong.

I have a client who hires me routinely every year for the most straightforward physical test of their office. It is so basic and easy that I have sent other people to do it once or twice because, despite my carefully pointing out their numerous security lapses every time, they never remedy their issues and as soon as they have their budget in April they ask me to do the same thing as last time all over again. It ticks their compliance box, we get paid and it's easy. What can you do?

On this particular site, they take a name at reception and as long as you are a 'visitor' you are issued a pass and allowed into the building. However, all we ever do is send everyone on site an email asking them to donate to a charity page (on a broken link) and just wait to see which staff members are out of the office from their replies. Then, we call reception on the day of the visit and tell them that X (who is on vacation) has a visitor booked who is clear to be allowed past. I often send one of the crew to do that bit (as some of the security team know me by now) and they walk through the building straight to the furthest door on the site and unlatch it. This lets me inside later that evening with ease and away we go.

We have used other non-destructive methods of entry in the past, picking locks and climbing through windows – it's a huge sprawling site with frequent staff rotations and is never particularly difficult to get inside. Once I'm there I wander around, have a rummage in people's desk drawers, make my way to the upstairs offices and generally see if anything that constitutes a potential security risk might be left lying about. I've found all sorts over the years from car keys and passports to credit cards and large amounts of cash. I pick them up, log them and give them back to the individuals along with some awareness training and security recommendations. People are generally a bit shocked but glad for the heads-up and tend to behave less carelessly as a result.

The client in this case, in common with many others, isn't really bothered how I choose to carry out the test. They are delightful to work with and happy to book me year on year, even though they never really improve things beyond the most obvious of issues. They just can't grasp that security is a mindset, rather than a single exercise. You can't give people training once a year, tick a box and say it's done, any more than bringing professionals in to test your site now and again and then thinking you are safe.

Security is an ever-evolving entity, and people need to be constantly reminded of their individual role in keeping them-selves and their workplace safe. If you put an alarm on a door so you are alerted if it gets left open, that deals with that door, that symptom of slack operations. If you don't address why the door was left open in the first place, why someone didn't close it or think it was an issue, then a different door, literal or metaphorical, will be left open tomorrow. The causes of poor security must be continuously addressed in a holistic way through relevant and consistent education, otherwise it's a game of whack-a-mole in terms of vulnerabilities and attackers.

I return to this client most years, on their insistence, and do what I can to improve their site and understanding, always recommending several other providers and solutions they should use to try to vary their testing and give them new angles. It might seem counterintuitive from a business perspective, but I actively try to move them away from just using my company all the time, because it is really important to get a range of different perspectives in security. It's one reason why diversity of all types is such a necessity in the security industry, to avoid complacency and consider alternative views.

This raises another point that I often mention in talks, one that surprises people given my history, and that is that I must be the *most* moral and principled person in the room. In my profession there is no excuse at all for stealing anything for real – ever. Not one penny. If we take something to show a vulnerability, we bag it up the first chance we get and seal it to give back. I then put it into a paper envelope (or bag if it's a uniform or similar) and hand it back *directly* to the owner. Not the business. Exceptions include guns, knives and knuckledusters, illegal drugs and anything that constitutes danger to another human. If it's illegal, we speak up and ask for confirmation that law enforcement have been contacted.

No stealing, no showboating, no eating. Red lines we shall never cross in case we curse the job. Which brings us back to my careless client and the physical penetration test of their insecure offices.

I was on my way out and things had gone well. As usual,

no one had challenged me, and I had hardly seen a soul for the hour or so I had been wandering around the site. My driver, Bianca, was waiting for me in the car park. I had just texted her 'Jalfrezi' which meant 'I'll be out in fifteen minutes' when I noticed the remnants of a large and rather marvellous-looking cake on one of the shared tables in the office.

Thou shalt not eat . . .

It had clearly been freshly cut and the icing still spelt out half a message in corporate colours on the top of the cake. This place was always having office parties, so this was probably for some anniversary or company celebration, done to get pictures for their social media feed as they finished the day's work. The cake looked expensive and fresh. It was right in front of me and I was starving.

Thou shalt not eat anything at the client site . . .

Fuck it, I thought. 'Stupid rules, anyway, why are you so silly about these things? Superstition is a chain, a manacle,' I muttered to myself and took a napkin. 'It's fine; no one will notice,' I continued my little monologue, swooning as I tasted vanilla sugar icing and sponge. 'One tiny piece of cake can't curse the job.'

And then I distinctly heard a window slam and the sound of a cat meowing. I swore aloud, an alphabet of curses and threw down the remains of the cake with some force as I turned towards the noise and paced across the office, licking what was left of the icing off my fingers.

'Ate the cake. Cursed the job,' I said out loud and texted 'MANGO', which means *potential fucking issue* as I wandered towards the noise to check what it was and whether it was something that impacted their security or would otherwise need documenting on our report.

The office floor was massive and, as I turned a corner, I saw a window had blown open, blinds swaying erratically in a brisk wind, fluttering papers on desks and all making a considerable noise. There was quite a storm brewing outside. I reached across to try to reattach the window to the latch just in case it smashed as it slammed into the frame, but it pulled away again and wouldn't stay shut. This was 'the curse': an unpredicted incident likely to draw attention to my location and perhaps summon a security guard or cleaner.

I decided to get out as quickly as I could and texted 'POP' (short for poppadom: *Be ready, I'm making my way out*). Then, out of the corner of my eye, I saw something dark scoot under the desk to my left. I've seen plenty of mice and rats in my time at night in buildings. I'm not a fan. However, I got the feeling this was bigger and remembered the mewing noise I had heard.

I got down on all fours and looked under the desk. Staring back at me was a scared-looking little tabby cat. A kitten really and a cute but very scared one at that. What the hell was it doing in here? It surely couldn't have come through the window as we were a few floors up.

It ran away towards the cake and stopped to look back at me. I took a step towards it and made some vague shushing noises. I like cats. I've always owned them, can't resist them in fact, and I strongly felt that this little chap was lost and probably in trouble. If he went towards a window he could fall out, jump out, be blown out. My mind went straight to disaster, and I felt this was fate. I had to save the kitten, the job was already cursed.

'Pss pss pss,' I said sweetly, holding out my hand. After a minute or so, curiosity seemed to get the better of it and it approached with only slight hesitation. I stroked its ears and before long it was happy, licking some stray icing from my fingers. It had a little collar with a mobile number and a name. I said the name and the little chap relaxed. What to do?

I had to get out. I'd already texted to say I was on my way and the still-slamming window would eventually attract attention. I made a snap decision, opened my rucksack and grabbed my reversable fleece from inside. I wrapped it around the cat, who didn't protest much. Getting closer, I noticed it wasn't in great shape, a little damp and thin compared to my own cats at home. I swaddled it a bit tighter in the fleece and put it gently inside my rucksack, zipping it fastened but leaving a tiny gap for the kitten to breathe easily. I quickly made for the door to the staircase, the bag bouncing a little against my back as I moved. The motion rattled the cat and it began to whimper a little and scratch against the side of the bag.

I rushed down the stairs, moving as gently as possible, muttering to the kitten in an attempt to soothe it. Four floors high, so eight flights down, with Bianca waiting in the car park, my phone beeped as she asked me to confirm, and I wasn't replying. I had two more flights to go down and was on the first-floor landing when a door flew open with absolutely no warning, and a large woman in a brightly coloured cardigan stepped out into the staircase in front of me. She looked up, seeing me immediately and jumped in surprise. I stopped abruptly so as not to charge directly into her.

'Who are you and what are you doing?' she asked loudly, going straight for the jugular, clearly having no crap at all.

Cursed. Five years and not a challenge. Five times in this place and no one – *no one* – had ever so much as questioned me. But I broke the rules and cursed the job and now, with a cat in my rucksack, I bump into someone whom I could tell, from a lifetime of reading people and working a thousand different persuasion routes, was unlikely to be an easy con.

'I've been checking the canteen,' I tried, for who knows what reason. It made no sense, and the canteen was on the first floor anyway so why would I be pelting down the stairs? It was a bad start.

'What?'

'Er, not the canteen actually, the little coffee-making kitchen, you know . . .' I nodded and smiled, trying to think as my phone beeped again. 'I've been working late with the procurement team, Dave's team, and I needed a coffee.'

She put her head on one side: 'I think I heard about that.'

Was she biting? It seemed unlikely.

'Anyway, I'm just on my way out actually and—' A loud and mournful 'meow' emanated unmistakably from my rucksack which was moving independently on my back.

'Oh my God! Do you have a cat in your bag?' she gasped, confusion spreading over her face.

This was a bust. Time to come clean. 'Look,' I squinted for her name on the rainbow lanyard around her neck. 'I've lied to you, Carol, and I'm sorry.'

She looked shocked. 'It's just . . .' I continued. 'It's just that I suppose you are aware of the vermin problem in the building?' I said in conspiratorial tones.

'The vermin?' She pulled a face. 'Yes, I am.'

'Good, good. Well, you see—' I started, but she interjected with some volume.

'It's that fucking stupid bitch Lucy in accounts, isn't it? I hate her so much I've spat in her sandwiches.'

Despite everything, my own jaw dropped. 'Er, what? I mean no, yes, eh?'

'Oh, she knows I did. *She knows*. I told her. She just never washes up or anything, the kitchen stinks and then, well, she labels the milk [she did air quotes] "FINANCE MILK" and I just lost it.'

I was, for once, speechless. The cat was becoming more

agitated. '*Filthy, horrible dirty pigs.*' I was genuinely horrified at the sheer hate in her voice. '. . . and you just know that once we put in all the effort to fucking clear it out, they will *still* not clean it up.'

'Er . . .'

'So I'm not surprised at all we needed pest control. *Not at all.*'

I gathered myself. 'Yes, *yes*. Exactly,' I stuttered, rolling my eyes. 'So, er, I'm just going back to the lab and hopefully all sorted.' I stepped towards the last flight of stairs.

She walked in front of me and held open the door, suddenly the picture of corporate politeness and professionalism. 'Thank you, Carol,' I said as I stepped out. 'And Carol?'

'Yes?'

'Obviously, this isn't something to be shared with the wider team. Until we can find the, er, cause.'

'Of course,' she said and gave me a conspiratorial nod, her lips pursed, as she let me out of the building, and I walked towards Bianca in the car.

'Drive,' I said, and we left the car park.

'You've stolen a cat?' said Bianca, with less surprise than might have been expected, as we pulled out.

I spent a lively twenty minutes calming the cat down inside the rucksack before being able to read the number on the collar well enough to call it. The owner lived only about ten minutes away, and we had found the cat on the local Facebook lost and found page before she even picked up the phone. Pulling up outside her house, I handed her the cat still inside my rucksack. Otherwise empty, it was rather soggy as kitty had peed inside it, but the cat seemed more or less fine and happy enough to be reunited with the owner.

'Where did you find her?' the owner asked.

'In an unexpected place. Near a birthday cake,' I replied, and smiled at her puzzled face as we headed off for wine and chips.

13

FALLING

I'd had time to ponder my life as I fell off the roof. I've fallen off more than a few roofs in my time, although never so far as to seriously injure myself, and I can tell you that sometimes it happens so quickly that, as soon as you realise you have slipped or whatever, you have already stopped and are looking at the world from the wrong angle. Other times, like this one, things seem to run in slow motion, and you tend to observe some idiotic detail like the distance between the bricks being so even, or a piece of litter in the guttering, that makes you think *That abandoned shoe must have been up here for years*, or *Who dropped that pen up here?*

Then pain happens, you get up again and the day/night continues . . .

The roof in Transylvania was high enough, maybe twelve metres from the ground. It was a four-storey building, and I was tucked away behind a sizeable chimney on gently sloping slate tiles. About two metres below me there were short railings with ornate spikes framing the wide ledge that ran alongside the top floor. The climb from there had been a matter of standing on the window ledge, pulling myself up and swinging my legs onto the roof slates. It hadn't seemed particularly dangerous, and the ledge looked as if it had been designed so that someone could use it to walk around the exterior of the building, perhaps as a safety measure. I had stopped briefly on my pre-job check to admire the clarity of the air in the approaching Romanian night, the foreboding castles on the horizon, fingernail moon and the silence of the city below.

The hotel had been chosen for its view of the target, a small café-bar in the street below, directly opposite my room. However, when I had checked in I'd realised that I had a limited view to the street from the front window, so I had opened the large side windows and found the wide ledge.

I had a booking for a standard training in the city the next day which had been in the diary for months. However, about a week before I was due to fly I had been contacted by a second client and was asked if I could do some surveillance work to help catch a rogue employee who, they thought, happened to be in the same city that week. I didn't need to know much more, and I didn't want to know why the information was important, although I had been told they had evidence of corporate espionage, coercion and threats. The client paid well, asked politely for help and it fitted with my schedule. It also doubled the pay on the trip, so the job was on.

They asked me to verify a lead they had been given that their employee would be in a certain bar on the evening before the first day of my course. If I saw him, I was to take a picture to prove he was there and send it through to them. The next day I would be picked up by the other client who would drive me to their offices, where I would teach their top team about non-verbal communications and deception for a couple of days, before making my way, somehow, across country and through the Carpathian Mountains to Bucharest for a boozy catch-up with a friend before flying home. I was yet to work out how exactly to do this as my transport options were limited, but I was taking one challenge at a time and the first job was to grab a picture of my target.

As per any normal business trip, I went and had pizza and a glass of wine in a beautiful medieval square near to my hotel. Sitting at the table I looked like any other tourist, or businessperson, enjoying a moment of quiet while I ate my food and took in the general atmosphere of the place and the beautiful surroundings. I took a few shots with my phone and was relaxed, texting home pictures of the food and trying to find the name of the church opposite me online.

Suddenly, something felt wrong, I got a wave of worry for no reason and quickly put down my phone and looked around me. It's hard to describe exactly what this sensation really is, but many people are familiar with the sudden feeling that they are being watched. This was like that but turned up to maximum volume, and I have learnt not to dismiss it when it comes over me. I switched from relaxed to alert and fought the instinct to look around me in a more thorough but also more obvious way.

I picked up my sunglasses and pushed them onto my head, then reached for my water and, as I sipped, looked methodically around the square for anything that stood out as unusual. On the edge of my peripheral vision, among the crowd of people wandering around, I noticed a huge guy with a lumbering gait walking in my direction. He was taller than most of the other people, and I had the distinct feeling he had just been looking in my direction but had turned away and doubled back on himself. Not good. Years of watching my back on various jobs in different cities have made me wary of feelings like this and apparently insignificant details and I tend not to ignore them.

I mentally assessed my options. I was in a good position, fully public and with a good view of any approach from across the square. I could sit and watch from here, and the restaurant was busy so that help was on hand if anything happened, but I needed to be able to move quickly, so I gestured for my bill while keeping a casual eye on him and on the general crowd.

He continued towards the restaurant, ambling along but pointedly avoided looking at me or any of the tables as he walked past. I turned away for a second to sign for my tab, and when I looked up again, I couldn't find him. He had disappeared. In a matter of seconds I'd lost him among the milling people in the square. Blending like that is difficult, especially if you are his height and build; I thought he had probably had training. Maybe law enforcement?

I waited a while longer, but I saw no more signs of him, or of anything else that caught my eye. Time was pushing on and I needed to return to the hotel and get to work, but I couldn't shake the strange feeling and wasn't happy that I'd lost him so easily. I hurried nervously across the square, checking around me as I walked and telling myself to stop being so dramatic, but also with strange vibes and 'Spidey senses' tingling all over the place.

I crossed the square quickly and headed down the little street that led to my hotel, walking past the café-bar I'd be scoping later on my left. I stopped to cross the road, turned my head to check for traffic and there he was, on the same side of the pavement as me about twenty metres away. Lumbering up the street and huge, there was no mistaking it was the same guy. I started slightly and looked again to cross the road, but it was suddenly alive with mopeds and cabs and there wasn't an opportunity. The guy got closer but was looking away from me, and I stepped further into the road, pointedly staring ahead, and hoping he would walk right past. Now with a bad case of the jitters, I couldn't help turning my head as he got closer, and then he was directly behind me.

It was then I noticed, my jaw dropping, that he was wearing a red and white Liverpool football scarf. I did a double take, jumped, and breathed in sharply. He looked me right in the eye, gave me the merest nod and continued past me without breaking his stride and was quickly at the top of the street, re-entering the square.

I dashed across the road, dodging the mopeds, and fumbled stupidly with the key as I let myself into the courtyard at the rear of the hotel. I climbed the stairs to my room, carefully closing and locking the door, sat down on the bed and breathed out heavily.

I hadn't needed any crew for this job, and I had felt no need to bring anyone but myself and the client into the frame. This wasn't big or especially difficult, it involved no infiltration or complicated planning and I had assessed that I didn't need any help. I was just taking a few pictures, after all, and apart from my office, and my friend in Bucharest, no one outside of the clients knew I was here. But who the heck was scarf man?

I was sitting on the bed, feet dangling and pondering the situation, when I noticed it was getting quite late, and it was time to get into position to try to see if the target was in the café. I told myself to get focused and made my way back downstairs to the courtyard, paused near the wooden door to the street and listened for a moment.

Beyond the door, I could hear noises of people gathered, presumably in the café, with some background music and the occasional passing car. I walked outside onto the pavement and smoked a cigarette while pretending to take a call on my phone and keeping watch for scarf man. If someone wanted to approach and talk to me, give me new information or warn me off, whatever, then I wanted to give them a window to do it and better here, in public, than in the courtyard or in my room. It wasn't lost on me that I wasn't the only person who could use that ledge as a pathway should clandestine access to any part of the building be required. It wasn't exactly ideal.

This little cigarette break on the pavement was about me giving myself the best chance I could think of for some help, or at least some witnesses, if something sinister was about to go down.

The café-bar was busy. People filled the interior and were spilling out in and around some little tables on the pavement outside the door. The crowd within had a happy, noisy buzz about them that was congenial, and there was the sound of plates and cutlery and glasses clinking in the background.

A set of double doors at the front of the café opened and I half-turned away as a few people stepped out onto the street and lit cigarettes. Glancing around for scarf man, I melted back a little more towards my hotel door and nodded vigorously at the fake caller on my phone while looking more closely at the people from the bar.

They were a young crowd; the men had beards, piercings and tattoos and most were wearing predominantly black, jeans, T-shirts and hoodies. I could see only a few women, but they were similarly casually attired, a few with bright colours in their hair. Most tellingly, there were a lot of laptops on tables. Expensive laptops covered with stickers. Hackers. I knew this type of crowd. Under different circumstances I might even have joined them, got chatting. I probably even knew one or two of their Twitter handles, and they mine. I watched as carefully as I could. If I could catch the guy from this position, I wouldn't even need to climb onto the roof.

I waited a little longer, but none of the crowd whom I could see inside the place, or spilling into the street, resembled the person I was looking for. He had a distinct physical feature (I cannot mention here) that would make him easy to spot, so I was pretty sure I wouldn't miss him. That said, I couldn't keep up the phone-call pretence much longer, I'd risk being noticed. My position was too obvious, and the target had good reason to be more suspicious and observant than the rest of this crowd, if he did ever arrive. I grabbed a few sly general shots of the café from my phone and moved back through the door to head to the roof.

The noise of the gathering grew faint but was still audible as I climbed the stairs and made my way to my room. It was a still, crisp evening and sound was carrying a long way. Overall, this city was one of the quietest I'd ever been in, and it continued to feel a little eerie. The square itself was completely pedestrianised and the traffic in the street outside the hotel had died down almost completely. The place was undoubtedly beautiful and yet it had a disconcerting, otherworldly vibe about it and I couldn't shake that feeling of being watched.

As I got back to my room, I pondered what was going on. While it was undoubtedly true that I had been a little spooked by the setting, and it was also just about possible that scarf man was a weird coincidence, I was reluctant to ignore my gut feeling that something unusual was afoot. I felt as though more was going on than I knew about, and I didn't like it. I don't like surprises. Especially when I can't summon help up easily if required.

I thought momentarily of abandoning the job. I could always claim some confusion or problem, a migraine or similar. I could legitimately claim to have been spooked and return my fee. It happens. However, I have always been worried about doing that because in my line of work you deliver or risk not being hired again, and neither my ego nor my bank account would stand for that. I whitewashed the thoughts of quitting from my mind, walked over to the windows, turned the lock and took another look outside at the ledge. It was happening, I needed to get ready.

I took off my smart jacket and shirt and changed into a long-sleeved black T-shirt, black jeans and my chunky black work boots. Lacing up to the knee and with thick rubber soles, they are my uniform for physical infiltrations and have the type of weight and grip that comes in useful if I have to climb anywhere.

I could smell the yeasty aroma of cannabis as I opened the window fully and stuck out my head and shoulders. I grabbed the ornamental railings with both hands and hauled myself out of my window and onto the ledge, where I paused to check that no one was in the courtyard below or peering out of the open windows on my floor. All clear.

My earlier recce had shown me the best place to climb up onto the roof, and I retraced my earlier route, edging along towards the front of the building where the ledge widened a little at the corner of the building overlooking the street. Using a little cornice as a handhold, I swung one leg upwards and pulled myself messily up onto the roof. I intended to crawl behind the chimney, which would give me some cover as I lay flat on my stomach and got into position to take the shots.

I scrambled awkwardly, pushing down with my foot to get higher. It was not easy. The grey tiles were not exactly slippery, but there were no other handholds and the edges of the slate were sharp. I was worried I would dislodge a tile and I ended up planting my left foot into the guttering for the final push onto the roof. Guttering of any kind is notoriously precarious and, as it isn't designed to take the weight of a human being, should never be relied upon as a climbing aid. It made a loud crumbling noise and I stopped dead, expecting bits of it to fall and smash down on the ground in the courtyard below and give me away.

I finally managed to crawl into position, the roof feeling surprisingly warm through my clothes. I lay down flat and spread my arms and legs outwards into a star shape, inching forwards slowly on my belly to the front of the building behind the chimney. From there, I was able to look around the chimney stack and directly down onto the street full of beaten-up cars, neatly stacked rubbish sacks and mostly domestic-looking buildings. The café looked out of place here with its liveliness and noise, and from this new perspective I could see it was rough around the edges, a bit run-down and shabby. There were now more tables and chairs outside, I could make out some garish signs above the door and around thirty or so people, nearly all bearded men, drinking bottled beers and smoking and chatting on the pavement outside.

I watched a while and took some shots of the crowd, musing that it was likely a local hacker meet-up of some sort. The cyber industry has lots of them and this seemed to be more of a semi-professional gathering than an actual party. I thought to myself that they could have a great logo for their merchandise, something with a vampire on it, or maybe blood dripping from a keyboard. Cool. I was also starting to think about the large glass of wine I would sink in the bath when I got down from this roof and finished the job. Hopefully I wouldn't have to wait too long, it was getting dark, and I was relying on the light from the café to give the pictures enough definition for us to identify the target in the crowd if he showed up.

I was getting cold and my legs were starting to feel numb. I shuffled around a bit to try to get more comfortable, moving closer to the chimney stack. As I straightened myself up slightly, I glanced back down to the café and then I saw him. Clear as day, and no mistaking, the guy I was looking for walked out of the café and lit up a cigarette at one of the tables. They'd have to enhance the pictures, but I had the clearest view, and he was standing in the light of the window so hopefully it wouldn't be too much of a job to make him out. Relieved and happy, I pointed my phone downwards, took a few shots and then reached around my back to slide it into the back pocket of my jeans. Then, quite suddenly and quite violently, everything turned upside down.

To this day, I've no idea whether I slipped, or mistimed something, or what, but I know I stifled a yell, the world upended, and I was aware of myself rolling down the roof, slipping off and outwards, bouncing against the railings and landing heavily and painfully onto the ledge a little way along from my still-open bedroom window. If I had fallen outwards even a little further in any other direction, I would have dropped four floors into the courtyard of the hotel and certainly died.

I somehow caught my finger on the railing as I landed, twisting it badly and bending my wedding ring so that it never did fit me properly again. I ripped a hole in my trousers above the knee, knocked my head hard and caught the lacing on my boot on the railings, ripping the laces through the holes on one side and scattering rubble on top of me and down into the courtyard below. I felt a dozen little explosions of pain all over my body, as various cuts, bruises and grazes appeared.

Groaning, I knew I had to hide quickly in case anyone had heard me, and I crawled, shaking painfully, along the ledge and dragged myself into my bedroom. I flopped through the window and onto the rug beside the bed, dizzy with pain and nearly peeing myself as the shock came in waves over me. Then, and only then, did I scream out loud, trying to keep a low volume but unable to control it. 'Ow! Fuck! *Ow! Fuck! Ow!*'

I kept on shouting for what seemed like a very long time, before standing up, staggering to shut the window and careering into the bathroom, locking the door behind me. I plonked down on the toilet and sat for a long time without moving, despite now being desperate to pee. When I got myself together to try to urinate, I weirdly couldn't go at all, my legs had turned to jelly and nothing else was working properly. Plus, I had a blinding headache and was starting to feel sick.

When I finally felt able to move a bit, I sat down drunkenly on the floor and pulled off my boots. They were useless and would have to be dumped. I peeled off torn and filthy clothes with aching, cut hands, stood up and rinsed my dry mouth with cold water. I wrestled for a moment with the taps before running myself a very hot bath, watching motionless as the water filled the tub. After what seemed a very long time, I grabbed a couple of paracetamol from my make-up bag and swallowed them, drinking from the tap, and then started to inspect the many cuts and bruises that had appeared in both obvious and non-obvious locations about my person.

I saw a nasty graze on my left elbow with bits of thread from my T-shirt, dirt and what looked like black paint mixed in with the congealing blood. I picked a flake of paint out and flicked it into the sink. A wave of nausea hit me, and I turned, almost casually, and threw up pizza and paracetamol into the toilet bowl.

I fell asleep in the bath and woke to cold water and stinging cuts on my arms. The headache was pounding, and I had a large bump under my hair. I got into bed and fell asleep quickly, without checking in with the client or sending through any pictures, stopping only to set my alarm for the course the next day.

I woke up ahead of the alarm and looked at the bed. It was covered in little patches of blood and grit. I walked over to the mirror and groaned. I looked awful, I'd have to shower and hope for the best. I took more painkillers and logged into my laptop, then sent the pics from my phone to my email and then through to the client with the message: 'It was him. I hope the pics are clear enough. All fine.'

I finished breakfast and went outside to wait for the cab the client had booked for me, very glad that this training was one I had done a thousand times and enjoyed giving without needing much effort on my part. The bump on my head had gone down and with any luck they'd be a lively group and would make me forget all of this for a few hours.

It was then I noticed the café-bar, or rather the lack of it. I was standing exactly where I had made the fake phone call the previous evening, directly opposite the café. But the café was gone. The building was there, and there were cigarette butts and a few beer bottles on the pavement, but the place was boarded up, the sign was gone and it looked more or less dere-lict. No one would have guessed that just a few hours earlier there had been thirty or more people socialising in that space.

I was about to cross the road and take a closer look when a cab pulled to a stop in front of the hotel, and the cheerful driver got out and put my case in the boot, holding the door open for me to get in. I sat down awkwardly, my leg and arms still throbbing away, and I decided not to think about it any-more and switch my focus, as I have done so many times, into corporate training mode.

My group was lovely. Clever, young and eager to learn, but every time I raised my arms or made a sudden movement my clothes rubbed against all my cuts and my bruised limbs ached. During the first coffee break I found a confirmation email from my client and a notification that the payment was already in my account, with thanks. I was trying to google train and bus times from where I was into Bucharest and having no luck, seriously pondering whether to book myself into a different hotel and try to change my flights, when one of the group, a guy in his twenties called Stephen, approached me and asked me if I was OK.

I explained that I'd fallen at the airport and was a little achy, but that my main issue was that I had to get to Bucharest the following night and was struggling to find the best way. I told him I was supposed to meet a friend and then find a flight home from there the following day. It was a long way, and I could find nothing obvious transport-wise. My friend had offered to come and get me, but it was a five-hour drive each way at least and I felt it was too much to ask. I looked for business chauffeurs or some sort of shared lift, but the best I was coming up with was a bus. A bus that would stop a lot and take over seven hours to get to the capital. My friend told me not to do that.

'I'll think about it later,' I said, more to myself than to him.

He smiled at me and said: 'We can give you a lift if you like. Marta, my girlfriend, and I, are heading up to a spa for the weekend. We leave immediately after the course.'

I looked at him. He was young and had been friendly, polite and fun throughout the course. He saw me hesitate. 'It's no trouble, and you'll struggle to get to Bucharest any other way. It's a beautiful drive as well, you must let us help you.'

I was extremely grateful and found myself agreeing as it seemed like the only option. I offered him the petrol money but he wouldn't entertain it. With some relief I texted my friend, but she didn't come back as she was probably in the middle of her working day. I asked again if he would let me at least contribute to the fuel. 'No, no,' he had replied in his youthful, accented English. 'You just have to sing for the supper, yes? You have great stories Jenny; we love to hear them.'

Had that been just a flash of something across his face?

What did he mean about the stories? I had told a few tales on this training, I always did, but people who normally said that knew me through the security role and this job was a corporate training gig. Weird.

I was professionally suspicious most of the time, and I had to check myself occasionally for being a tad paranoid without cause. But, just for a moment there, I thought I had noticed a strange expression across that baby-face of his as he spoke. If I had to label it I'd have put money on 'anxious excitement', but I was tired and in pain and decided to think about it later and watch for it again, meet the girlfriend and see if I saw anything weird. I also chastised myself for being ridiculously spooked on this entire trip that probably, I reasoned, led to me nearly crashing into a courtyard in bloody Transylvania in the middle of the night.

It turned out that he had some friends in a place called Râmnicu Vâlcea, which we would pass through on the way to the capital. Dubbed 'hackerville', it was a surprisingly affluent area just beyond the Carpathian Mountains known for a cluster of cyber criminals as well as some legitimate tech firms. He was something of an aspiring hacker himself, it turned out, and had recognised me from an interview on social engineering I'd done a few months before. He'd been surprised that I'd turned up to do the corporate training, but was excited to have the chance to give me a lift and perhaps chat to me a little about some common interests. Most of all, he wanted to surprise some of his friends in hackerville, who also followed my security posts, by having me turn up at their birthday party and deliver the cake.

Partly due to language barriers, but mostly due to the girlfriend's indifference to his geeky friends and aspirations, his explanations of what was going on were sketchy at best. I was unclear as to the plan and wondered vaguely, and with some alarm, why I was being ushered, exhausted, into a house in the middle of Râmnicu, holding a cake, in the middle of the night.

He had also pushed me for information about who I worked for, clearly assuming I was some sort of spy. While untrue, it wasn't an entirely ludicrous assumption and people often probed me about my affiliations to various agencies. On this occasion, his questioning seemed to be fuelled by the fact that he himself had been approached in the past for some sort of government work and while the job had never materialised, he was still very excited about it. I'd checked in with my friend on the way and was extremely pleased to see her in Bucharest, where we drank champagne and gossiped and I gladly put a long and rather strange day behind me.

She dropped me off at the airport the next day and, as I waved her goodbye, I was very glad to be heading home. I dropped my bag and turned towards security when a chap wearing a stab vest and an official-looking lanyard stopped me and said my name. 'Oh, for fuck's sake! What in hell now?' I said, rather unprofessionally.

'Oh no! Jenny, don't worry,' he said. I raised an eyebrow, did bloody everyone know my name? 'It's just that we have instructions that you will not need to go through security today.'

The guy was smiling at me and gesturing for me to follow him. Hung-over, tired and still aching from the fall, I had no idea who might be aware of my presence in Romania, or why someone else might know my name, or need me to do something for them. The variety of the job had always appealed to me, but it seemed my reputation reached further than I had suspected, and as a consequence I was going to have to be more careful about who I worked with and what I agreed to do in the future.

Right now, in that airport, I had no choice but to trust this apparently friendly guy who wanted me to follow him. I was done with this job and done with surprises. I'd think about it all tomorrow but for now I just needed to get home. I looked up at him and he smiled. 'OK,' I said and nodded, and with that he led me past every single check in the airport and directly to my gate.

When the wheels touched down at Manchester Airport, I closed my eyes and exhaled in relief, never having been so glad to be home. 'Learn to say "no"', I said to myself and grabbed a cab back home.

14

HAMBURG

I'd been asked to speak about persuasion techniques in high-stakes crisis negotiations at a conference in Hamburg. It wasn't a paid gig but the networking opportunities were good and my expenses were being covered by a new contact I'd made – we'll call him 'Knox'. He was a lying, narcissistic, predatory former pilot with a world of insecurities to keep him occupied and a ton of money to spend. I'd been introduced to him by a lawyer friend who had told me he wanted to learn more about lie detection and non-verbal communications. 'He knows a few things already,' she had said. Don't they all.

Like others I have met before and since, he really didn't know much on the topic, but he was a great bullshitter and had got himself and me onto the speaker's stage at a couple of different events. He had also asked me to help him with a client he was protecting, a billionaire who had a team of twenty-two close protection staff circling him constantly in separate teams while he was in London. I'd met the twenty-two and they were professional and friendly. That job was going to be well paid, so I agreed to Hamburg to keep things cordial, figuring I could mostly avoid him in the conference crowd and swearing not to be too scathing when he said

241

stupid or misogynistic things. It would be an exercise in self-discipline.

The conference went well, as did my talk, and Knox stayed close to me as people came and asked me questions about related topics. I sipped decent wine for a while but decided to call it a night quite early and head off for a solo dinner in my room. Knox, as per his fashion, wasn't staying at the same hotel as me and was drinking with the conference crowd, so I said goodnight and walked back the block or so from the conference venue to my hotel alone.

As I got to the front door of the hotel, I decided to take a look at the river and text home before turning in. I walked through the lobby, past the bar and into a little garden at the back of the hotel, picturesque and empty in the night air. I stood by a little fountain among the plants and was scrolling through my phone, when a voice with a Geordie accent hissed at me through the leaves of a large plant behind me.

'Jenny Radcliffe?'

I nearly jumped out of my skin but before I could think of anything to say or do, it continued: 'Jenny, we need to talk to you about a job you can help us with. Sorry if I made you jump.'

I exhaled and rolled my eyes. 'You really did! Are you with Knox?'

'Knox? No, no. I just need a burglar for a job on Friday. Here. It's all on the level; I've left you a message at the desk but then I saw you. Really sorry if this seems weird. I was at the conference – great talk! Can we talk a minute? Sorry I scared you.'

I relaxed a little. These security types did love their bloody theatre! I kept some distance but nodded for him to carry on talking as he proceeded to tell me that he worked for a company who had been asked to try to get past security at a bank across the city. He told me that all had gone well, but the best date for the physical infiltration was the day after next and they needed someone to help with it.

The main issue was that they all looked like what they were: huge former military men with short hair and lots of muscles. The chances of them sneaking in anywhere without being noticed were slim to none, and now they had forty-eight hours to come up with a decent plan. They were failing. They had realised I was in town, asked a few questions about me back home, and had decided to see if I wanted to make some quick cash and help them out.

I let him buy me a brandy and sat down. As he went to the bar, I texted the name of his company to a contact in the UK. 'Legit or nutcase?' I asked as I watched him walk over with the drinks.

He sat down and told me that the job was to get into the inside of the bank where the C-suite executives and general offices were located. They had a keylogger cable device that would transmit everything from the finance director's laptop to their tech team if they could get inside his office and plug it into the back of his computer. They also had to prove they had got into the offices by leaving a few business cards in the supposedly secure area. This was standard stuff if you could get in.

They needed me to somehow get past the security guards in the lobby and get behind the scenes into the inner office area. Plug in the cable, place the cards, and then leave via an alarmed fire exit on the ground floor. They would be able to pick me up, if we timed it right, in the car park behind the bank, although the alarm would ring once I opened the door, and then wallop, job done, and I would personally receive £3,500 the same day as a fee. Easy.

'Legit and LOADED!' the answer came back on my phone.

'OK, then,' I said. 'What have you got?'

He reached into his briefcase and handed me a fat brown file. They had done excellent reconnaissance and had good notes on names, photographs of the directors and some information about the general layout of the building. It was as good a set of information as I have ever had, and I could see immediately that provided I got into the corridors I could find the right office easily enough. If it was empty, it could be fish in a barrel, but I had no kit with me and would be flying solo until the pick-up point when I would open the door and all hell would break loose.

I mulled it over a while; there were a few variables here that wouldn't be easy. I didn't speak German for a start, which made verbal persuasion techniques more difficult. I was also going to need a very good back story to bail me out, should it be required, and playing dumb was unlikely to work well. No bank is exactly lax in terms of security and the keylogger cable they wanted me to use wasn't going to be disguised in any way.

Normally, if I am going to drop a USB with an executable file inside a client premises, I generally try to make it look more innocent than a standard business thumb drive. I've used cartoon characters and other novelty shapes in the past, like a slice of pizza or a flip-flop, so that when someone sees or finds it, they tend to assume it belongs to a child or is for personal use. The more benign it looks, the less likely people will think it is dangerous, a principle I've relied upon for some time. The cable for this job, though, was a simple grey line as anything more elaborate would draw attention. I just had to plug it in and leave it running on the target's computer on his desk in his office.

He saw me hesitate and began to speak but his phone beeped, and he glanced at a text. 'Good job checking us out!' he said, eyebrows raised. 'I'm impressed.'

I sighed. 'Just checking you were on the right side of things. OK, I'll do it, but I'll need your briefcase and a few bits and pieces. I've not got much kit with me, and I want a "get-out-of-jail-free letter" that is rock solid. *Rock solid*, mind you, in case I get stopped.'

He reassured me. We finished the brandy, shook hands and the con, as they say, was on.

The bank was not the normal high street affair. In fact, it didn't really look like a bank at all but more like a luxury hotel lobby. It catered for very rich people, ultra-high net worth types who did not rock up and wait in a queue to deposit money or arrange their affairs. The security should be excellent. We would find out.

My boots sank into plush carpet as I strolled through elaborate monogrammed front doors, and I was immediately aware of a subtle floral scent, soft background music and a pleasant temperature increase contrasting with the crisp morning air outside. Without hesitating, I walked towards where the file had told me the staff door would be. It looked like just another polished wooden panel in a wall of polished wooden panels. The difference was that this one was actually a door, indicated only by a discreet biometric lock next to it. If you were a senior staff member, this was your way into the inner part of the building. Your thumbprint would have been scanned acting as a key when pressed against the little screen. A match would open the panel door and allow access into the inner sanctum of the staff area beyond the public lobby. My thumbprint had, of course, never been scanned.

Despite the early hour, the place was busy. Some smartly dressed staff were greeting a few people I assumed to be customers, while a cleaner gathered the cable from her vacuum and got ready to disappear out of the sight of the front-of-house staff and customers. I avoided eye contact with anyone, but noted the security guard had spotted me and was following me over. I was, if you will excuse the pun, banking on it. I stopped at the panel and took a deep breath. Here goes.

I placed my thumb awkwardly over the pad for the biometric lock and waited for the low beeping noise that would certainly come when it didn't recognise the pattern. 'Boop!' A red light came on. No dice.

'*Shit!*' I said loudly, and felt a movement behind me as, from over my shoulder, the guard said something to me in hushed and somewhat alarmed German. I turned to face him and had to look up to make eye contact. He was tall, in a starched khaki uniform. My initial exclamation had broken the relaxed vibe of the place and I could see he was anxious for me to speak softly and preserve the tone. He was quite young and looked more worried than angry. He looked me up and down, his eyes resting on my right hand.

The day before I had purchased some bandages and tape from a pharmacy. I had tightly bandaged my right hand and wrist so that my skin tone was a little bruised, and I held my thumb awkwardly as if it was injured. I had looped hotel guy's briefcase over my bandaged arm and was holding a bunch of cardboard files filled with meaningless documents I had printed out the night before in the other.

'*Hello*,' I said, far louder than necessary, and feigning frustration. 'I see this thing is *still* broken?'

'Madam?' he exclaimed, quickly switching to English.

I exhaled and rolled my eyes, turning to put my thumb against the pad again. It beeped another 'no' and I looked him right in the eye. 'Oh, for fuck's sake!' I said loudly and then added: 'Why is this *still* knackered? We pay *somebody* to sort this!' I finished with an angry frown and looked pointedly at my bandaged hand.

The guard was mortified. My general demeanour and noise were disturbing the calm ambience of the hallowed halls, and as for swearing at volume?! He hissed at me. 'It has been working, madam, all morning. May I?' He took hold of my hand and pushed the thumb onto the pad.

'*Ooooowwww, fuck!*' I exclaimed, as several little groups of customers and staff turned to look at us. '*Stop!*'

'I think it is because, madam,' he was speaking quickly in calm low tones which he clearly wanted me to emulate, 'it is because you cannot put your thumb down flat against the pad properly, and—'

I interrupted him: 'Well, I can hardly help that, can I? Stupid bloody thing, it wasn't working yesterday, and it *still* isn't working. Ridiculous. And *watch* my sore hand, please. *Danke.*'

Of course, the guard should have been unfazed by such tactics, removed me from the situation and respectfully, but firmly, refused to allow me to go any further without thoroughly checking my credentials. The issue is that so many staff members, including security teams, are very often working in a blame-based culture. Often people will rather not challenge a suspicious person on site because they are at risk of annoying a customer or a senior colleague and getting into trouble as a result. I was banking on the guard dismissing me as harmless while simultaneously being worried that he would be blamed for the fuss around the biometric lock. I was raising his emotional responses (anxiety and embarrassment) and giving him a task (letting me through) which would end the problem. He had a choice to make based on the consequences of letting me through that door. He had to decide which was the bigger problem: letting me cause a fuss in the lobby of the bank or letting a seemingly harmless, if rather grumpy, woman through a door. The fact that he chose the latter told me a lot about the culture of that bank, and about the training, or lack of it, that young security guard had done.

I was glad we always insisted on non-punitive remedial measures from our clients. The guy would hopefully be properly trained in the near future, to help him handle things better if this happened again for real.

Right now, though, he was panicking and was glancing around for help, which wasn't coming. The absolute last thing this place expected or needed was anything to break the carefully constructed veneer of calmly maintained order and opulence. In this scenario, and especially in front of those rich customers, confusion, noise and disorder were especially unwelcome and, as I had correctly assessed, as good as weapons. He needed me gone or at least much, much quieter. Not going to happen.

'Try the other hand.'

'Fine.'

Beep. No.

'Honestly, I don't think they even scanned that one,' I said, switching my tone to irritated anxiety, 'and, I just, I just need to—' and then I dropped the files from my left arm over the floor, scattering papers in a large, messy pile. Swearing some more and sighing loudly, I bent down awkwardly to try to pick the papers up with my 'good' hand and thrust the remaining files at the guard with an air of defeated irritation. He stooped to help me, and I made a mental note to make sure he wasn't blamed for letting me through once we had finished the job. He stood upright, files in hand and I heard a cushioned hiss as the panel in front of me opened inwards, revealing a dark corridor, flanked by glass doors.

'Look, just go in!' he said, handing me back the remaining files and motioning for me to walk through.

'Finally! *Danke!*' I exclaimed and gave him a weak smile, gathering my stuff and walking through into the corridor with an air of relieved impatience. I heard the door close behind me and looked around properly. I was standing at the end of a dimly lit, carpeted corridor, flanked on either side by glass panelled offices and yet more glass doors. I paused for a second, half expecting someone to emerge from behind one of them and offer to help me, at which point my rather thin cover story about a training meeting would come into play, but no one came.

I walked quickly up the corridor, glancing through the doors as I went. The glass was patterned and frosted, with blinds beyond obscuring any view into the offices. I could make out muffled voices and hear telephones ringing, but apart from the odd silhouette beyond the glass, this was every bit as tranquil and controlled as the lobby was supposed to be. I turned left at the end of the corridor and saw a sign for restrooms up ahead. Like the rest of the building, it was more wooden panels. Unisex, private cubicles. *Nice.* I made for the nearest cubicle and locked the door behind me. Gentle music started to play and air freshener subtly sprayed into the room. *Loaded.*

I worked quickly, tearing off the bandage with my teeth and dropping it into the bin. I reached into hotel guy's briefcase. Although I'd acted as if it were full, it was almost empty apart from a couple of items I'd gathered in case I needed them. There was a pair of round oversize glasses which I immediately put on and I tied my hair back into a loose ponytail. There were also some little smoke bombs. I'd found these in the bottom of my own suitcase. These were always useful in case I had to create a diversion and I kept them hidden inside tampon applicator tubes in sealed packets, so they wouldn't be found if my bag was searched unless the security guard was especially thorough. There was a reversible fleece so I could quickly change my appearance and the keylogger cable the security guys had given me to plug into the laptop. I also had my phone and some crumbly mint sweets I could use as chalk if I got lost, these are more easily explained to a security guard than a packet of actual chalk might be. Lastly, I had some business cards from the security company that had hired me and one of my silver octopus charms.

I listened at the door and, apart from the music playing in the cubicle, there was nothing much to be heard, apart from the very faint normal office sounds of muffled conversations and phones ringing. I opened the door fully and walked out into the corridor, taking a right at the end and looking for the stairs. Past the lift and through a door into the staircase. I noted the basement exit door a flight below, which I was to leave through at the pick-up in forty minutes, the target's office being on the second floor four flights above me now. That was where I was headed and I turned and climbed the stairs, stopping outside the door to the second floor.

I went through and emerged into another carpeted corridor. This floor was slightly fancier than the first with fewer, much larger offices and with glass display cabinets between every door. The first had photographs of former employees, framed certificates, awards and trophies. The next displayed a huge antique lock and an explanatory plaque in German and English which I didn't stop to read, thinking it was probably from the first vault or building or something. This place was like a museum.

I needed to dump most of the meaningless files. The bin in the restroom had been too small for me to dispose of them there, so I'd slotted them into the briefcase. I only needed a couple as back-up if I had to use the training story and the rest constituted unnecessary weight and were taking up space I might need. As I walked down the corridor, I kept my eye out for a bin, but before I saw one I came to the office of the finance director that I was looking for, his name clearly etched on a very large glass door next to yet another glass award cabinet.

Dump the files.

Reaching up on my tiptoes I lifted most of the files onto the top of the cabinet and tried to push them to the wall out of sight. They hung precariously over the edge, but I turned the briefcase over in my hand and reached up, using it to push them to the back. They disappeared and I caught my reflection in the glass and grinned, imagining them being found by some cleaner a month from now and the puzzlement they would cause. *Done.*

Of course, the second you lose focus something happens, and I heard an office door open further up and quickly walked back and through the door to the staircase and waited, listening at the glass panel. I heard footsteps approaching and grabbed for my phone, putting it to my ear so I could fake a conversation and deter any questions. Soon, the door burst open and a well-dressed man walked straight through and dived swiftly down the stairs, clearly in a rush. He didn't so much as look around to see me as he dashed past, so I put the phone in the case and walked back through, glancing into the corridor, which was empty again as I moved.

I walked quickly, passing the glass cases and along to the finance director's office, hoping it wasn't locked or occupied. I hesitated in front of the door, listening. Nothing. I tried the handle, but it didn't give. Locked. I stepped back and glanced at the door to the stairs and then at my watch. Rendezvous was thirty minutes from now. They would wait in the car park for five minutes, then return exactly one hour later. After that, if I was still in the building, there wouldn't be a ride and it was up to me to leave on foot. A bad idea.

I walked slowly along the corridor looking for options, but the opposite office had a closed door and was occupied. I could see a figure through the glass hunched over a desk. However, the next one was in darkness. I tried the handle, which opened, and I stepped in. I was now inside a small and comfortable office with the obligatory wood-panelled walls, a few tasteful pictures and a polished wooden desk. A window took up most of the exterior wall behind the desk and I could just see the city skyline through ivory blinds. *It's nice*, I thought. A little luxury cell.

I tried the desk drawers, which opened, so I grabbed some papers, a few keys and an expensive-looking pen, shoving them into the briefcase for bagging up later to show the client the perils of leaving the place unlocked. I then moved back to the door.

I waited, peering through a clear line in the frosted glass and into the corridor beyond. In passing, I mused that the dim lighting and wood was intended to give an atmosphere of calm and opulence, but I found it all dispiriting and oppressive. I was thinking how dreary it was when the door to the next office up opened and a figure emerged and trotted past my room. Then the office opposite opened too. I quietly moved the latch into the locked position and stood well back from the glass so no one would see my shadow. The corridor was emptying. Perhaps a meeting?

Pretty soon another door further down opened as well and a woman on a phone rushed past me following her colleagues. The place was emptying out but the door I needed was locked. If I didn't get into the target office I would fail the test, miss my lift, and have to hang around in this luxury gloom for another hour. I looked at the lock on the door in front of me inside the office. I needed my lock pick hook, with it I could likely lift the latch from inside the gap in the door. But I didn't have my hook with me – it doesn't travel well through airport security – so I needed something similar to pick that lock. This is never ideal. You can't explain away lock picks easily and if anyone catches you fiddling with a lock the jig is almost always up.

I wondered if the keys from the desk in this office might be a universal one that opened all the doors. Maybe I could try that or otherwise persuade someone somehow to let me into the room. I was turning over the possibilities in my mind and glanced at the countdown on my phone. Twenty-three minutes until pick-up.

The corridor was silent, I creaked open the door and glanced up and down. I'd try the office on the other side of the target first, look for a master key. Look for something. I quickly slipped across the corridor, past the target office and tried the door of its neighbour. It was open, empty, and I slipped inside and closed the door quietly behind me, so it didn't slam. I looked around and on the desk was a large bunch of keys. I made my way over and looked at the neatly written labels on the plastic keyrings. *Dammit. German.*

I leaned against the wall, folded my arms and tried to think. Standing in the corridor and trying every key would be obvious, time-consuming and difficult to explain. While I never admit defeat until it is unavoidable, I was close to calling it inside that fancy office that day. I cursed inwardly and swore I would stop accepting the constant stream of crazy jobs that came my way. I had to get out of the habit of saying yes and then getting involved in some disaster or other. I looked at the countdown: eighteen minutes. I sighed and leaned back against the wooden wall. Just on the other side was the office I needed to get into. So near and yet so far. I folded my arms and made my mind up. Abort. I'd try again, head back in the future and bring my hook.

Then I saw it.

A large square cardboard recycling bin was pressed up against the furthest panel on the wall. It was ugly and bulging with papers and somehow out of place in this plush setting. I squinted at it and thought I'd shove the remaining files inside and leave, but there was something else.

There are times when something just looks wrong. Glancing at my phone I could see I now had just under fifteen minutes to pick-up. I moved towards the bin and shoved the papers in and then I pulled it back and took a quick peep behind it. Around the solid wooden panel there was a small but definite gap, and I could see a frame of daylight! I pulled the bin back a bit further, surprised it moved so easily, it was clearly not as full as it looked. I pulled harder, moving it a few inches into the room, and exclaimed out loud. 'No way. You beauty!'

The wooden panel behind the bin was not in place and was only leaning against the wall. I grabbed the top and was able to move it easily to one side and found myself looking at the back of a duplicate bin in the next office, the target's office.

I listened, breathing hard, and then slid the loose panel fully to one side revealing a space big enough to crawl through and enter the finance director's office. I poked at the bin through the empty panel space trying not to push too hard and topple it. It slid forward easily enough, letting in more daylight from the office next door. I waited a heartbeat then pushed harder and could see the carpet and chair of the office I was looking for.

I stopped to consider what I had found.

For some reason, the owner of the office I was kneeling in

had gone to a lot of trouble to sneak into the finance director's office undetected. At a passing glance the loose panel wasn't obvious and the bins hid the gap very well. While it all might well have been harmless, my internal security radar was screaming in my head that this was suspicious as hell. I thought back to the eighth floor all those years ago – every building has its secrets. I was pretty sure that someone was spying on someone else, and I could only speculate at the reason. Corporate espionage maybe? Extortion? But it was a clear case of insider threat if I ever saw one, less obvious than an arrogant footballer with a hundred girlfriends, but insider threat just the same. This would make an interesting page in my report!

Without waiting anymore, I crawled through awkwardly and made straight for the computer at the desk. There was a tangle of wires and cables, many of them bunched together inside a sort of plastic tube. A clock on the wall caught my eye. No time to ponder. Ten minutes to rendezvous.

I reached back through the gap and grabbed clumsily at the briefcase in the other office, pulling it into the room. Still on my knees I opened it, found the keylogger cable, and crawled to the back of the desk where I could see the computer ports. Three to choose from. If I picked the wrong one, the computer would register a fault, the finance director would call IT, and the logger would be found. Mission failure. I went for the one in the middle, but it didn't fit. *Focus.* I moved to the port on the left and had no problem plugging it in. I took a quick shot with my phone and then one of the office as proof. I shoved a business card under the monitor and glanced around the room as the monitor blinked briefly to life and then returned to silence.

There was no time to do any more searching, so I grabbed a framed picture of a corporate team from a shelf, put the recycling bin back into place over the gaping panel and moved to the door. My lift would be almost there, parked up a street or two away and waiting to come and meet me in the public parking area beside the door on the lower floor.

I snapped the latch unlocked, opened the door an inch and waited, but I could hear no noise. Moving quickly and feeling adrenalin surging, I grinned as I slipped out into the corridor and walked quickly to the door to the staircase, when I hesitated. I needed to leave the octopus. There was just enough time to do it.

I moved to the glass cabinet outside the door, to place it alongside the files I pushed to the back, but even on tiptoe I couldn't reach to do it. I paused. The place was deserted. I could probably get away with quickly dumping it in the adjoining office. I could just slip in, place it down and push the recycling bin back up against the missing panel. I'd be gone in a few minutes, and it would be better if they didn't immediately notice the gap had been found. I paused again. It was risky. My phone beeped a text: 'Standby – 5.'

No, no. We had eight minutes left according to my phone not five! They must have had to move quicker; if nothing else the Germans kept good time. I had to run for the door on the staircase now or I'd be stuck here another hour. Not good. I turned in the direction of the staircase when I heard the door at the other end of the corridor squeal open and a cacophony of loud German voices as a large group of people deep in conversation came through the door and began moving along the corridor. I turned and walked as casually as I could towards the staircase door, trying not to panic and knowing they had seen me. I pushed it open and stepped through slowly, scrambling down the flights immediately as it closed behind me. I had to time this right because as soon as that bottom door opened the alarm would sound and security would appear.

Standing on top of the briefcase I squinted through the safety panel on the door, looking for the car. Nothing yet, but they must be right outside. Wait for it.

A text. As I raised my phone to read it, I noticed my fingers felt sticky. I looked at them and they had some still-tacky red paint on them. I had noted, somewhere in the back of my mind, that the staircases smelt a bit of paint. *They probably paint a place like this regularly,* I had vaguely thought, but now it was all over my hands, my phone, and yes, marvellous, on my trousers and shirt. *Oh well, I'll buy some more with my fee,* I thought, realising it would be another thing that would be hard to explain if I was caught.

'Standby. Black Mercedes turning in now.'

That's it, time to go. I pushed the crash bar on the door, but it didn't move. I tried again, slamming my sticky hand against the metal bar as hard as I could. Still nothing, it was fast shut, and then I realised why. The red paint freshly painted on the door was still tacky and had seeped into the crack, effectively gluing it shut. I thought I could hear the car engine just outside waiting for me.

I slammed the bar again, as hard as I could, making a huge bang in the stairwell. It gave a little, bits of red paint scattering to the floor, but it held. I stepped back and aimed a hard kick at the bar with the full force of my boot, more paint spatters and it budged a bit but it did not open. My phone beeped and I reached for it to text 'Wait! Give me thirty seconds', but I heard the car engine start again.

I threw the briefcase on the floor and stood on it again, jumping up so I could see through the panel at the top of the door. At the same time the sticky phone in my hand beeped with another text, but it was too late. Through the grid of safety glass, I watched a large black car, my lift, slowly leaving the car park.

I grabbed my phone and glanced at the text, still standing on the briefcase. 'No show. Report back. RV2 in 1 hour.'

'here3doorglue comeback' I texted frantically.

'????RV2 in 1 hour'

For a few seconds I just stood there, trying to suppress the panic that was rising in me. Stupid door, stupid paint. With some effort I pulled myself together and picked up the briefcase. I needed to move, right now, find a restroom, wash my hands and regroup.

I sprinted upwards to the second floor and glanced through the door, but I could hear voices and spotted the group from earlier still chatting in the corridor. I went up again to try the next floor. The restrooms would likely be in the same position throughout the building. The third floor was much noisier, I could hear it before I even got next to the door.

Worker bees, I thought. 'Try the next one,' I muttered aloud. 'Running out of options.'

The next floor seemed to be the last floor accessible from the stairs, and I could immediately see it was different to the office floors below. It had different, bigger double doors and some posters apparently warning about carrying heavy things and running written in German, but it seemed quiet. I recalled from the reconnaissance documents the team had given me that the canteen area was on the top floor of the building with only maintenance and roof space above it. A canteen wasn't bad. There would surely be restrooms to clean up and maybe grab a knife or something to loosen the paint up inside the cracks on the door.

I had to stand on tiptoe again to peer through the little windows at the top of the doors. I pressed my face up to the glass and through the grille I could see a large bright floor space with tables scattered around, I couldn't hear anything. Perhaps it was still a bit too early for mid-morning coffee crowds. In the absence of a better option, I decided to go through and look around for a place to lie low for the next hour or so, but only when I really had to move from the relatively safety of the stairs.

I had an hour to clean up as best I could, find a knife or similar, keep from being noticed and then get the hell out of there. Also, as almost an afterthought, it occurred to me that as I was going to be hanging around a little longer, it really would be a good idea to go back into the first office and just push the other recycling bin back against the panel.

After ten minutes I heard a door slam a couple of floors below and footsteps on stairs, so I moved through the doors which opened with a noise like the scream of the damned, and stepped through into the brightly lit space beyond. I walked briskly towards a table in a corner, sat down unhurriedly, although my heart was pounding, and gave myself a good view of the place. Dammit, it was exposed. There were a few plants and some bins, but otherwise just tables and chairs, and on the left wall some vending machines and a long glass food counter with some ladies in hairnets and uniforms bustling behind it and chatting away happily. I was the only other person in the room, and now I noticed red fingerprints on the table in front of me. What if it was also on my face?

I decided the best thing to do was to pretend I was supposed to be there, a visiting colleague perhaps, without an allocated desk. I could pretend to be busily working away and hope they wouldn't notice me, then gradually move down back into the stairwell, try the restrooms again and, if I had time, push the bin back and maybe, plant the octopus. I pulled my phone out and looked studiously downwards, trying to appear like a busy executive looking for a quiet corner to make a few calls.

I texted the pick-up team. 'The door was painted shut. It will give if I go back. Can you make it earlier?'

'20 minutes. Location unchanged. Confirm. Are you OK?'

'Confirm pick up in 20. OK'

Hanging around for twenty minutes was better than an hour. I sat there quietly for a while, keeping an eye on the ladies behind the counter. Although they knew I was there, they were busy and seemed not to be curious about me, presumably preparing for the lunch crowd. After five minutes or so, one of them emerged from behind the counter pushing a trolley with sandwiches, coffee pots and fruit on it and made her way to the lifts, making a delivery to some catered meeting, I assumed.

I tracked her across the space and for the first time noticed the cutlery racks at the end of the counter. I could go up and grab a knife to loosen the paint and then head for the stairs again, try to get back to the office on the second floor and move the bin. A quick look at the countdown and we were on sixteen minutes. Time to make a move.

I watched for the ladies to bustle behind the counter, but they didn't really give me a window, moving back and forth and laying out lunch items behind the glass. After a while longer, I had to make a move or give up and, even though I knew they would notice me, I got up and walked over to the cutlery trays. Sure enough, one of the ladies saw me and shot me a quizzical look. I smiled and muttered something like: 'Just need this for fruit. For the meeting.' I smiled broadly and picked up a knife and fork. 'I'll bring them back,' I said and kept walking.

I noticed a look of confusion on her face, but she didn't say anything, so I kept going and through the door to the stairs. Down to the second floor, I listened and could hear people. Eleven minutes. I was going to be out of there at any moment. It was such a gamble. I could get caught going to straighten the bin, but if people were about, they might see it anyway. I waited, trying to decide.

I settled on a no. It was too risky. I didn't have long to wait and with any luck no one would spot me on the stairs. I began to walk down the flights of stairs to the painted exit door on the bottom floor. I took out the knife and thought I would try to crack the paint while I waited. I was almost there when I heard voices from below me, near the door. Although I couldn't understand what they were saying, they were speaking with some urgency, and I wondered if my trying to open the door had attracted their attention. If they were still there in a few minutes I would have to give up, hand over my 'get-out-of-jail-free' letter and confess all. Then one of them started to walk up towards me.

Without really thinking about it, I turned around and walked back up the stairs, stopping on the second floor and striding over to the door. If I was going to be caught, I would plant that octopus first, dammit, and be caught in the office, not on the stairs. As I walked along the corridor, aiming first for the restrooms, I noticed that now almost every door was open and the offices were mostly occupied. I looked straight ahead but felt people glancing at me as I walked past. Reaching the restrooms, I gratefully bolted the cubicle door behind me, threw the fork into the bin and looked in the mirror. Sure enough I had a couple of smears of red paint on my face. Nothing much but very noticeable with even a casual glance.

I turned on the tap and washed my hands. The paint stayed. I tried again. It still stayed. I took a dry paper towel and rubbed my face. This stuff wasn't budging. Fine.

'Five minutes. RV2. Standby.'

No choice, I would have to improvise on the way. I took a deep breath and left the restroom. Walking hurriedly down the corridor I slowed pace outside the office with the missing panel. Door still closed. With horror I realised that the target guy, the finance director, was now in his own office next along and talking rapidly on his phone. It was loud. He seemed angry. He had probably found his door unlocked and the picture gone. Maybe he had noticed the cable, although I doubted it – it blended well with the others.

In a split second, I decided to go for it. I opened the door to the missing panel office, walked straight over to the bin and pushed it firmly, as quietly as I could, back into position hiding the panel. Then I paused and bent down. I shoved the little octopus under the bin and braced myself to leave. Through the gap I heard him suddenly go silent.

I walked out of the office, into the corridor and past his door without glancing inside. A few more steps and I heard him start talking again, this time louder and then closer as he got to his door. 'Warten,' he said, but I was almost at the door. 'Fräulein.'

I let it shut behind me and then bolted down the stairs, my phone beeping in the briefcase, but I didn't have time to look at the message. I kept going down the stairs, past a guy in uniform who swivelled as I ran past. 'Danke!' I gasped, without looking back and heard the door above me open.

'Warten! Fräulein!' And then louder, rapid German. I got to the door and without glancing at the phone I took a run at the bar, slamming it with my full right shoulder. Nothing. Footsteps above and shouting. I slammed it again and it gave a little. I stood back and took a deep breath, I spun around and kicked it as hard as I could, connecting with the bar and stumbling with the force of the blow. It finally gave way with a loud bang and an explosion of tacky red paint flakes, fresh air and light pouring into the stairwell. The air immediately exploded into loud alarms and shouting, the emergency lights flashed on and the mayhem that I always knew was coming began.

I scrambled to my feet, aware of shouting and many footsteps behind me. I looked up and with some relief saw the car, engine rolling, about ten metres away. I ran over, grabbed the handle and dived headlong into the back seat.

'*Quick, mate!*' I gasped and hotel guy put his foot on the pedal and screamed away, his colleague in the passenger seat already on the phone to the contact at the bank, telling them not to panic, but they had just failed their physical infiltration test.

A little olive oil did a good job removing most of the paint, and I was in the airport lounge less than two hours later. A little frayed around the edges and with a horrible jarring sensation in my right leg, I sat down at the bar and ordered a rum and Coke. Then, I heard a familiar voice behind me. Knox. 'I thought you'd left yesterday morning, little lady.'

I gritted my teeth and side-eyed him. 'No, no. I thought I'd do a little sightseeing. We spoke about it, remember?'

'Ah yes, yes. You said that. You meant shopping, though.' I sighed. 'Anyway, we may be back soon, I have a job that might come up I'm thinking of you for.'

'Oh.'

'Yeah. It's in an organisation that are leaking information and they need someone to dig around a little and find out what's happening. They think the finance director is selling stuff on, but they can't find a thing on him internally. He's clean but the information is definitely leaking from his office.'

My ears pricked up. Surely not.

'It's quite a posh place, though, so I might do it myself. It is probably very well secured, bio locks and all that, might need me on the crew. No offence.'

'None taken.'

'What do you think, though? It's a bit of a mystery. I think I know the answer, but always happy for your ideas, see if you have a clue.'

My gate was called and I got off the stool, draining my drink and looking at him. He'd never catch up enough to be a threat, and I was done with this town.

'Tell them to check the walls of his office,' I said.

'What for?'

'I don't know. Sea life,' I said as I walked away, waving without looking back.

'See you in London, Knox.'

15

TURNING OUT THE LIGHTS

We pulled up into a lay-by about two miles away from the job, early on a bright summer morning. My friend Anthea was accompanying me on this one, partly as it needed more than one person and also to be the corporate contact for the client, who was a tad excitable and beyond my patience. Anthea could be extremely diplomatic.

He was meeting us for a final update before we made our move and did a physical penetration test on a large energy facility in the middle of the UK. What scant communications had filtered down to me as principal contractor did not bode well for a smooth day ahead. The client team, and especially our contact, were way, way too excited about the job, and had given us a couple of pointers as to what could, or could not, be done on the job.

This is never good. Sometimes people get entirely carried away by a romantic, Hollywood idea of cat burglars and heists and either try to help out in some way or, worse, try to take part in the job themselves. Interest creates interference and almost always slows us down. Apart from any necessary safety advice and some basic protocols, I would always prefer to work independently of any internal assistance.

Additionally, too much information or help from internal teams means that the test itself isn't a true replication of a real attack. The bad guys wouldn't have help, unless they recruited an internal contact perhaps, and the exercise consequently lacks authenticity and impact if we are given access to details an outsider would otherwise not find. The contact's interest in our plans that day may well prove to be an issue. I was unimpressed and expected problems.

This guy, Gecko, as we had codenamed him, was a piece of work. On the scoping calls, he had wanted to chat to me about some stories he had heard me speak about in podcasts and interviews. He was excited that 'a really famous thief' was going to try to jinx his system and told me repeatedly that it was a job he thought he would be excellent at himself. He didn't want to make things easy for me and, if we failed, he could claim victory over 'the great Jenny Radcliffe'. If we succeeded, then it was no problem as he had hired 'the great Jenny Radcliffe' and she always got past. I was extremely uncomfortable and if Anthea and her associates hadn't been involved I'd have pulled out.

I was tired, I'd had months of travelling and had recently completed a couple of intensive and dangerous tests in Europe. I was also part of a wider team looking after a very demanding, high net worth celebrity client. My profile within the industry had never been higher, I'd done dozens of keynotes, webinars and interviews, and I was mentally exhausted and physically wiped out. This job was the last one I was going to do before a long summer break.

Anthea came to me firstly because she could see the job was going to be awkward. She had mentioned a potential need for a lead social engineer to the client who, aware of my work, subsequently requested my involvement and was willing to pay for me to lead the infiltration team. She had done several physical penetration tests herself and realised that this was unlikely to be straightforward. It was a large site: well resourced, with guards, alarms, cameras and well-trained and alert staff. The place was also of significance to the infrastructure and security of the UK. Any breach, including a simulated one, was taken extremely seriously and subsequently reported to the security services and powers-that-be in Westminster. This wasn't going to be easy.

Anthea sat in her little car, full of papers, clothes and discarded coffee cups and texted Gecko our location. I stood watching in the lay-by, staring at the blue sky. I was in no mood for this job.

Her phone rang; it was Gecko on the line. She spoke to him for a short while, polite and patient, then hung up and gave her phone a middle finger. 'God, he's into this,' she said. 'On his way with [she formed air quotes] "updated intel" for us. The colossal arse.'

I laughed. I was glad she was here. Anthea is a clever, funny, former soldier, and she has more hutzpah than almost anyone I'd ever met. She was experienced enough to be a good wing-woman and would follow any lead I gave her without skipping a beat. She knew me well enough to back up when required or leave me alone and distract people if I was on task. I was glad to have her by my side, as we had had many adventures together.

Just the night before we had scammed drinks and cigarettes from a team of men who were drunkenly showing off in our hotel. We had played the part of naive HR consultants on a training visit, delivering emotional intelligence training. They'd picked up our bar and food bill and proceeded to tell us far more than was safe about their company software and security.

'Are there really, you know, hackers in real life?' I'd asked, wide-eyed, and she'd snorted, spilling her wine. She joined in the charade, helping me lead them along and extract information, taking over when I nipped to the ladies and following my lead seamlessly without a word between us. They had told us what systems they used at their company. They had outlined some of the most common mistakes their staff made on the system, as well as describing some of the previous times they had been hacked, telling us that they hadn't had a chance to patch the issues yet.

They were the IT team of a global motoring company and what we now knew was enough to at the very least get started on a plan of attack. We were only warming up for the real job though and had no interest in breaching them. We would never use the information we got, but the ease with which we hooked them with the helpless female act was worrying. Once again us not appearing to be a threat, alongside their guard being down in a social situation, could have been very dangerous. They needed to watch their backs and be more careful in future. Seeing them at breakfast the next morning, I handed over a business card, giving them the option to look me up online. If they did they would regret the loose lips of the night before when any security precautions they may have taken at work had been forgotten after a few beers and some good company. Like many people, their shields were lowered when they felt they were off-duty, a fact that many criminals exploit to the cost of their victims.

If they don't bother looking me up or don't care about what they had revealed, then fine, I thought. They weren't my client or my problem and I only had one last job to do then I would be away for the summer. In the lay-by, I could almost taste the first cocktail.

After a few minutes a large, new, black Mercedes pulled up in the lay-by. Gecko got out.

'Morning girls! All set?' he said, grinning and rubbing his hands.

I forced a smile. 'Of course.' I looked at him. 'Anything I need to know?'

He grimaced. 'Well. A couple of things, really,' he said. 'Firstly. I've got you some badges and lanyards, so you should be able to tailgate in.'

He handed us some passes and I looked at mine. It had a picture of a middle-aged Sikh man on it with a turban and beard. Anthea's was also that of a middle-aged man, with a shaven head and facial tattoos.

'Sorry they don't match your looks!' He was chuckling with glee. 'Also. We have had to stand down armed police response for the test.'

'Armed response?'

'Yes. Obviously,' he continued. 'We are a high target as you are probably aware, so we have an armed response unit based near the site. They respond in two minutes *if* we give the alarm. So I didn't want to have you ladies shot! Ha ha! So we have stood them down.'

'Well, that's something,' I said through gritted teeth.

'Yes, well, we aren't allowed to do it for long, though.' He avoided my eyes. 'So, you'll have from 11.49 until 12 p.m., *on the dot*, to get into the secure area. Or it all gets a bit frantic.'

'Eleven minutes?'

'Yes. I mean you can access the rest of the site for as long as you like if you don't get rumbled, but for the target area it's just that eleven-minute window. That OK?'

I frowned and took a breath, but Anthea stepped in. 'Of course. Eleven minutes or it gets a bit clicky-clicky-shooty-shooty! We get it. Anything else?'

'Well. I'm your on-site contact and will be around if you

need me. Our head of security is also aware, so shout for him if anything happens.'

I was displeased but managed a thin smile as we arranged to meet in the canteen, just after midday, regardless of the outcome of the test. He drove away a bit faster than strictly necessary and I looked at Anthea.

'Terrific.'

'It's why we pay you the big bucks,' she replied and looked at the passes. 'Not an exact likeness, is it?'

We went to a supermarket on the way and got some passport photos taken, carefully sellotaping our own pictures over the ones of the two men on the passes. The names couldn't be changed but they might work if someone only gave them a casual glance. We'd been stopped on a previous job with similarly unsuitable lanyards. That time a very pretty and very switched-on female security guard had firmly but politely turned us both away with a grin and a 'Not today, ladies'.

I'd gone back to shake her hand after the test, and it emerged that the entire security team on that job had known that an infiltration would be attempted that day and were consequently on super-high alert. Hardly fair and hardly realistic, but we had still got past many other guards and it was only she that had stopped us. From that day forward we referred to her as 'the Valkyrie'. I am often asked whether being a woman gives me an advantage in the job, and as I have already said, a lot of the time I am overlooked because I don't fit the picture of what most people imagine a criminal or malicious hacker looks like. That being said, the question does often presuppose that the security team on the lookout for me are men. When the security team has women on it, as in the case of the Valkyrie, I have found that the likelihood of being challenged increases. This is very welcome from a security perspective and is yet another excellent argument for encouraging as much diversity in the industry as possible, different perspectives give broader coverage and that leads to a more secure site.

At Gecko's site a few days before, we had spent time watching his security team and getting to know the site. There were no women guards that we could see, but we had noted that at the front gate they did have some very capable-looking guards and dogs. We wouldn't be easily talking our way past those. On top of that there was a high perimeter fence bordered by trees and plants, vast car parks, and very few access points, all of which were heavily guarded and monitored by CCTV. We would need a subtle approach to get in; fence hopping or somehow sneaking in was unlikely to work.

We visited a rear gatehouse instead, just as the shift was changing over. We gave Gecko's name and said we were there for the onsite security check. While this hadn't been cleared with him, we figured that he was the type of person that likely *had* told several people that a test was going on that day, just like had happened on the site with the Valkyrie. Odds were that some of his ground staff may have got wind of some sort of security test, but not be aware of details. We were banking on them simply hearing the words 'security test' and his name, and letting us through. We did have another, more elaborate approach lined up if this one didn't succeed, but working on the principle that he wasn't the type to keep a secret and that the guards must have been told that armed response was standing down, we tried it.

The client hadn't wanted the expense of a larger team, and we had discussed this with them. If they had funded a bigger team, we could have spoofed passes ourselves and mingled with the employees at the start of the working day, buzzing ourselves in. With working staff passes the odds of our being stopped on a site this size would have been slim. Spoofing passes isn't especially difficult with the right kit, but our fees were already high and it was an extra cost. So we clutched our passes with taped pictures and decided to try the security check story. Once inside they might work on internal doors, but I didn't want to chance a close inspection from one of the exterior guards, so we went with the security check story, crossing our fingers that the guard would be conspiratorial and let us through.

'What company, please?' said the guard.

'No, no,' Anthea smiled broadly. 'We are from the other site. Gecko knows, all good.' They called Gecko, who didn't answer, but waved us in and gave us a specific parking spot.

'Too easy,' I said to Anthea. 'Security definitely know we are on site.'

She nodded: 'This will be interesting.'

We parked up and walked to reception, who signed us in as colleagues from one of their other sites, only glancing at the passes with our hastily shot passport pics, and giving us a safety leaflet to read. We decamped immediately to the ladies' restroom behind reception.

'This is too easy,' I hissed under the cubicle. 'They know we are here. Someone has blabbed.'

'What shall we do?'

'Go with it,' I replied. 'They are really only interested in us getting into the control room and not being shot. I suspect our friend has told quite a few people to let us through.'

'So, we carry on.'

'Yes. Have a wander. See if you can find where that room is, I couldn't see it on any of the plans you guys passed me. Take shots of anything of interest and meet me at the smoking shelter in thirty minutes.'

'Roger that,' she replied and left first.

I set my phone to a thirty-minute alarm and waited a while before leaving the restrooms and walking into the interior of the building. It was a busy modern space, with shared working areas, lots of light and many workers bustling around the site in smart office clothing. It had an atrium structure, with the canteen at the centre of the space framed by rows of offices several floors high on all sides. It was clever, because you could quickly move around the building, crossing the atrium to reach any point. You'd be visible to everyone in the offices, but that usually didn't matter.

I set off in a clockwise direction and spent the next thirty minutes wandering around purposefully, stealing various bits and pieces as evidence of entry into supposedly secure areas and writing vague words on a pad I'd brought with me, appearing busy if anyone stopped and looked at me. I walked through office spaces, kitchens and meeting rooms, a gym, some first aid areas and a training suite. While a few people noticed me walking through, no one stopped or approached me, and many people held doors open for me or smiled as I passed by. It seemed like a pleasant enough, busy working environment and with the badge facing inwards and the right lanyard I wasn't anyone's problem and didn't stand out at all.

Initial walk done, I found a door and walked to the smoking area, a little shelter near a fountain in the gardens. Anthea soon emerged from another exit and walked over to join me. There were a few people already there, chatting and gossiping in their morning break. We smiled and turned to each other. 'So, I think it's OK to start checking the cameras,' I said pointedly.

'Yes, I agree,' she followed. 'All good so far?'

'Lovely,' I replied. 'Much bigger than our site.' I continued and watched as our companions left.

'Did you find the location of the control room?' I asked.

'No,' she said. 'It's a bit of a maze, this place. I walked through loads of places but there is no sign for it.'

'Yeah. Me too,' I said, pursing my lips. 'It's got to be quite big, though. Basement? Did you get onto the upper floors?'

'No,' she said. 'I thought I'd try that next.'

'OK,' I said. 'Can we get a quick look again at the layout?'

She opened a screenshot on her phone and squinted at the building plans we had been sent from the reconnaissance. 'Not labelled.'

'Anything that might be it anyway?' I asked, hoping we'd see a blank area that we may have missed when we scrutinised the plans the night before, but nothing obvious presented itself. 'It's clever,' I said. 'Good practice, this, if it's intentional. The building plans are online, but they make sure the sweet spot isn't marked. Got to hand it to them.'

She nodded and looked up. A guy in office trousers and shirt was walking slowly from the exit I had left, towards the next one that Anthea had used. He was staring pointedly in our direction. She looked back at her phone,

'Uh-oh. One o'clock, looking square at us, Jen,' she said, turning away from me, so that at a distance we didn't look like we were chatting.

'Shit. He is definitely interested!' I said.

He carried on walking slowly towards the exit door and, glancing back a couple of times, went through.

'Let's move,' Anthea said. 'Canteen in thirty?'

'Yes. Avoid him if possible. Blue shirt, grey trousers, walking with an odd gait. Maybe a limp.' It was hard to be sure.

We split up again and I saw Anthea walking up some central stairs in the atrium, as I began walking around inside again. I decided to venture down some of the side corridors and look for the control room. I knocked on some doors and if the room was open or occupied, I went in. I looked around once inside, apologising if I disturbed anyone, telling them I was 'checking the security cameras'. I maintained a busy, uninterested air and was allowed into many rooms and offices and subsequently ignored completely or politely allowed to carry out my fictitious survey as they carried on their business.

One team asked why I was disturbing their (highly confidential) meeting and I used the same reason. 'But there aren't any cameras here,' came the reply.

'Exactly!' I responded in a serious tone and got out of there before they could think of anything else to say.

Anthea, meanwhile, had passed the guy with the limp from outside several times and had been trying to shake him off. He definitely knew we were up to something and yet did not challenge or disturb us. He just kept staring at her and she was annoyed as this could easily give the game away. We later found out he was the head of security, who clearly needed some practice at stealth.

For all the ground I had covered I still had no clue as to where the control room was situated, another thirty minutes was up and so I strolled into the canteen and saw Anthea waiting on a relatively secluded table. 'Let's get a coffee,' I said, conscious that we weren't eating like everyone on the other tables. It was already 11 o'clock, only forty-nine minutes before our window to infiltrate their secure area, so we didn't have long before we had to make a move or declare a fail. When she came back, I spoke in hushed tones. 'I can't find any sign of that room,' I said. 'Do you think he is playing games with us? Maybe it doesn't exist?'

'No. I'm sure this is the place,' she replied. 'I've found lots of bits and bobs, but nothing yet.' She sipped the coffee and sighed. Then, I saw her straighten up and point her head down. 'OK. Guy from outside approaching.'

Damn. This was it. We'd been made. He was about to call us out. He walked past our table, looked pointedly at both of us, smirked slightly and gave a tiny bob of his eyebrows and then carried on, glancing back as he left the canteen space.

'What the hell?'

'He's going to get someone,' I said. 'Dammit. Gecko has told a bunch of people about us. We don't look that suspicious. No one else has so much as given us a second glance. This guy is in on it. They are wasting their money!'

She nodded and then immediately looked up again and hissed: 'Gecko! Coming over.'

'What?!' I said in disbelief. 'No!'

But, sure enough, here he was, sitting down next to us and smiling: 'How's it going?'

'Fine,' Anthea said. 'You sitting with us could give the game away, though. Couldn't it?' she added in honeyed tones.

'Ah, yes. Well, I'm afraid our head of security already did that,' he said. 'I *told* him not to say anything, but he told most of his team, I think.'

'If you tell one person, then they tell someone else,' I sighed. 'It's fine, but y'know it's not a real test if people know we are here.'

'Well. The gate team didn't know but I covered for you. Neither did reception, so good job there. We are really concerned about the control room to be honest. Found it yet?'

'No,' I said.

He chuckled. 'Well, good luck. Tick tick.' And pointed to his watch as he got up from the table.

Pfft.

'God, he is annoying.' I looked at Anthea.

'What now?'

'OK. Where can it be? There must be lots of people in and out. It must be a big room? I can't give him the satisfaction of failing. Let's think and get this job done.'

Anthea scrolled through her phone, checking the plans again. I rolled my neck back and forth, I ached, fading injuries still giving me pain in my shoulders. Then, almost at the same time we looked at each other. 'Wait,' I said. 'What's on the other side of these windows?'

'I was just thinking the same thing,' she replied, her voice registering a touch of measured excitement.

'There are blinds over every window looking into the canteen,' I said.

'But it's not the offices,' she went on. 'They are set back a little, at least on this floor.'

'So we are in the middle of a doughnut, and the offices are on the outside of it. But what is inside the ring?'

'If you like.' She giggled at my clumsy description. 'Something is behind these windows. And it would be the right size. And it would be hidden.'

'But very accessible.'

We watched for a few moments, looking at each other. My eyes came to rest on an older guy in more casual clothes walking across the canteen. He walked towards the serving counter, but went past and disappeared. I beckoned Anthea to sit beside me.

'Over there. They walk behind the counter but don't come back.'

It was a few minutes, but sure enough, the first guy never came back, and we saw a couple of others disappear down there too. It was smart. If this was the control room, then a casual observer might never suspect it was hidden behind the counter.

'Jen. It's nearly time,' she said, looking at her watch. 'Mate, it's twenty to.'

'OK,' I replied. 'Go to the counter quickly and see if you can see anything.'

She popped up and headed back quickly after pretending to peruse the menu. 'Definitely a corridor. I reckon we are on.'

'Text Gecko. Tell him to stand armed response down at 11.49 but otherwise radio silence,' I said. 'I'm doing it. It's a go.'

'Now?'

'Right now. On schedule,' I winked at her. 'And then let's get the fuck out of Dodge.'

She grinned.

I walked to the counter and hesitated by the menu, glancing about. I could see the corridor curving around and behind the tills. I began to walk towards it and then stopped. I pulled out my phone and saw the time. Ten to twelve. They would have stood down by now; I was on the clock. I glanced back at Anthea. She subtly gave me a thumbs up while still holding her coffee. I needed something else. I needed to give them a reason to let me in. Hmmm. I walked quickly to just beyond the canteen area and into a shared space on the left. I looked around for something to carry and made for a photocopier in the middle of the workspace.

'Do you need a code?' said a woman's voice behind me.

'Just some paper, actually,' I said, smiling.

'It's 007 if you do.' She smiled at me – was that sarcasm? I'd no time to wonder. I approached the copier and looked to grab a ream of paper, so my hands would be full. Perhaps someone would open the door for me, like in Hamburg, like in a thousand other jobs when the human instinct to be polite and friendly overrides the obvious security issues with holding a door open for a stranger.

Then I noticed a bundle of flyers on the side of the machine. They were leaflets concerning a graduation ceremony for a bunch of apprentices to be held in the reception area later that day. I grabbed them and walked straight to the canteen. Making for the serving counter, I looked over and immediately registered both Gecko and the head of security sitting with Anthea, who was trapped and looked uncomfortable. Oh, for goodness' sake, how much more obvious could he be? No time to think about it.

I waited, just for a minute, and then followed a woman in a cardigan carrying a cardboard takeaway food box as she walked down the corridor. She turned left into a smaller space, and I followed her there as well. 'Hi, hi. Shall I let you in?' I said and raised my hand to an electronic keypad on the wall beside the door.

'It's OK, I've got it,' she replied and switching the box to her other hand, punched in a six-digit code, and opened the door. 'Cloak and dagger.' She raised her eyebrows.

'Always,' I smiled and walked right in behind her. 'Just shoving these leaflets on desks, for the grads later,' I said. 'Try and come, they've worked hard and there's not much interest.'

'Ah, I will,' she said and smiled again as she walked away.

I had entered a large, multi-level room, one wall of which was a giant map of the UK with strategic points marked out with flashing lights. It was bustling, but noticeably quieter than all of the other offices I had been into that day. At the centre, on an elevated platform, was the casually dressed guy I'd seen disappear into the corridor earlier. From his desk he could effectively redirect or even cut off entirely key elements of UK infrastructure with a few keyboard strokes. It was clearly very important that no one should get to that desk who wasn't supposed to be there; you could bring the country to a standstill with the flick of a few switches. What power that would be, in the wrong hands, even momentarily. The damage could be catastrophic.

Time being short, I worked quickly. I did a quick circuit of the rest of the space, entirely uninterrupted as people concentrated on their screens and spoke quietly into phones. Then I walked up behind him, waiting a second and watching his screens.

Then I made my move.

I tapped him on the shoulder, and as he turned around, he smiled. 'Hi!' he said. 'What's this?' Then he seemed to immediately realise what had happened and followed up with 'Oh shit!'

I grinned. 'This is a security test and all is well. I'm a paid consultant and Gecko knows I am here. My name is Jenny. Thanks for your help.'

He nodded resignedly and said: 'I was warned this might happen, this is a big problem. How did you get in?'

'All in the report. Thank you.'

I turned around, stepped down from his podium, walked out of the exit, and back into the corridor. I walked over to Anthea and Gecko.

'Never mind, Jen,' Gecko said, grinning victoriously at me.

'It's done,' I said, and his face fell. Anthea smiled but showed only mild surprise.

'When?'

'Just then,' I said and reached for a bottle of water. I glanced at a clock. It was exactly midday.

'Oh. How?' he added, looking very disappointed.

'All in the report, mate. All in the report.'

He rallied. 'Would you like lunch? You could try a few more things afterwards.'

The expression on my face must have been telling. 'I think that's enough for today. I think we hit your specification, didn't we? Anthea?' She nodded. 'Then we are off.' I stood up and looked at him.

'Thank you, Gecko,' I said. 'Don't be hard on anyone for letting me through, it's a pretty secure site, they do a good job. Overall.'

'Not good enough,' he said.

'We can all always improve,' said Anthea.

We thanked reception and said goodbye, walking over to the car. 'Wait until we are clear. Hold it in,' I said.

She drove out of the car park, and we came to a stop in the lay-by after a few minutes. We looked at each other, squealed and punched the air, she slammed on the radio and we made for a local pub for lunch, as, rather fittingly, 'Another One Bites the Dust' by Queen blasted at volume from the crackly speakers.

16

GORILLAS AND DEMONS

I was sitting in a car park, sipping coffee and looking at a faded picture of a man who knew enough information to bring down the worst person in the world. He lived about five miles away from our current location in a normal house that was under surveillance from at least three different security agencies, none of whom wanted the seemingly easy job of passing him a burner phone. He was undoubtedly a criminal with a chain of fraud and fake businesses to his name, but he looked like your average moderately successful businessman and, as far as we knew, he had no idea he was being watched. I'd taken a call from an old contact who needed someone like me to do the job. The target was super-paranoid and regarded everyone with deep suspicion. The operation needed someone who looked innocent, someone he wouldn't suspect until it was too late.

I winced as I sipped the coffee. I'd handed back the file without opening and reading it. I didn't want to know more than the few details needed to convince me to help to do the job, and my contact reeled off a list of crimes that were enough to make me feel sick. She reassured me there was much more if I had the stomach to hear it, but I didn't want or need to know more. This guy was violent and cruel, scary enough in himself; however, his unofficial boss, the person everyone was interested in stopping, was as bad a person as anyone I had ever heard about. The guy our target could lead us to was responsible for ending or ruining many innocent lives, as well as political stuff indirectly involving hundreds of thousands of people and billions of pounds. There was apparently corruption and terror on a global basis. This was another level. It was scary and I did not want to know any more than I needed to help stop it – no names or nationalities, no locations, no numbers and only a vague description of the target so I wouldn't pass the phone to the wrong person.

Beyond that, I was very happy to be kept in the dark, ignorant of details and unable to identify anyone if pressed in the future. What I was told, though, was that he was about to be allowed to walk away without so much as a parking ticket if he helped get the other guy caught. If he was persuaded to help stop his boss then that would help end a world of pain and misery, and in return the piece of shit would walk.

My contact had pressed upon me the urgency of the job. Time was a factor and we had to move over the next forty-eight hours for reasons I didn't need or want to know. The plan was for me to wait until the right moment at some point over the next two days and approach him when his guard was down and he was, even momentarily, on his own. I was to hand over the phone, say a phrase he would recognise and tell him we would call him the next day. I was to leave quickly and get into a car and be driven away by a personal protection guy or 'gorilla' assigned to protect me and get us both away as fast as we could and before he had any time to respond. If anything else happened whatsoever, the gorilla would step in and get me out of there.

It sounded like a plan. Thin, dangerous and weird as hell, but a plan just the same.

Gorilla and I went to a hotel, grabbed some food and decided to do some night-time reconnaissance on the area immediately surrounding his residence. We parked up in the seaside town near where he lived and headed to a pub where it was thought he sometimes socialised. The place was packed out, as there was a county fete planned for the next few days and there were lots of tourists and exhibitors staying nearby and enjoying the local countryside and beaches. The crowds made great cover for us but would make it hard to spot him if he ventured out.

We discussed it briefly and concluded that he likely would avoid such an atmosphere, so strolled towards his address instead, weaving our way through throngs of tourists and exhibitors enjoying themselves ahead of the next day's events.

We couldn't get close to his house, though. He had chosen an apartment on a small and affluent private estate with a few houses and other buildings set back from the main road and accessed only by a single, private drive with security cameras clearly visible on the road going in. Any car would be clearly seen as soon as it rolled up the drive, which was surrounded by woods and enclosed by a low wall.

It was a great choice if you wanted to hide, or if you wanted to know if anyone was getting close to you. Nonetheless, there was a public right of way running around the entire place, and it was well used by dog walkers and people out for a picturesque evening walk. I took Gorilla's hand and we strolled leisurely along the full path, chatting like a couple out on an evening walk, taking sly photographs with our phones and trying to get a look through the trees at the properties beyond.

The footpath curved around the property boundary and we had almost walked full circle when we saw that it also forked to the left, behind the main road, and could take us more or less

285

directly around the back of the residential part of the estate. It was late now, almost dark, and we were debating whether it was too risky to stroll past the houses when we heard voices and a young couple with two large dogs approached us from the other direction and walked straight through. 'Lovely evening!' the man said and, making vague sounds of agreement, we smiled and followed them through, asking questions about the dogs and giving them our cover story.

Back at the hotel we discussed the site. There were lots of cars at the front of the property, two of which belonged to our target, while at the rear we had confirmed two identical large black vehicles. The lights had been on in the kitchen. He was certainly home.

The next day we parked in different spots on the outskirts of the village, covering the main roads and watching for any of his vehicles moving. We had two further teams in and around the area for surveillance, protection and to help get me into position if he popped up somewhere convenient to do the drop. We waited for hours, sometimes together, sometimes apart, Gorilla occasionally leaving the car to pee in some under-growth. I tried to make conversation as best I could, but he wasn't the most verbose individual I'd ever worked with and spoke only a few words about football and rugby, if pressed. Eventually I gave up trying and we sat in silence. I was grateful when we separated again and took up different positions.

We had been many hours in place when my phone lit up from the main team. 'Wake up and get plates of the 4×4s about to go past you. Just entering the village now. You'll have visual in about two minutes.'

I looked up and sure enough in fairly quick succession three brand new black 4×4s zoomed past me on the main road exiting the village. I'd been ready with the phone but was trying to stay mostly hidden and had got only blurred shots; Gorilla had been in a better position and confirmed one of the plate numbers in full and the others partially. Somebody somewhere ran them through something.

'Back to base. Right now,' came the order over the phone and we headed to yet another hotel.

In the room we were told that the plates were unregistered. Our lead added that she was very uncomfortable and suspected that another team, possibly hostile towards the target, was also in the area. We were stood down for the night and I stared at the hotel ceiling for a long time wondering what the next day would bring, my imagination presenting awful images, filling in the gaps from the list of crimes I'd heard about the day before.

After breakfast, we stood in the car park and the lead told us that they now had details he would move today, possibly suspicious that the other team was in the area and would likely try to kill him. I tried not to flinch and acted as if this was a common occurrence, but I didn't pretend not to be rattled when she asked me if I was OK. I said that I was but that this job and its associated dangers were something of an escalation to my usual breaking-and-entering. Especially as she made it clear to me that if they approached him and I was there they wouldn't think twice about hurting any of us to get to him. Lying in bed the night before, I'd already worked this out and decided I'd see it through until the end anyway. If it stopped all that misery then it was worth it, and I'd had a good ride so far. Blaze of glory and all that. I was in to the end, but once it was done I was saying no from there on.

The target was heading to a local station to catch a train, before travelling into London for a meeting. There would be a team watching the house and we were going to wait at the station and try to approach him there as he parked his car. In broad daylight and full view of anyone else around.

'Do we know who was in the 4×4s?' I asked.

'Yes,' came the answer, offering no more information. I didn't ask any more questions.

We sat in the little station car park for a couple of hours, waiting to hear that he was on his way, but after a while we got a message to head back to a rendezvous point outside the village. He had changed his plans, it seemed, and was still in his house. Apart from the obvious danger the job was uneventful so far, which is often the case. At the rendezvous our lead told me that we would wait here until another team saw him move, however long that might take.

Sometimes surveillance like this goes on for days with nothing happening, apart from endless waiting. The hours ticked by at a glacial pace until finally, at around 4 p.m., we got a message that he was on the move. He was in one of his cars and was heading into the village. Gorilla cranked up the engine and we headed there, too. Our man, usually paranoid and reclusive, had inexplicably decided to visit the village shop and the car park was as good a place as any to do the handover.

We pulled up and waited, parked about three spaces down from his own car in the tiny car park flanked by trees and recycling bins at the back of the shop. He was taking a long time. 'Wait for the signal, Jen. Do *not* move unless you get GREEN.'

'RT,' I replied and pulled up the hood on my jacket. I'd removed all my jewellery and wore no make-up. I was wearing a pair of dark sunglasses and had practised my phrases many times so that my distinctive accent and voice weren't obvious enough for him to remember. I had made myself as unmemorable and anonymous as possible, because the last thing anyone needed was him to be able to identify me later, even if it was from my accent and especially as I was now speaking on stages all over the world and occasionally on television.

We waited for another five minutes or so and then Gorilla's phone rang at the same time as mine. 'Pull back and abort. Now!' came the order, and Gorilla drove us out of the car park and away immediately and at speed. Another false start.

It transpired that our man was no longer in the shop. He had somehow parked up, walked into the place and disappeared, likely on foot into the village, leaving his car in the car park. This wasn't good, and while we ate sandwiches at a picnic spot a few miles out of the village we agreed he knew someone was tailing him, but exactly who, apart from us, was still unknown and time was running out.

It had been made very clear to me that unless this handover was done in the timespan I'd been told about, the opportunity would be lost. Although I didn't know the details as to why, I got the impression that the chance to do this, to recruit him grudgingly to turn on his boss, might never arise again. In the meantime, who knows what was going on in the background, what deeds would be done, what people might suffer as a result. Additionally, if he had realised he was being tailed, he might disappear altogether or alert the other guy and the entire job could be lost. It was frustrating and stressful to put it mildly, but if you get the order to abort, you abort. Immediately and without asking any questions. I had no idea what had led to that command, some new information perhaps, some added variable or complication. I didn't want to know, but it was starting to look like the job had failed and we were never going to catch him.

'We will give it one more go,' said the lead. 'We'll get you two back into position at the house. If he goes back, you can doorstep him.'

'Doorstep him?' I said, incredulous.

'It's the only way, Jen.'

'Well, OK, but surely that's the most dangerous option. I mean, who else is at the house? Who was in the cars at the back? If he is already spooked, he will definitely react if someone rings his doorbell! I mean, if I was going to fight back, I'd do it there.'

'I'll do it,' said Gorilla. 'She's lost her nerve,' he growled.

'No,' said the lead, addressing him directly. 'The only person cleared to approach is Jen. Do you understand?' She was tiny but she had such commanding presence and was so senior that she was used to being obeyed. I found her impressive and quietly terrifying, and though I doubt the Gorilla was scared, he was used to taking orders.

'Yes. Roger that. Understood. No worries.' He took a huge bite from a tuna sandwich, tiny in his great paws, and looked down and away from me.

The lead turned back to me. 'If you want to pull out, Jen, now is the time. It's fine. No one will think badly of you. It's a scary situation and you are right. He is prepared at his home and will be on his guard. Speak now if you are done with this.' She smiled at me.

'I'm good,' I said. 'Can I just confirm that Oscar Wilde here will be very close by.'

'He will be. And so will I.' She grinned. 'You won't get hurt, I promise.'

I'd known our lead a while. We had done two other jobs together, but nothing so dangerous as this. I'd never known anyone so disciplined and skilled. She had told me about a couple of things she had done over the years, and I also knew some stuff about her by reputation on the industry grapevine. I believed that if anyone could handle this situation and keep me relatively safe it was her and her team. I trusted her completely and knew that any immediate danger would be handled very well, but clearly it was still very dangerous and I could see the concern in her face and hear it in the increasingly terse comms that came over the radios from the rest of the team.

If I could have some tiny part to play in bringing down some-one who caused so much misery and pain, then it would be worth it. The rest was about holding my nerve and dispensing with ego. I wasn't important enough or involved enough for global criminals to bother coming after me. I knew nothing. I was, once again, just someone hired to help because I had a knack for getting where I wasn't supposed to be and looking innocent. If this house of cards did fall, I'd be low on the list of targets for revenge, I wasn't worth the bother, but doing this one would make up for all the times I should have asked more questions. It would make amends and balance the scales of anything dubious or questionable I'd ever been involved with. Therefore it *had* to be done regardless of the risks and, I told myself, for that reason, all would be well. This would not be a cursed job; the good guys had to win sometimes.

I decided to run with that narrative and put everything else out of my mind.

We'd been in position for a couple of hours when confirmation that the car was returning to the house came through. 'Just give the guy the phone and you are done,' she messaged. 'Then you can get back to office roofs and emails, Jen.'

'I'll grab him as he goes to his door,' I told Gorilla, who agreed and communicated it to the lead.

'Agreed,' came the response.

'It's a go. Move the car into position behind number six.'

Gorilla inched the car into position in the drive. The target's car came into view a minute or two later, headlights illuminating the estate's shared parking area, wheels crunching the gravel. I got out and closed the door quietly, walking on some grass at the side and moved towards the target's house.

However, as I crouched in the shadows at the side of the house, I watched him move the car as close as he could to the front porch, instead of halting in the parking space, and, without switching off the engine, jump directly out and straight into the house. There was no time to intercept him or move close enough to speak.

Dammit! I thought and stayed where I was. Glancing back at Gorilla, he was sitting in the car with the engine and headlights off. I waited and watched the target's car, engine running and door still open outside his little stone porch and front door. I felt my phone buzz in the pocket of my coat. Pushing myself further into the wall of the building, I carefully pulled it out and looked at it, shielding the light with my coat and ducking down behind some bushes to the left of the front door. I had good cover here; a matter of five steps or so and I would be at the car.

'*Green. Do it,*' came the message from Gorilla. I didn't respond but stayed in position and put the phone away, dropping the old-fashioned simple phone I was supposed to hand over in my other pocket. Somewhere behind me, I heard a very quiet tick as Gorilla switched the engine of our car back on. I heard him get out of the car and creep up behind me. Give him his due, for an enormous guy he could be very quiet. He came to a stop a few paces behind me and crouched down against the wall. I looked at him in the dark and saw him give the thumbs up through the gloom.

Then I heard voices and footsteps and the target emerged from the house and got back into the car. For a minute I thought he might just drive away again, but something had changed.

He was moving more slowly, seemed relaxed, and he drove the car in a wide curve, straight past us, coming to a stop and reversing, bringing it to a standstill with its rear directly in front of me hiding against the wall. He turned off the engine and got out. I stepped forward and he jumped in surprise then immediately raised his fist.

'Back the fuck off!' he shouted, and Gorilla stepped out behind me, enormous and threatening from the shadows. He shouted a name and looked to the front door, taking a few steps forward ready to hit me. I stepped back and said the first phrase. It had the desired effect and he held a hand up to a man who had appeared at the front door. I held out the phone and said my other line as a third man's face came to the front door.

'It's OK,' he called out, and looked at me. I repeated the line again and put the phone into his hand.

Gorilla moved in between us and pushed me in the back. 'Car.'

I was moving but he pushed me over to the car giving me more speed, and I got into the back seat as we had planned. The wheels screamed on the gravel as Gorilla drove quickly away without turning on his lights. I lay in the back and started to shake with adrenalin, feeling my phone buzz in my pocket. I fumbled for it in my horizontal position, struggling with flaps on my pockets and clumsy as my body reacted to my fear. Gorilla's phone beeped in the darkness, mounted on a phone holder on the dash. He extended a gigantic finger and said, 'Go on.'

'Abort! Abort! Do not complete!' came a voice down the line. *'Do not hand that guy that phone. Pull her back. Do you copy?'*

I was holding my own phone with a shaking hand and reading more or less the same message. 'Too late,' Gorilla replied. 'Mission complete and en route. Ten minutes. Over.'

By the time we made the rendezvous I was in full panic mode. 'It was too late,' I gasped. 'It came too late, we'd done it. I'm sorry. What happened? Oh no, what did I do?'

Our lead was calm. 'It's OK. It's OK, Jen. Calm down. They have him another way, it was no longer required,' she told me soothingly, but I wasn't sure I believed her and it showed. 'You did well, Jen. Calm down and thank you. We can take it from here. Don't worry.'

It took her a while to bring me down, but in the end I let myself be convinced. There wasn't much I could do now anyway and if they had already got him some other way then it didn't matter. I asked for no details and was very happy to grab my little hire car from the hotel car park and point it towards home. As the miles rolled away, I didn't listen to music and barely watched the sat nav, very much on autopilot. I had done a good thing, at great personal risk. Regardless of the outcome, I had given it my best shot and the people I worked with, professional people, were happy with my work. That was all I had really wanted. That, and doing some good in the world.

As I had done many times before, I resolved not to take the crazy jobs anymore, to ask more questions and play it safe. I was done with the drama, the escalating danger and the myriad people who contacted me, finding many uses for this weird skill set I have acquired over the years. I would talk about it, educate, take a few jobs here and there to stay in the game, but the mad ones, the dangerous assignments were in the past. I could hardly be a burglar or perform clandestine operations if I carried on speaking in public anyway. My profile was growing, and I was set to move in another, much more public direction. The physical work would likely dry up as attacks relied more and more on purely technical means to succeed and I would, finally, really start to say no.

I'd achieved a lot more than might have been expected given where I started. I'd seen and done things that had made a difference. I had no need to take so many risks or prove myself to anyone any more. If it all ended tomorrow, I couldn't complain, it had been an interesting and significant career, and I had helped a lot of people, I'd done a lot of good. That was all I could really control, and it was the only way forward that I felt I could commit to from now on.

I thought back to my eight-year-old self, trapped in that house with the neighbour. I remembered how frightened I had been as that little kid, helpless at the hands of someone intent on harm. Maybe today, in some small way, I'd managed to stop that happening again, to some other little kid, or their family somewhere far away. Maybe, the chances of some child being trapped and frightened by bad people had been somehow diminished by my handing a phone to a bad person in a driveway, and trying to stop someone who did much worse things than I had experienced, worse things than I could even imagine.

Maybe not, but I'd done what I could and had to move on.

I'll never know exactly what happened after that job, and it is difficult to quantify how much good is done by my work, how much of a difference, if any, it really makes. But one thing I knew for absolute certain as I drove home that night was that I'd definitely chosen a side. If I ever met the devil on the roof at some point in the future, I doubted even he would have to ask me that question again, and if he did, I'd know the answer.

I smiled to myself and focused on the motorway in front of me. It was more or less empty. I drove on into the night, tired but calm enough, looking forward to seeing my family and getting back to the cosy mundanity of domestic life.

I pulled into a service station for a break and reached for my phone. Turning off airplane mode, I noticed a new message from an old client.

'Are you free next week? It's a tricky one. You up for a job in the sun, Jen?'

ACKNOWLEDGEMENTS

There are many people who I need to thank for their help in writing this book.

I want to thank my agent Trevor Dolby, who is clearly a genius and one of the most generous and interesting people in the world. Your patience and humour are as legendary as your talent. I'm so lucky to have worked with you.

To Max Metzger, without you this book wouldn't have happened, thank you for everything you did.

To the teams at Aevitas, Leading Authorities and Simon & Schuster; thank you all for your help and encouragement, I appreciate everything you all do and your patience.

I also want to thank Helen Cockram. There was no one else scary enough and kind enough to knock me into shape the way you did. You are amazing and this book wouldn't exist without you.

Thanks to Lilly, Nick and Jo-Anne who are never, ever too busy or too tired to be my cheerleaders. I adore you all.

To all the crews, thank you for the good times and all your help. Never stop being pirates, be careful and don't eat on the job! It's all fun and games until you fall off a roof.

To my many clients who over the years gave me the jobs and paid for the drinks, you gave me the work that made me and you have my sword, always. I bet you think this song is about you.

To every security professional, guard or employee I've ever fooled. Apologies, it was of course likely an off-day and I probably just got lucky. If it helps, we are all on the same side; stay frosty.

To the numerous friends in the security industry, too many to mention, stay wild and never change, thanks for the community and the craziness.

To the plagiarists, critics, pretenders and fakes, you only ever succeed in making those of us who actually do the job stronger. Keep going by all means, try and find your own swag. May you one day realise that being yourself is always better than being a thinly disguised version of someone else, In the meantime, avoid me and yes I know.

To all the colleagues I worked with over the years who shared meetings, drinks and flights with me but never realised what I was actually up to. I apologise for never giving you the full story, you'd never have trusted me with the day job if you had realised what the sideline was. We had the best times anyway, I'll explain in person when we meet again and I'll buy the round.

To the incredible, resilient, funny and rebellious city of Liverpool. You helped make me. I am for ever in your debt. I'm not English, I'm Scouse. For ever.

To my children and extended family, here and passed. You are the reason I do all of it, I love and thank you all for everything. None of it matters without you. Thank you most to my husband. My glass never empty, the home fires always burning; coming home to you, laughing and talking trivia meant I could carry on. You and me against the world, let the heavens fall. Thank you and all my love.

Finally, to every social engineer, hacker, mischief maker, pirate and rebel, there are more of us than you think. Stay curious and do no harm, the world needs people who think differently.

We aren't the weakest link, nor the strongest defence, we are all just human. That will be our downfall but it is also our one shot at salvation.

Thanks for flying JennyAir.